LOVE AND MARRIAGE IN THE GREAT COUNTRY HOUSES

Also by Adeline Hartcup

ANGELICA
MORNING FACES
(with John Hartcup)
BELOW STAIRS IN THE GREAT COUNTRY HOUSES
CHILDREN OF THE GREAT COUNTRY HOUSES

Love and Marriage
in the
Great Country Houses

ADELINE HARTCUP

SIDGWICK & JACKSON
LONDON

First published in Great Britain in 1984
by Sidgwick & Jackson Limited
Copyright © 1984 by Adeline Hartcup

Picture research by Deborah Pownall

For Jason and Victoria
this description of loves and marriages
so different from theirs

ISBN 0-283-99002-3

Printed in Great Britain by
Biddles Ltd, Guildford, Surrey
for Sidgwick & Jackson Limited
1 Tavistock Chambers, Bloomsbury Way
London WC1A 2SG

Contents

List of Illustrations

Acknowledgements

Once again I am grateful to the owners of the nineteenth-century family archives I have enjoyed using, and to the erudite librarians and archivists who can so quickly switch between their two functions – at first alert watchdogs, then helpful guides.

Unpublished material stored away in the great country houses and the county record offices has been included in this book by kind permission of the Duke of Devonshire and the Trustees of the Chatsworth Settlement; the Earl of Derby, who holds the copyright of the fifteenth Earl's personal diary; Lord Egremont; and Mr T.D.G. Sotheron-Estcourt, whose family papers, the Sutton-Estcourt correspondence, are held by Gloucestershire Record Office, reference D1571, F207; and the Kent Archives office and the Trustees of the Chevening Estate.

The staff of the Kent Archives Office and the Cheshire, Gloucestershire, Liverpool and West Sussex Record Offices have all been helpful, as were Mr Michael Pearman at Chatsworth and Mr John Eyre at Uppark. At Knowsley Mrs Iris Young, the Librarian, her predecessor Mrs Kay and Mr Anthony Mason-Hornby were as welcoming as they were knowledgeable. A useful clue was given me by Mrs Margaret Harcourt Williams, who remembered the Sutton-Estcourt letters she once catalogued at Gloucester. No one could have been more helpful and careful on major and minor points than my editor, Libby Joy, and Deborah Pownall has been so successful in tracking down illustrations that many splendid ones have had to be left unused.

The London Library is a labyrinth as well as a bran-tub. So my acknowledgement is not only to its resources and its willing staff but also to Mr Douglas Matthews, the Librarian, who is always ready to guide members up the Library's many metaphorical ladders – as well as down a few unavoidable snakes.

It is nearly a hundred years too late to acknowledge one of my greatest debts. On 23 March 1885, my husband's great grandfather, William Hartcup, was given a very fine birthday present by his wife. It was that year's edition of *Burke's Peerage, Baronetage and Knightage*, and she inscribed an affectionate message in spidery copper-plate lettering on the fly leaf. Without that weighty crimson volume, gold-lettered and coroneted on its stalwart six-inch spine, it would have taken infinitely longer to research this book and to find a way through the tangles of nineteeth-century genealogy.

A.H.
Swanton, 1984

PART ONE

1

The Rules of the Game

Ways of loving and failing to love – what the French call *la vie sentimentale*: why is there no equivalent catch-phrase in English? – are revealing characteristics of every age and every group of people. Those who belonged to the top layer of society in nineteenth-century England, the Upper Ten Thousand as they were called, are rewarding to consider in this context because their ways and many of their feelings were as different from those of their contemporaries in other classes as they are from ours in the twentieth century.

To get a sharp focus on even one class during rougly one hundred years is not easy. Attitudes and manners changed – from full-blooded sexual permissiveness in the early years of the century to a contrasting strictness in the middle, then back to *fin de siècle* laxity towards its end. Through all the varying ups-and-downs, sexual freedom, and unorthodoxy were condoned so long as there was no whiff of scandal or publicity. When this was not avoided, it was the woman in the case – whoever she might be, however unjustly smeared – who paid the fine.

It was a peak period of aristocratic power and affluence. The great families still formed a self-contained, exclusive social group, intricately linked by intermarriage and inter-adultery. Between them they owned vast acres of town and countryside. The great country houses were the homes of most Members of Parliament, most members of the government, and most Prime Ministers. So politics, land and money were usually all considered when it came to planning a marriage. The pattern of society had not changed much since Dr Johnson's pronouncement that 'chastity in women is all-important because the whole of property is involved in it'. A Victorian aristocratic marriage settlement, with its great pages of hand-written parchment, its formal calligraphy, unpunctuated endlessness and its handful of signatures of dukes and eminent statesmen as witnesses, has something of the grim gravity of an international treaty between nations which only recently may have been at war. Often vast family estates and hundreds of tenants as well as substantial sums of money changed hands when such transactions were made. It might seem that the child of a hugely wealthy family could afford a free choice of partner, but that was not how most of the nineteenth-century nobility saw things. Great houses and estates needed invigorating shots of new money to keep them going. Daughters of ancient families were brought up to steer clear of the débâcle of marrying 'beneath them'.

For the girls, even in the park-walled shelter of the great country houses, love and marriage were the only two acceptable options unless they were exceptionally strong, independent characters like Florence Nightingale or Hester Stanhope. The game consisted in trying – often against heavy odds – to get love and marriage into line. Today it seems little short of miraculous that they sometimes succeeded. The ones who lost out, the victims of the system, were daughters without much in the way of looks or dowry, and 'younger sons' who were unlikely to inherit anything substantial and were untrained to earn their own living. One match-making mother made no bones about her attitude to younger sons. She called them 'detrimentals'. 'Though you may try hard you cannot invariably keep detrimentals at a distance,' she said. Some of the girls felt differently. Why was it, they asked each other, that younger sons were often so much more attractive than heirs with brilliant 'prospects'?

It was a curious dance, sometimes as cruel and ruthless as that of a primitive tribe. Pressures of money and rank put the lives of the younger generation fairly inexorably in the hands of parents who planned, decided, or vetted their choice of partner and wielded their purse-string power to make them comply. The case against matrimony was eloquently pleaded by Byron: 'Though women are angels yet wedlock's the devil' was his famous battle-cry. Marriage in his eyes was an unnatural institution which not even angels could survive. The prospect for them was bleak indeed.

A thankless husband, next a faithless lover,
Then dressing, nursing, praying, and all's over.

Ladies walking abroad, escorted by a footman. A drawing by Gavarni, the French caricaturist, who was in England from 1847 to 1851.

'Is it Friendship? Is it Love'? A problem for the ballroom vigilante.

There was no escape.

> Some take a lover, some take drams and prayers,
> Some mind their household, others dissipation;
> Some run away, and but exchange their cares,
> Losing the advantage of a virtuous station.

Byron was spoilt, cynical and embittered, but his attitude was shared by others. His friends advised him that his 'best chance of steadying his mind without weakening his genius' was marriage, and he agreed, but without any illusions. 'As to Lady B.,' he wrote, 'when I discover one rich enough to suit me and foolish enough to love me, I will give her leave to make me miserable if she can. Money is the magnet; as to Women, one is as well as another, the older the better, we have then a chance of getting her to Heaven.' Perhaps in fairness it should be added that Byron was writing to his adored half-sister Augusta, whom he loved but of course could not marry.

London ballrooms and drawing-rooms during the summer season were the jousting-ground, and girls hoped to triumph by receiving and accepting a proposal before it was over. Old Lady Stanley in 1847 commiserated with her daughter-in-law, who had had to bring her eldest girl back 'out of Town without a husband'. Not till six years later did she marry – none too brilliantly, by family standards – and her mother still had five younger girls to shepherd through their initiation rites. Sixteen years later, in 1863, the youngest of these (Rosalind, who married the future Earl of Carlisle in 1864) was lamenting that by the end of the season she had not 'found the real happiness that was to come to her'.

So it took courage – it must often have seemed reckless and even suicidal – for a girl to say no to a 'good offer' for no better reason than merely not being in love. The conventions – what Thackeray called the 'grim workings of marriage capitalism' – did not give young people much chance of getting to know each other. Girls were escorted everywhere by chaperons, and they could commit the unpardonable offence of 'drawing attention to themselves' and consequently being considered 'fast' if they had the same dancing partner more than twice in an evening. When the music stopped her partner escorted the girl back to her mother or chaperon, where she sat demurely by her until invited to dance again.

The young Queen Victoria appreciated the quizzical wisdom of her first Prime Minister, Lord Melbourne – he was wiser in retrospect than he had been in his own life – on personal as well as state affairs. A woman needed to marry, he told her, for she could not 'stand alone for long, in whatever situation she is'. He agreed with the Queen that twenty-three was a suitable age. 'But girls begin to be nervous when they are past nineteen,' he said, 'and they think they'll never marry if they are "turned twenty".' Why did so many marriages come to grief, the Queen wondered? 'Why, you see,' Lord Melbourne explained, 'a gentleman hardly knows a girl till he has proposed, and then when he has an unrestrained intercourse with her he sees something and says, "This I don't quite like".' The Countess of Bessborough saw the problem from the girl's point of view. 'In the way Girls are often married', she wrote in 1807, 'hardly knowing their Husbands or what marriage is, how many there must be who would gladly separate, and still more gladly chuse again, if they could do so without ruining their characters.'

But a broken engagement left a lasting smear – on the girl, of course – and once the matrimonial machinery clanked into action it was difficult to switch off. A few dances together, a few words, and two lives were irrevocably riveted together. The man could get away from time to time if he wanted to, and might have Parliamentary or other work to interest him away from home; but for most wives everything depended on the quality of their marriage. 'I wonder if a different husband would have made her a different woman,' one mother wondered about her daughter. It seemed unlikely. 'Perhaps not if she had as many children for she seems almost worn out, poor thing.'

The repeated agonies and dangers of childbirth during the last century are hard to imagine today. Diaries kept by married women often tell of little else but pregnancies, miscarriages, illnesses, and births and deaths of children, many of whom wasted away by slow painful stages while their distraught parents could only watch and pray by the bedside. There was occasional success in limiting the size of families, but methods were risky and uncertain, and much of the religious teaching of the day ruled out as plumb sinful any attempt at contraception – let alone abortion, of course, although there were also do-it-yourself possibilities of that. Gradually, however, the idea gained ground. In 1826 Richard Carlile, author of *Every Woman's Book* and *What is Love?*, advised inserting a small sponge, soaked in a solution of quinine and water, in the vagina. It was an important advance on previous methods of limiting inter-course to the safe period and on withdrawal, as it did not depend on the man's carefulness or even on his being aware that it would be used. But even as late as the 1890s there was general fear and disapproval of contraceptives. When Bertrand Russell married in 1894 he was warned that his children were likely to be either epileptic or imbecile, but even so he met with strong opposition on medical as well as religious grounds to the use of contraceptives. The orthodox view was that sex was for the procreation of children by married couples, and that it was abnormal, improper and disgusting for a woman – unless she were a prostitute – to experience sexual pleasure.

Not everyone, of course, was orthodox. Extra-marital affairs sparked off a wide range of different reactions. Some accepted the infidelity of a husband or wife with philosophy and resignation; others saw it as calling for a duel or divorce. William Lamb (the future Lord Melbourne) certainly did not imagine what lay ahead of him when as a young man he declared that if he ever felt a 'growing passion' for another man's wife he would 'fly to the further end of the earth to resist the danger'. Emily Eden's sparkling novel about an aristocratic marriage, *The Semi-attached Couple*, tells of a character who sees the situation in a different light. 'I shall always suppose,' she says, 'that when a man makes love to a married woman it is entirely her fault.'

Strict rules drive people to rebellion and humbug. Foreign visitors to London were struck by the numbers of prostitutes brazenly accosting men in West End streets, and there was an élite of captivating courtesans who prided themselves on relationships with aristocratic and wealthy admirers. Harriette Wilson's *Memoirs* were written as a profitable counter-offensive to the sixth Duke of Beaufort when he defaulted on the annuity he promised her for giving up her liaison with his son. Undependable as they are, they give a lively picture of the affairs of Harriette and her sisters with a succession of noble lovers. The girls were alluring and greatly sought after, and their accepted code of behaviour is interesting. Harriette, daughter of a Swiss watch-maker, insisted on consorting with none but 'men of the very highest fashion'. She had been very young when she launched herself on her career. The provocative

An illustration from Harriette Wilson's scandalous, best-selling
Memoirs showing her with Lord Ponsonby.

opening sentence of her *Memoirs* refuses to tell how this happened. 'I shall not say why and how I became at the age of fifteen the mistress of the Earl of Craven,' it reads.

But there was not much else she would not tell. Harriette flirted openly at the opera with her crowds of titled admirers, walked out alone – as of course no respectable young woman should – and sent inviting letters to men who interested her, among them even the Prince of Wales. She had her scruples, however, or at least so she claimed. She would not dally with a new lover while she was still living with his predecessor; and her description of her passionate affair with Lord Ponsonby gives the credit for their discreet behaviour to Harriette's admiration for his beautiful (but stupid and deaf) wife, and to their resolve not to hurt her feelings. Harriette used to meet Ponsonby in the Park after dinner almost every day, but they took care not to speak – only to gaze at each other. When they did spend an evening together, to put off the dreaded moment of parting they would drive to the House of Lords in a hackney carriage and there Harriette would wait for hours 'merely for one more kiss, and the pleasure of driving with Ponsonby to his own door'. To 'the crime of attaching myself to a married man' she later attributed many of her troubles, and she believed that if she had not indeed loved Ponsonby she would have accepted one of her unmarried suitors, who might have offered her marriage and respectability as Lord Berwick eventually did to Harriette's sister, Sophia.

Marriage and respectability meant acceptance by society and the law, but the law laid its icy hand very unjustly on marriage, and on married women in particular. Until the 1870 Married Women's Property Act, only a wife who was wealthy enough to have a marriage settlement had any rights to her own property. Other wives were in common law held to possess nothing; their property, money and even earnings belonged to the husband, who could do as he liked with it. The day after their wedding Byron told his wife that they must separate, if possible after she was already on the way towards producing an heir for him; he would then use the fortune she had brought him, he said, to enable him to live abroad, far away from his wife and child in England. A wife who lived apart from her husband was entitled to no support from him, no right to keep her children with her, no claim on any of the property or money she had contributed to the marriage. Even for a happily married couple the law made things awkward. Lady St Helier married in 1871, just after the Married Women's Property Act became law, but it was not yet in operation and her marriage settlement had been drafted on the old lines. Later she described what this had meant.

What money I had was settled on my husband, and no part of it was reserved for my private use. . . I still did not possess a cheque-book, nor was I able to get any money except by asking my husband. He was kind and generous. . . and endeavoured to minimize the anomalies of the position. He paid all my bills, he kept my bank-book, and gave me a small allowance for my personal expenses.

Gradually it came to be realized that the law must change. Step by slow legal step, women were granted rights to money they had earned, to own and dispose of property, and to instigate legal proceedings without their husband's permission.

The other great grievance was the indissolubility of marriage. Until 1857 it was only by a special Act of Parliament, an expensive matter which was out of reach of all but the very wealthy, that a marriage in England could be dissolved. The Matrimonial Causes Act of 1857 aimed at making divorce more generally available, but even then – and until as late as 1923 – the wife was heavily handicapped. Adultery – commonly referred to as 'Crim. Con.' (Criminal Conversation) – was sufficient grounds for a husband to petition for divorce, but a wife had to prove such additional wrongs as cruelty, incest, bigamy, rape, or desertion. And a woman who had been unfaithful risked losing much more than her marriage; her home, her children, and her acceptance by society were also at stake. There was a general assumption, with special repercussions of course in aristocratic circles where titles and inheritance were involved, that guardianship of children should be vested in the father. Ludicrous as it now seems, it was only for an illegitimate child that a mother could have full legal responsibility; the father had the right to make decisions about all legitimate children. And even a widow, after a happy unbroken marriage, was not the legal guardian of her children unless her husband had explicitly provided for this in his will.

Here again the law gradually changed. In 1869 it became possible for a wife whose husband had been convicted of assaulting her to be granted a judicial separation, with custody of children under the age of ten. In 1886 a deserted wife and children were entitled to contributions towards their maintenance. An Act of Parliament in 1895 made it possible for a wife to be freed from the obligation to live with her husband, to have legal custody of children under sixteen, and to claim payment of a small sum from her husband.

What now seems strange is the resistance, sometimes quite violent, of intelligent people to these changes in the law. John Stuart Mill had blazed the way for reform in 1869 with his book, *The Subjection of Women,* and two years before that he had introduced a Bill for Women's Suffrage in the House of Commons. Bertrand Russell's mother, Lady Amberley, was among its supporters, but the Queen saw the Bill as 'mad, wicked folly' and appealed to various influential people to stop it. 'Lady Amberley ought to get a good whipping,' she went so far as to say.

The Church backed up the law in settling the pattern of marriage and divorce, and nowhere more than in the prevailing biblical taboo on marriage between certain relations. The question often came up for discussion in the closely intermarried country house world. When the seventh Duke of Beaufort's first wife died he married her half-sister, but this was considered improper until 1835, when the Deceased Wife's Sister Bill was passed, declaring all such existing marriages to be valid but forbidding any future ones. It was one of the questions that puzzled the Queen and made her ask for Lord Melbourne's opinion. 'Spoke of Miss Pitt, and of our fearing she was attached to her brother-in-law,' she jotted in her diary. 'Lord Melbourne said such a marriage could not take place now.' But he was not dogmatic about it. He explained the workings of the recent Act, weighing up the pros and cons, but said he did not know if it was right or wrong.

Not everyone was so open-minded. A long time later Lord Hugh Cecil went into action against the reformers who aimed at getting rid of the taboo on marrying a deceased wife's sister. Such a marriage in his view was 'an act of sexual vice'; it was 'incestuous and unlawful' according to the canons of the Church. Himself unmarried, he wrote off adultery as no less a crime than murder or theft, and considered a man who divorced his unfaithful wife to be 'an accomplice in her adultery'.

The conventions of the day were almost as rigid a straitjacket as the law and the Church. The stiffness can be felt in the way Lady

Stanley of Alderley (who died in 1863) always referred to her husband – even when writing or speaking to members of her own family – as 'my Lord'. Unmarried girls, of course, were heavily loaded with restrictions; wherever they went their chaperon had to go too. To walk or go in a cab alone was out of the question. One cautious father gave instructions that his young daughters when they were out with their governess must cross to the other side of St James's Street to avoid walking past the famous bow window of White's, where they could see and be seen by all the dandies. Sometimes a female escort was not enough: a young lady travelling with her maid needed a manservant as well, to avoid the risk of being 'squeezed' in an omnibus. Even when an engagement had been announced, there were still some young couples who were not allowed to be left on their own together.

The men were freer, of course. The Queen told Lord Melbourne that she could never marry a man who had loved another woman. Her Prime Minister did not hesitate to disagree with her. One affair before marriage was nothing, and should be permitted to anyone, he considered. Well, said the Queen, for her part she was very pleased that Prince Albert did not pay attention to other women. Once again Lord Melbourne gave a straight answer. 'That sort of thing is apt to come later,' he said.

For a young girl, even if she was at home in that world, it could be daunting to marry into one of the great families. In 1894 Lord Edward Cecil's fiancée received a letter wishing her well in her marriage. 'It is such a delicious family (I think) to marry into,' it read. 'Such a large wholesome free life about it – in spite of orthodoxy. You'll find it rather like going to a nice public school when you go among them.' She was taken to Hatfield, the Salisbury family home, on a day when the family were away. In a phaeton drawn by a pair of splendid horses they drove round the park and down to the vineyard where the peacocks were. An outrider cantered alongside to open the gates.

As the social field gradually widened to allow Americans and other 'outsiders' to marry into the aristrocracy, the culture-shock must have been very sharp. Duties as well as privileges were involved, restrictions as well as freedoms. At Hatfield it was taken for granted that sons and daughters-in-law should spend several months there every year with Lord and Lady Salisbury as well as going to France during the summer holidays and turning up at dinner parties in Arlington Street, their London home, when they were needed. And there were other intrusions on a young couple's privacy and quiet home life. Many spent their first years together in a rented town house or even as the guests of one or other family, fitting in to the parental pattern of life without a chance of being on their own. The future second Marquess of Westminster, Richard Grosvenor, and his wife Elizabeth both belonged to the wealthiest and most eminent families of the day, and when they married were given an income of £100,000 each as well as large country estates and a palatial London house. Yet during the first years of their married life – and thirteen children were born to them between 1820 and 1840 – their only country home was with the Grosvenor parents at Eaton Hall in Cheshire. Not until 1831 was it suggested that they might like to have their own home in Dorset, and even then they were expected to pay regular visits to Eaton Hall.

It is also surprising to find how often newly-married couples had difficulties in making ends meet. When Lord William Russell married in 1817 he was serving on the Duke of Wellington's staff. His father, the sixth Duke of Bedford, offered to pay any debts he had and to buy him a Lieutenant-Colonelcy, and he also gave him some carefully thought out financial advice. He would do well, he said, to rent a furnished house near his headquarters. 'You will not be rich, but with prudence and economy, you will have *de quoi vivre*,' he wrote. They would not need an expensive honeymoon, as they could stay as long as they liked at Woburn after the wedding. During the next few years when they were living on half-pay in London, they were often glad to make use of the rooms that were always ready for them there. Even so, shortage of funds was one of the reasons that decided them to join the growing number of English families who found life cheaper and more enjoyable on the continent.

A society marriage was assessed according to the rank and wealth involved, and the Queen and her court endorsed those values. When one of the Grosvenor girls became engaged to Prince Adolphus of Teck, the Queen was enthusiastic about the match. 'It is a vy *good* connection,' she wrote, adding an important rider, '& she will doubtless be well off.' Rank was even more important than wealth. When debutantes were presented to the Queen at one of her 'Drawing Rooms' at the Palace, daughters of peers were honoured with a royal kiss while the other girls were allowed to touch the

Caroline Norton, one of Lord Melbourne's devoted women friends. A drawing by Queen Victoria's official portrait painter, Sir George Hayter.

'Susanna and the Elders': Queen Victoria with Lord Melbourne and Lord Grey in the year of her accession.

Queen's hand with their lips. There were other grades of royal favour too: widowers who had remarried were received by the Queen, but widows who had taken a second husband could not expect the same privilege. Nor, of course, could women – like Lady Holland – who had been divorced.

For the most part such invidious distinctions were accepted, but sometimes they were questioned. When Lord Melbourne was dangerously ill, Caroline Norton, who had been at least his intimate friend – a charge of adultery was rejected in court – called to enquire after him, on several occasions in the company of her husband. A leader in *The Times* protested that it was only her social position that saved her from criticism in doing this. 'Countesses like Kings can do no wrong,' it thundered, 'and Marchionesses may visit when and where they please, and afterwards sit in judgment on the morning calls paid by the wife of a poor squire. In the one case it is the occupation of an idle hour, and in the other one of the principal proofs in a case of divorce!' Caroline was neither a countess nor a marchioness, so it was a rather silly protest; but it tells of a certain discontent that was felt at the freedom of behaviour enjoyed by the privileged classes.

Equally if not more unfair was the difference between the effect of the court case on Caroline Norton and on Melbourne. Against her the doors of society were firmly closed, at least for a time, and her children were not allowed to live with her. Melbourne, on the other hand, was still welcomed by the hostesses of the day and, far from being disapproved of as a bad influence on the young, within a few years was enjoying a uniquely close relationship with the seventeen-year-old Queen, who has been seen to value his wordly-wise judgements on moral issues. It was a remarkable intimacy, for a time filling the foreground in each of their lives. The diarist Charles Greville analysed it shrewdly. 'The Queen's feelings are sexual though she does not know it,' he wrote. 'I have no doubt he is passionately fond of her as he might be of his daughter if he had one; and the more because he is a man with a capacity for loving without having anything in the world to love.' Melbourne, still handsome, attractive, witty, and well-informed, was then in his late fifties.

Greville took Caroline Norton's victimization as a matter of course. Although the case had resulted in 'a very triumphant acquittal' for Melbourne, there was, he said, 'a determination in many quarters to run down the woman. . . . Nobody ever imagined that She was a pattern of propriety and decorum, and the question was, not whether She was refined and scrupulous in her manners, but whether She was chaste in her conduct. . . . But such are the ways of the world; malignity must fasten upon something, and if the man escapes they have nothing left for it but to turn upon the woman.' It was a cool, masculine reaction, and a warmer sympathy for Caroline was shown by the Duchess of Sutherland, who made a public display of her attitude by driving in her barouche with her in Rotten Row at a time of day when everyone would see them together and, she hoped, follow her example in forgiving and befriending her. Caroline herself set to work indomitably to get the law changed, so that women who were separated or divorced might be allowed legal custody of their children. Her efforts and her writing did eventually achieve this as well as fairer property and wage-earning rights for married women.

The splendid ball given at Chiswick House in 1820 by the sixth Duke of Devonshire had something in common with the Duchess of Sutherland's drive in Rotten Row, for it too was aimed at persuading society to receive an offender back into its ranks. The Duke's cousin, Harriet, had recently married a German count after some flighty escapades and the birth of an illegitimate daughter. But kindly intentions were not enough. Mrs Arbuthnot, the Duke of Wellington's friend and another of the great diarists of the time, described the ball and explained that it was given because Harriet's father-in-law would not make a settlement on her unless she was once more 'received in society here'. The ball was 'very fine but not very gay,' Mrs Arbuthnot wrote, '& the occasion of its being given kept many persons away.' It was attended by 'most of the town', but as nobody spoke to poor Harriet, it did not seem likely that it would 'assist much in patching up her broken reputation'.

Harriet's fatal mistake had been that she was still unmarried when she had her baby. One or more illegitimate children could be forgiven when the mother was married; all the more so, of course, if she had already provided her husband with a son and heir. A wife would slip away discreetly to the continent with a sister or mother to keep her company, and several months later would come back to her family in England, bringing the new baby to join his or her legitimate half-siblings in a welcoming nursery like the famous Chatsworth one at the end of the eighteenth century. Tolerance

27

levels varied from family to family, from year to year. The genial and popular third Earl of Egremont sired a plentiful illegitimate brood at Petworth as well as in other nurseries; Lord Melbourne was almost certainly his son – and not unduly concerned at knowing this – but at least two of Egremont's Petworth children were lastingly haunted by the knowledge of their illegitimacy. The eldest son, George, married a strictly evangelical woman and after her death became a paranoid recluse; and the younger son, Henry, was condemned by the family for deserting his wife and living with his mistress at Cockermouth Castle, in Cumberland, another family home. Local society refused to open their doors to them until the family led the way, so they too had no escape from their lonely, remote partnership.

The attitude of society to love and marriage fluctuated and varied as the century went on. Lady Charlotte Bury, who was Lady-in-Waiting to Princess Caroline, the Prince of Wales' estranged wife, wrote a diary which was scandalous and unreliable, but it describes the feelings of the day as well as uninhibited conversations with the Princess. 'Married love never lasts,' the Princess decided, 'dat is not in de nature.' But her Lady-in-Waiting thought it was worth risking, for if 'a married woman found herself obliged to resign the sweet illusions of passion, she had yet the sober consolations of esteem from others . . .; whereas, a woman who was a mistress was always in danger of losing her lover, and with him she lost everything.'

As for how a husband should react to his wife's infidelity, Lady Charlotte found it hard to be consistent in answering that question. Should he go to law? Or challenge his rival to a duel? Was it better perhaps for a man to accept 'a compensation in money for his wife's guilt' than to insist on 'the blood of the offender'? On the other hand, when Lady Charlotte put herself in the shoes of the injured husband she decided that 'nothing but fighting to the death would satisfy me; for how can *gold* be a compensation for wounded honour?' But perhaps after all, she felt, the noblest line for the wronged husband to take was that of Christian humility and forbearance, pardoning both his faithless wife and her guilty lover.

Lady Charlotte's diary dates from the first decades of the century. During its last years there was still as much insistence on chastity in unmarried girls, but extramarital affairs between married couples were an accepted feature of society life. Elinor Glyn, the novelist, a neighbour and close friend of the Countess of Warwick who was famous both for her liaison with the Prince of Wales (later Edward VII) and for her socialism, described the scene. It was, she said, 'quite normal in Society circles for a married woman to have a succession of illicit love affairs, during the intervals of which, if not simultaneously, intimate relations with her husband were resumed.' The love affairs took place and were encouraged during country house-parties, and certain agreed rules were observed. There was no touching in public, and no singling-out of possible partners until after dinner. At bedtime a rendezvous might be suggested or the servants would see that a discreet note was left on a certain breakfast-tray. The hostess would stage-manage things by sending couples on little walks through the park.

It was a perilous, inflammable scenario, and many of the actors and actresses were well-known, leading members of society, Parliament, even the royal family. Occasionally things got out of control and the Prime Minister, Lord Salisbury, was called upon to advise and adjudicate. His own way of life was very different and it is interesting to see what guidelines he had to offer. He wrote in his own hand to Lord Charles Beresford, who had been the lover of Lady Brooke, the future Countess of Warwick, but had left her and been replaced in her favours by the Prince of Wales. 'If you have stood in a certain relation to the anonymous lady,' Lord Salisbury wrote, 'you are consequently bound, according to our social laws, so far as you can help it, not to let that relation with you be a cause of injury or obloquy to her.' It must have been difficult for the straight-laced and straight-living old statesman to find the words which would guide the younger man, whose politics but not his morals were in line with his own. He reminded him of the *esprit de corps* of their caste. There was, he said, 'no point that the public opinion of our own class would take up more warmly' than the betrayal of a former lover.

Disraeli was another Tory Prime Minister who knew how to write about love and marriage. When in 1870 Princess Louise, the Queen's daughter, became engaged to the Marquess of Lorne, was it wisdom, the lessons of his own experience, or just a platitude that he sent to the Queen? 'There is no greater risk, perhaps, than matrimony,' he wrote, 'but there is nothing happier than a happy marriage.' He was certainly wrong, as has just been seen, in the married happiness he foresaw when the future Earl and Countess of

Warwick became engaged. The 'approaching event' seemed to him to possess 'every element of happiness . . . romance, youth, wealth, beauty and love, a lofty rank and an historic name to sustain and inspire'.

So it must have seemed, and in some cases so it was. But the coin had another side. A realistic assessment of upper-class wives at the end of the century was made by Mrs Gerald Paget, sister-in-law of Lord Charles Beresford who had been Lady Brooke's lover. 'We were bad cooks because it was coarse to take any interest in food; we were bad cows because nobody, for goodness sake, must breathe a word about the realities of motherhood. As cultivated courtesans, we practised upon other men the arts which had been taught us by our husbands.'

Everyday realities no less than outworn conventions throw their light on the lives and feelings of the past inhabitants of our much-visited great country houses.

2

Breaking the Rules

So many rules and taboos, backed up by religious training and considerations of property, inheritance and rank, inevitably threw up some notable rebels and mavericks. Victims too. At this distance it often seems that those whose feelings were strong enough to crash the conventions and face the consequences were perhaps more emotionally alive than their more conformist contemporaries.

Lord Byron, of course, was the great rule-breaker of his time – if not of all time. And he describes his feelings so willingly and entertainingly that is is impossible to resist quoting him. Although his earliest, very precocious loves had been for young girls, and his nurse went to bed with him when he was nine, the taboo of homosexuality was the first one he broke. It loomed large in the boarding-schools where the sons of country house families were sent, and it was not only the boys who indulged themselves. The headmaster of Harrow, a married man with a family, had to resign in 1859 because he was having an affair with one of the boys; and at Eton William Johnson, a brilliant master who became well-known as a poet – he changed his name to Cory – had romantic attachments to many of the boys, among them the future Prime Minister, Lord Rosebery, and William Wood, the future Viscount Halifax.

Byron never forgot his schoolboy loves. The most lasting of these was for Lord Clare, one of those he called his 'juniors and favourites' at Harrow, and years later he wrote that even then he could never hear the name Clare 'without a beating of the heart'. At Cambridge he was also devoted to a chorister, two years younger than himself. When he died a few years later Byron mourned him as 'one whom I loved more than I ever loved a living thing, and one who, I believe, loved me to the last.' In the wider world after school and university Byron was always drawn to relationships that had the added spice of guilt and taboo. There were plenty of other tensions which pulled his marriage apart, but it is worth mentioning that at least one close friend of Annabella Byron believed that it was her discovery of his homosexuality, quite apart from his aggressiveness and his incestuous relationship with his half-sister Augusta, that was the main cause of their break-up.

The upper-class attitude to homosexuality can be judged by the very different experiences of two Prime Ministers. Just before Queen Victoria came to the throne Lord Melbourne had survived two mud-slinging lawsuits, with angry accusations of adultery both in court and in the Press; but in 1822 a blackmailer's trumped-up threat to provide evidence of his homosexuality drove Castlereagh to kill himself. Happily married and very attractive to women, he was so far from any tendency in that direction that his friendships with married women like Princess Lieven, the German ambassador's wife, and with Mrs Arbuthnot had struck sparks of jealousy in Lady Castlereagh. What actually happened is not quite clear, but it seems that a trap was laid for Castlereagh and he went into a brothel with a young man dressed as a woman. Other gang members followed them and added threats and accusations. Castlereagh, exhausted and ageing, was broken by his persecutors. A few days before he killed himself he told both King George IV and the Duke of Wellington what his accusers were saying. There are some tantalizing gaps in the story. Would the Prime Minister have laid himself open to blackmail merely by being known to have followed an ordinary prostitute into a brothel? Presumably not, or the gang would not have taken the trouble to dress one of them as a woman.

Homosexuality sometimes provided a curious bridge across the class gap. Just as the Gaiety girls and other actresses attracted and occasionally married aristocratic admirers, there was a parallel band of errand boys, stable hands and male prostitutes – known as 'renters' – whose rough charms were no doubt enhanced by the elegant drawing-rooms to which they were invited. Working partnerships provided opportunities for other homosexual relations, actual or merely suspected. One incongruous appointment that led to some awkward questions was that of Alfred Montgomery, maternal grandfather of Oscar Wilde's calamitous love, Lord Alfred Douglas. What qualifications had he, people asked, when he was only sixteen and given the job of private secretary to the Duke of Wellington's brother, Richard Marquess Wellesley? Was he perhaps Wellesley's illegitimate son? But other queries were prompted by a touch of effeminacy about the boy and by his having said – with some truth, it was to turn out, in his own case – that 'to marry is to enter Inferno'.

The middle years of the century threw up some sensational homosexual scandals which implicated members of the aristocracy. Lord Arthur Clinton, the fifth Duke of Newcastle's son, was a Member of Parliament who lived with two male transvestites, one of them commonly taken to be his wife. In 1870 they were arrested, but before the trial took place Clinton died of scarlet fever. The eighth Duke of Beaufort's family were also involved in a scandal. Two of the sons were homosexuals. Lord Henry Somerset married in 1872 and duly sired an heir, but because he was having an affair with a youth of seventeen his wife won her suit for separation and was granted custody of their child. However, she had brought matters into the open, so that her husband felt bound to leave the country and she, although innocent and wronged, never recovered socially from the implications of his offence. She was no longer received in society and had no chance of marrying again, so she went off to live in the country and devote herself to the care of alcoholics. Lord Henry lived in exile in Italy, writing (and publishing) poems to the young man in the case, although they never again met. He, for his part in the story, was packed off to New Zealand and there he died.

The Duke of Beaufort's third son, Lord Arthur Somerset, was one of the customers who frequented the notorious male brothel at 19 Cleveland Street. In 1889 there was a sensational case about the goings-on there, of interest here mainly because its outcome was influenced by the aristocratic rank of many of the men involved. Lord Arthur Somerset had been a Guards officer and had had a court appointment as assistant equerry to the Prince of Wales, who regarded him as a close friend. The scandal broke when the courageous but unwary editor of a local newspaper, the *North London Press*, reported that the Earl of Euston was among those who frequently visited the house. Lord Euston brought a case for criminal libel against the paper, won it and received an apology from the editor. Lord Arthur's name was also mentioned, and during the hearing of the case some of the boys from the brothel identified him as having had sex with them. The Lord Chancellor's influence, added to that of the Prince of Wales, saved him from prosecution and he too went to cover on the continent.

It was in the 1890s that the eighth Marquess of Queensberry's two sons provoked him to uncontrollable frenzy by giving him reason to suspect that they were active homosexuals. The old story of Alfred Montgomery, Lord Queensberry's father-in-law, suggested a parallel when his eldest son, Viscount Drumlanrig, was appointed secretary to the fifth Earl of Rosebery, then Secretary of State for Foreign Affairs in Gladstone's government. Once again people began to ask why Drumlanrig had been chosen for the job. Lord Rosebery had been happily married, but after his wife's early death damaging rumours about him began to circulate. He had a villa near Capri, already known as a homosexual centre, and Lord Queensberry was not the only one to have his suspicions. But for him suspicion meant action, violent action, and on one occasion he travelled to Germany, turned up at the hotel where Lord Rosebery was staying, and had to be restrained by the police from carrying out his threat that he would flog the elderly, eminent statesman. Once again it is not clear whether Queensberry had grounds for his suspicions, or what led to Drumlanrig's unexplained death when he was about to become engaged.

Lord Queensberry was a vindictive, stop-at-nothing psychopath whose outbursts reached extremes of embittered shrillness; they are worth playing back today as evidence that such animosity could be provoked in a man by the suspicion that his son was homosexual. 'If I thought the actual thing was true, and it became public property,' he shrieked at Lord Alfred Douglas in 1894 about his son's relationship with Oscar Wilde, 'I should be quite justified in shooting him at sight.' And when his suspicions had been confirmed and he had metaphorically shot at sight by delivering his fateful note to Wilde at his club, his words were even more agonized and agonizing in their echo of Lear and Cordelia. 'What could be keener pain than to have such a son as yourself fathered upon one?' he ranted.

After such a catalogue it is refreshing to remember that it was in fact possible for a nineteenth-century aristocrat to be a respected, unoffending homosexual. Lord Ronald Leveson-Gower, son of the second Duke of Sutherland, was one of Wilde's Oxford friends and is said to have inspired the character of Lord Henry Wooton in *Dorian Gray*. A Member of Parliament and a trustee of the National

Gallery, he lived openly with a man friend and seems to have achieved the rare distinction of sexually unorthodox respectability.

While male homosexuals attracted litigation and publicity, the lives of their feminine counterparts were befogged by modesty and reticence. It is well known that the Queen's unawareness of the existence of Lesbians led to a strange anomaly in the law, and she cannot have been the only one to be ignorant of those particular facts of life. There must have been many women of Lord Ronald's class who suppressed or sublimated their homosexuality, many who never fully admitted it, even to themselves. But one couple were exceptional in their self-awareness, honesty and courage. The passionately loving relationship of the much-discussed 'Ladies of Llangollen' began in the previous century, but flourished on into the nineteenth. The older, masculine-looking Lady Eleanor Butler played Rosalind to the Celia of Sarah Ponsonby, seventeen years younger, 'polite and effeminate, fair and beautiful'. That adroit commentator on the social world of his day, Prince Pueckler-Muskau, described the pair as 'the two most celebrated virgins in Europe'. Celebrated for what? For their romantic elopement, the charm of their conversation, the distinguished visitors and admirers they attracted to their remote Welsh hide-out, and for their remarkably happy and devoted relationship.

Was it partly the assurance that came to them from being daughters of the landed aristocracy that enabled them to live so openly and lovingly together? It had not saved them from strong opposition in their early days: Sarah had been locked away in her room, and outriders had been sent to the Irish port where the couple planned to embark for England and freedom. Both were in men's clothes, Sarah was then twenty-three and 'determined to live and die with Miss Butler' (as Eleanor then was). The geometrically half-timbered house in Denbighshire where they chose to live can still be seen. They were happy to retreat together into the wild and beautiful Vale of Llangollen, with its historic memories. The ruins of an ancient castle look down on the house from the hill behind it, and those of the thirteenth-century Cistercian Valle Crucis Abbey are not far away. Once they were launched on their fifty-year honeymoon at Llangollen they put aside their inhibitions. They slept together in a four-poster bed, and spent their days reading, drawing maps, and learning Latin and Italian. Together they welcomed a stream of visitors – among them the Duke of Wellington, Wordsworth, Southey, Darwin, and Scott. 'My beloved', 'My heart's darling', 'The Beloved of my Soul', 'The Delight of my Heart', 'The Joy of my Life' was how they referred to each other in letters to their friends. Their clothes were out of fashion as well as masculine, although they were displeased by the innuendoes implicit in a newspaper description of their appearance. 'Miss Butler is tall and masculine,' it read, 'she always wears a riding habit, hangs her hat with the air of a sportsman in the hall, and appears in all respects as a young man, if we except the petticoats which she still retains.' An acquaintance described them in their later years looking like two old men, dressed always 'in dark cloth habits with short skirts, high shirt collars, white cravats and men's hats, with their hair cut short.'

Although travellers went miles out of their way for the pleasure and privilege of meeting the Ladies of Llangollen, those who had only heard about them were incredulous and uncomprehending. Many agreed with the Princess of Wales in deciding that the couple must be mad. Lady Charlotte Bury had a knack of transcribing the Princess's curious English. 'I do dread being married to a lady friend,' she had said, with a backward glance at the miseries of her own marriage. 'Men are tyrants, mais de women – heaven help us! dey are vrais Neros over those they rule.' Lady Charlotte was inclined to agree. 'I never yet knew or heard,' she wrote, 'of female friendships answering completely to both parties, or enduring through life.' The Ladies of Llangollen were the exception that proved the rule.

Next to homosexuality in the list of nonconformities came incest. Here again no one could be more explicit than Byron, who passionately loved his half-sister Augusta and was happy to proclaim this in his diaries, his letters and the poems he wrote to her.

> For thee, my own sweet sister, in thy heart
> I know myself secure, as thou in mine;
> We were and are – I am, even as thou art –
> Beings who ne'er each other can resign;
> It is the same, together or apart,
> From life's commencement to its slow decline
> We are entwined: let death come slow or fast,
> The tie which bound the first endures the last!

'The two most celebrated virgins in Europe': Lady Eleanor Butler and
Miss Sarah Ponsonby in their later years at Llangollen.

Although Byron did not hesitate to affirm both in conversation and in verse that incest was no crime, public opinion strongly disagreed with him. A warning came from his close friend, Lady Melbourne – herself by no means a prude – when Byron planned to travel abroad with Augusta Leigh. (She was married by then.) 'You are on the brink of a precipice,' Lady Melbourne warned him, 'and if you do not retreat, you are lost for ever – it is a crime for which there is no salvation in this world, whatever there may be in the next.' If Byron's relationship with Augusta were known, even if (as Augusta asserted) they had not slept together after his marriage, their reputations and social acceptability would be lost for ever. It was a nightmare tangle. Byron enjoyed telling his wife, Annabella, that Augusta was 'the least selfish & gentlest creature in being, & more attached to me than any one in existence can be'. Annabella and Augusta admired and sympathized with each other until Annabella felt herself to be unforgivably wronged by Augusta, mainly because Byron made comparisons in Augusta's favour, sadistically proving to Annabella that he was well acquainted with Augusta's under-clothing and her menstrual periods. Augusta's reputation for a time depended on the discretion of Annabella, who after her separation from Byron was tortured by his threat that he could and would take their daughter from her and put her in Augusta's care.

Was this legally possible? Annabella was advised that only by offering to take his wife back could Byron regain custody of their child; but it was a terrifying threat, and the need to prove that Augusta was not a fit person to take charge of another woman's child prompted Annabella's attacks. However strongly she might suspect – or even know for sure about – Byron's incest, as his wife, Annabella could not give her evidence in court. The only charge against him would be one of 'brutally indecent conduct and language'. Certain though she was that public opinion would be on her side, it would be a death-blow to her, Annabella said, to have to speak in public about these things. Byron was unmoved by the world's disapproval. When people at a party turned their backs on him and Augusta he was impenitent and proclaimed this in 'Stanzas to Augusta':

> Still may thy spirit dwell on mine,
>   And teach it what to brave or brook –
> There's more in one soft word of thine
>   Than in the world's defied rebuke.

38

If only neither of them had married, he wrote to Augusta, they could have lived single and happy lives 'as old maids and bachelors' or as a nun and a monk. It is an unconvincing image. Byron in his time played many parts, but never a monk was he.

Incest in his family did not end with Byron's death in 1824. He was almost certainly the father of Augusta's second daughter, Medora, who when she was seventeen was seduced by her sister's husband and had two children by him. Henry Trevanion had married Georgiana Leigh in 1826, and three years later when their third child was expected, Augusta sent Medora to live with them and continue her education under Trevanion's supervision. That is one way of describing what in fact happened. Georgiana went out of her way to leave her husband and sister alone together, and for a time accepted Medora's consequent pregnancies and their *ménage à trois*. When eventually she decided to divorce her husband, the law of the land stood in her way: the Ecclesiastical Court dismissed her suit because there was such clear evidence of collusion.

Incestuous relations between parent and child were likelier to occur in crowded working-class tenements than in the spacious, liberally bedroomed great country houses. But a way of life which encouraged young women to marry and have their children when they were very young, and then freed them from the wear and tear of strenuous activity, had its logical outcome in some passionate feelings of adolescent sons for their still beautiful and young mothers. In the middle years of the century two sons of the Earl of Westmorland wrote amorously tender letters to their mother; one of them sent a tribute in loving verse every year on her birthday. His brother-in-law was so closely attached to his own sister that he pined away after she died. She had married, but no one meant as much to her as her brother. Much though she loved her husband, she wrote to her brother, 'I don't think anything can be the "all over" thing you are to me.'

Bigamy crops up in the law reports and the novels of the century as it did occasionally in real life. A dukedom and a great inheritance were at stake in 1838, when an action for libel was brought against a weekly paper which suggested that the Marquess of Blandford, heir to the Duke of Marlborough, had already been married at the time of his wedding in 1819. If this were so, the Marchioness's children would be illegitimate and the dukedom and the estates – because an Act of Parliament from the time of the first Duke of Marlborough allowed them to pass to a daughter, if there were no son – would be inherited by a girl who had been born in 1818. The story told by *The Satirist or the Censor of the Times* was that Blandford had gone through a mock marriage ceremony in 1817 with the girl he was then living with, Miss Susanna Law. Twenty years later, in 1838, at the time of the libel action, Blandford admitted this. It seems that he staged the ceremony to take place in her father's house, where they were married by Blandford's brother, an Army officer who pretended to be a clergyman. Blandford persuaded Susanna that the marriage must be kept secret for a while, but by the time their daughter was born she realized what had happened and pressed for matters to be righted. Scottish law, with its easier conditions, provided a loophole, and Blandford suggested that they should go with the baby to Scotland and be married there. They lived together in Edinburgh, as they had in London, as Captain and Mrs Lawson. The legal crux of the case was whether they had at that time been generally accepted as a married couple; the court, while accepting Susanna's account, established the Marchioness as Blandford's legal wife and her son as heir to Blenheim and the dukedom.

The Seventh Commandment was the rule of the game which the nineteenth-century English aristocracy – like many others – found hardest to follow and most often broke. Because usually they did so with panache and flamboyance, often taking flight to the continent for both the escapades and their consequences, the European view of English upper-class behaviour tended to agree with the one mentioned by Charles Greville. The Germans, he said, considered society in England 'to the last degree profligate and unprincipled'.

The Palace came in for some of the blame, if it did not actually lead the way. King George III's sons had hardly been models of chastity, and for the last nine years of his life Lady Conyngham was known to be George IV's mistress. When William IV came to the throne the first Marquess of Anglesey advised him not to draw attention to his illegitimate offspring. Queen Victoria was, of course, virtue and propriety personified, but even in her time the Lord Chamberlain installed his mistress as housekeeper to Buckingham Palace; and Lord Uxbridge, who was Lord Chamberlain after being Lord Steward, also managed to billet his mistress there as a member of the domestic staff. Palmerston, when he was Secretary of State for Foreign Affairs, was in the habit of spending the night with one of his mistresses on visits to Windsor Castle, and he got into serious trouble when on one occasion he burst into her bedroom and found a different lady in occupation.

What could be expected of the rest of the population if the aristocracy set such a bad example? The writer Hannah More called for better behaviour in high places, writing on 'The Manners of the Great' and 'Strictures on the Modern System of Female Education with a View of the Principles and Conduct prevalent among Women of Rank and Fortune'. The Evangelical movement also urged stricter standards in homes great and small, pointing the way to the Victorian ideal of women as 'Angels in the Home', virtuous, submissive, and devoted. But there was always plenty for the moralists to pounce upon. Lord Tennyson, the Poet Laureate, was criticized for taking as the theme of 'The Idylls of the King' the adulterous love of Lancelot and Guinevere, but he endorsed the general disapproval of adultery and gave to King Arthur some strong lines condemning complaisant husbands:

> I hold that man the worst of public foes
> Who either for his own or children's sake,
> To save his blood from scandal, lets the wife
> Whom he knows false, abide and rule the house.

Throughout the century there were plenty, among the most eminent of both sexes, who failed to clear that fence. Probably the best-known instance was the Devonshire House tangle, when both the fifth Duke and his wife Georgiana had extramarital partners and children as well as a legitimate family. The Duke's mistress, Lady Elizabeth Foster, and the Duchess were also devoted to each other and the closeness of their *ménage à trois* gave rise to a curious query. Doubts about the paternity of children were common enough, but the mother's identity might be expected to be easy to establish in the days before test-tube fertilization. Not so, it seems. A letter written in 1817 contained the disturbing suggestion that Lady Elizabeth was the mother of the Duke's son and heir. By then she was the only one of the trio still alive, the doctor who had attended at the birth of the sixth Duke having contributed to the mystery by shooting himself. The writer of the letter noted that the story was 'said to be hushed up by a promise on the part of the Duke, that he will never *marry*, or pretend to present an heir'. He never did, but the story is now known to be a fabrication.

41

In spite of Hannah More and the Evangelicals, there was no shortage of extramarital affairs among the country house couples. The Countess of Oxford (whose family name was Harley) had so many lovers – Byron, half her age, was one of them – that her offspring were nicknamed 'the Harleian Miscellany'. The first Viscountess Melbourne's lovers included the Prince of Wales (later King George IV), who was believed to be the father of her youngest son, as well as the fifth Duke of Bedford and the third Earl of Egremont. She was the mother of William Lamb, who married Lady Caroline Ponsonby and was the famous Lord Melbourne who was Queen Victoria's first Prime Minister. Lady Melbourne's daughter Emily, Lord Cowper's wife, had a longstanding love affair with Palmerston which reached a tidy and happy conclusion when after her husband's death they married. It was said that the striking resemblance of many of her children to their stepfather was either not noticed or not mentioned. She was so fascinating that it was said that all the men were 'more or less in love with Emily Cowper'. She was certainly not Palmerston's only mistress. 'Lord Cupid', as he was called, was also the lover of the beautiful Countess of Jersey, whose husband explained that if he once began to fight duels to defend the honour of his wife he would find himself fighting every gentleman in town.

It was a comfortable, easy-going attitude that was shared by many husbands. Because they had no choice in the matter? Because they were lazy or did not mind much either way? Perhaps because they too liked to do as they pleased. Lady Holland wrote to her son about Viscountess Pollington, whose 'very wild and gay' behaviour her husband put down to 'excess of animal spirits'. He was, Lady Holland said, 'perfectly satisfied with her youthful *joie de vivre* and maintained that her "Boys", as she calls her troop of suitors, are merely her playfellows'.

And so *la ronde* spun on. Not only husbands and wives but lovers and mistresses too had to be tolerant, setting their sweethearts free with a good grace when the moment came. No one achieved this more generously and feelingly than the Countess of Bessborough, who for years had been the mistress and devoted correspondent of Lord Granville Leveson-Gower. He was twelve years younger than she was, brilliant, attractive and handsome, and both knew that one day he would marry. In 1809, when he was thirty-six, he became engaged to Lady Bessborough's niece, Lady Harriet Cavendish.

Augusta Leigh, Byron's half-sister:

My sister! my sweet sister! if a
  name
Dearer and purer were, it should
  be thine.

From a miniature painted in 1833 by
James Holmes.

Lady Caroline Lamb,
who had a flamboyant
affair with Byron. A
portrait painted by
John Hoppner, RA.

'This is a subject I can say nothing on,' she wrote to him; 'it is one of too immense consequence to me even to bear resting my thoughts upon it. I only know you are both very dear to me, and that I think I cannot be quite wretched at any thing that makes those I love so tenderly happy.' Such loving selflessness must always be rare. Other relationships ended in a hurly-burly of angry scenes and letters, with sometimes even a duel or a fee paid to a thug for his professional services in beating up a mistress's new love.

Dramatic scenes were also staged while a love affair was in full swing. Not many could compare with the sensational arrival in Byron's rooms of Lady Caroline Lamb, William Lamb's eccentric and bewitching young wife, in disguise which she then theatrically doffed to disclose herself fetchingly dressed as a page; or for that matter the gift of her pubic hair that she sent to Byron with a request for a swatch of his in return. As Byron cooled off, Caroline's exhibitionism broke all bounds. Lady Oxford was so afraid of her crazy jealousy that she did not dare show herself in London for fear of 'being dragged herself into some scene, and put in peril by the scissors or bodkin of the enemy'. Caroline's frantic longing for attention, for everyone to know how Byron had loved her, made her want to publish the letters and poems he had written her and inspired her to write a novel about their intrigue. *Glenarvon* was a *roman à clef*, published in 1816, which gave a distorted picture of the whole incident with virulent, easily recognizable caricatures of the main individuals she saw as her enemies, alongside genuine letters to her from Byron, including even the last one which begged her from then on to leave him in peace. Several similar novels were written at that time: Lady Melbourne was taken to be the prototype of Lady Besford in the Duchess of Devonshire's novel, *The Sylph*; and *The Exclusives*, by Lady Charlotte Bury, introduced two thinly disguised characters based on Jane, the very publicly divorced wife of Lord Ellenborough, and her diplomatist lover, Prince Schwarzenberg. Then as now, adultery promised a good read and big sales.

And then as now a scandal involving a well-known public figure was sure to hit the headlines. The two that Lord Melbourne figured in – and survived – followed each other in close succession. In 1827, six years after his legal separation from his wife Caroline, he was appointed Chief Secretary for Ireland and there let himself be seen everywhere in company with Lady Brandon. There was no question of Melbourne having broken up a previously happy marriage: the husband in the case, the Reverend Lord Brandon, was often away from his wife and had been accused of being cruel as well as unfaithful to her. Thomas Creevey, another great letter and journal writer of the day, tells the story with characteristic punch. Lord Brandon 'got possession of a correspondence between his lady and Mr Secretary Lamb, which left no doubt to him or anyone else as to the nature of the connection between the young people'. Creevey was being sarcastic here, as Melbourne was forty-nine when his affair with Lady Brandon began. He enjoyed cutting people down to size. He went on to tell how Brandon wrote a letter to his wife announcing his discovery, adding that if she would 'exert her interest with Mr Lamb to procure him a bishopric' he would 'overlook her offence and return her the letters'. To this Lady Brandon replied with cool dignity that she would 'neither degrade herself nor Mr Lamb by making any such application; but thanks her lord and will give his letter immediately to Mr Lamb'. So in 1828 Lord Brandon charged Melbourne with having seduced his wife. Melbourne was acquitted, and for four more years the attachment continued. The most they seem to have attempted in the way of caution was for Lady Brandon to adopt an incognito when she visited London; there she went by the name of Mrs St John, and it was to that name that Melbourne addressed his letters. After they parted he paid her an allowance of £1,000 a year.

It was also in Dublin, before the end of his affair with Lady Brandon, that Melbourne began the relationship with Caroline Norton which – because on the whole that is where is seems to belong – will be described in a later chapter about Platonic friendships. Once again Melbourne was taken to court by an angry but unloved husband and once again he was acquitted. But there were outspoken suggestions in the Press as well as elsewhere that it had not been Melbourne's wish that the relationship should remain Platonic. Whatever the verdict, and whatever the truth may have been, such vicious attacks left behind them an imputation of adultery. Her brother insisted that the verdict had been 'as strong an acquittal of Caroline as the law can give', and that Norton had done all he could to 'harass, sting and humiliate his wife: it was most vindictive and unmanly'. Much of the Press was no less vindictive to Melbourne. One editorial asked: 'Is Lord Melbourne in that awkward predicament that, not to be convicted of adultery is to his lordship a triumph?' The paper accepted that he was innocent, but went on: 'we believe his innocence is not due either to *his* virtue, or *his* intention. It is indisputable that he laid close siege to another man's wife during five or six years . . . a passion most improper in an old man, burthened with high and responsible duties.' The newspaper's summing-up was that Mrs Norton's virtue was impregnable, her husband was wanting in caution and – a very harsh judgement, probably inspired by political partisanship – Lord Melbourne's behaviour was ridiculous and criminal. As Macbeth did not quite say of Lady Macbeth, poor Lord Melbourne 'should have lived hereafter'. Do we perhaps 'order this matter better' in the twentieth century?

The one point that met with universal agreement was that any touch of scandal damaged the woman in the case, while the man usually got off scot-free. Lady Bessborough, whose long love affair during the years of her marriage has just been mentioned, considered the question of adultery very seriously and objectively. She was convinced, she said, that 'the solemn vow given before God in Marriage' was a religious as well as a civil bond, and she was 'deeply impress'd with the great guilt of breaking it'. She also held that a breach of chastity ought to be discouraged in every possible way, partly for reasons of justice but also to save the woman concerned from the disastrous consequences which the man escaped but she did not.

Lady Bessborough was writing in the early years of the century. By its last years some people still held to the old ideas and tried to put them into practice, but many others – led by the Prince of Wales and his Marlborough House jet set – were known to have and to allow their partner a succession of passionate love affairs, often within the same social group. The famous country house Friday-to-Monday visits were designed to promote these goings-on, with auspicious bedroom alignments and little brass frames on each door to hold a card which announced the name of the guest in residence. A warning bell rang half an hour before breakfast so that the various pieces on the chessboard could make the appropriate moves back into their places.

Once again there were accepted rules of the game and once again these were sometimes broken. *Fin-de-siècle* behaviour reached a peak of crazy extravagance when Lady Brooke presented herself in the bedroom of Lady Charles Beresford, whose husband was then Lady Brooke's lover, and proceeded to tell her of their relationship and their plans to elope together. Lady Charles resolved to protect her husband's career (was that really all she resolved to protect?) from being destroyed through such an 'insane project' by taking him 'home with her on the spot'. But the insane project was not abandoned. Lord Charles attracted attention by publicly cold-shouldering his wife at a Newmarket race-meeting, though he later began to suspect that he was not Lady Brooke's only lover. Then when Lady Charles was expecting her husband's child, Lady Brooke considered that her lover had been guilty of unforgivable infidelity to her, and demanded that he should leave his wife at once and join her where she was staying, on the Riviera. The résumé is based on Lady Charles' telling of the tale, so there may well be another side to the picture. What is interesting is the fact that each of the ladies concerned was able to appeal for sympathy to a very eminent man. Lady Charles told her story of injured innocence in a letter to the Prime Minister, Lord Salisbury; and Lady Brooke told hers to the Prince of Wales. He showed his sympathy by receiving her kindly at Marlborough House and hoping that his friendship would be some consolation in her distress. 'Suddenly I saw him looking at me in a way all women understand,' Lady Brooke later recounted.

It was an extreme case, interesting to compare with the lives and loves of another society group of the day. The Souls, as their members were called, were a constellation of exceptionally bright stars, all of them (it seems) beautiful, intelligent, noble, witty, wealthy, loving, and loved. Although there was some overlapping between them and the Marlborough House set, their intellectual and artistic interests and achievements set them slightly apart. A glance at their roll-call finds many names that are still remembered today. Many of the men were or became eminent, amongst them a Prime Minister (A.J. Balfour) and a Viceroy of India (George Curzon). Adoring lovers orbited around the women of the group, both before and after their marriages. Their adoration was usually reciprocated, whether Platonically or sexually. The amorous pattern had an affinity with that of courtly love in mediaeval times; both allowed for fervent passions which dominated the lives of those involved – thousands of letters flew between the *inamorati* of the Souls – often without any hope of consummation. Lady

Desborough was described by another of the group, Lady Wenlock, as 'the most perfect type of womanhood' of their time. The great difference, she said, between her and the most brilliant women of their mothers' generation was that in earlier days it was not considered proper for a woman to be charming (did she mean seductive?) after marriage. Lady Desborough acknowledged her need for this freedom. She told Cynthia Asquith that she was 'not monogamous in the strict sense of the word', and 'had never been in love in the way which excluded other personal relationships. To be at her best with one man she must see a great many others.' Was it really enough just to 'see' them?

A comparison of the love affairs of the Souls and the Marlborough House set at the end of the century with those of their grandparents at its beginning points at once to another big difference: those early adulteries produced such crowds of illegitimate children. Take the third Earl of Egremont, for example, for most of his life one of the most celebrated of unmarried Don Juans – a kind of minister without portfolio for extramarital affairs. As well as the other children he sired, he had his own family at Petworth, where he married their mother privately, years afterwards, too late to make any of them legitimate. The marriage was not a success. They had been much happier before, when Lord Egremont's common-law wife was accepted as the lady of the house, without any of the usual slur and disrepute, by the many visiting painters and royal and other eminent guests who were entertained at Petworth. What Creevey called Lord Egremont's 'very numerous Stud' attracted wide interest, and accounts grew in the telling. One of Lady Bessborough's letters, written from Petworth in 1813, tells how she arrived there after staying in the Isle of Wight with Lady Spenser, who

> does, to be sure, contrive to believe the strangest stories. Nothing will persuade her that Ld. Egremont has not *forty three* Children who all live in the House with him and their respective Mothers; that the latter are usually kept in the background, but that when any quarrels arise, which few days pass without, each mother takes part with her Progeny, bursts into the drawing room, fight with each other, Ld. E., his Children, and I believe the Company, and make scenes worthy of Billingsgate or a Mad House.

Fanciful though this vision was, it is amusing as an indication of how the unconventinal Petworth set-up appeared to contemporaries. Creevey reported again on the family in 1828, when Lord Egremont was a vigorous seventy-seven, with an income of £100,000 a year. He was (as he could afford to be) very generous, giving each of his daughters £40,000 when she married. He was also open-handed to friends, to artists he had helped on their way, and to his mistresses who were, as Creevey put it, 'by no means the least costly customers'.

Allowances and bequests to mistresses were often made. The fifth Duke of Marlborough had several illegitimate children and he bequeathed all his personal belongings to 'Matilda Glover, now living in my family at Blenheim', who must have been one of his mistresses. At one time she lived in a lodge in the Park, and from there she used to drive to the Palace every day, clattering over Vanbrugh's splendid bridge in the gig the Duke had given her, taking their daughter to spend the day there and coming to fetch her home every evening. Three generations later his great-grandson the eighth Duke also remembered his mistress in his will, leaving £20,000 to Lady Campbell 'as a proof of my friendship and esteem'.

Another ducal mistress, Mrs Palmer of Curzon Street, was left a substantial sum to enable her to care for and educate the two children she had had by the fifth Duke of Bedford, who also left annuities to three women in Marylebone to whom he felt obliged. His brother the sixth Duke had at least two mistresses, and was believed for that reason to have taken a permissive line when his second wife – her stepson called her 'my father's worse half' – fell in love with the painter Edwin Landseer. The Duchess was forty-two and he was only twenty-one but their relationship lasted till her death, although when the Duke died she refused Landseer's proposal that they should marry.

Sometimes, however, there was no help for it and willy-nilly a marriage could not be avoided. One such 'extraordinary' match was described by Lady Bessborough. Lord Lansdowne, she said, was marrying Lady Giffard, 'a Vulgar Irish woman near fifty and larger than Mrs Fitzherbert (at least that is the account given of her)'. Then she adds the explanation. 'I suppose it is point d'honneur, for she has liv'd with him publickly as his Mistress for some years past.'

After such stories a reminder is needed that an extramarital relationship could be stronger and more lasting than many a marriage. One of these, at least one of the partners felt (both were Souls), ought in fact to have been a marriage. After May Lyttelton's death in 1875 Arthur Balfour never allowed himself to fall so deeply in love again. Eight years later Mary Wyndham, whose brother worked with Balfour, married Hugo Charteris, Viscount Elcho, and after the marriage the friendship between her and Balfour crescendoed into a passionate attachment. 'If only you had married me in '81!' she said to him years later. As it was, she had her husband, her children – for a time one more almost every year – and her friends, but she could not wrench herself away from Balfour. She could not live 'without a *certain love*', she declared, and she did not find this in her marriage. A.J.B. was devoted too but it was not the same for him. 'You care less! *feel* less!' she told him, although she appreciated that he loved her at least as much 'as a man can love a woman he has loved for ten years'. Balfour had been loved by many women in his time and he could not contemplate the upheaval of a divorce between Mary and the eleventh Earl of Wemyss (as he was by then), who was another colleague. He also had a distinguished political career, which was to take him finally to 10, Downing Street. 'Whether I have time for *Love* or not, I certainly have no time for Matrimony,' he said. Wilfred Blunt, an intimate friend and fellow Soul, assessed Balfour's sentiment as a *grande passion* and Mary Elcho's as a tenderness. 'But what their exact relation may be I cannot determine,' he wrote in his diary. He was not the only one to wonder, but scandal was avoided; it was an important point that 'all the house accepts the position as the most natural in the world.' Blunt felt that Balfour had been 'hardened by politics' and was probably by then a cynic in the affairs of the heart. He had kept their love affair within set limits, while she on her side remained faithful to Balfour, more deeply committed to him than to her husband, who accepted the status quo in return for her tolerance of his own infidelities.

Beatrice Webb was another onlooker who allowed herself to assess the Balfour-Elcho relationship. The 'beautiful-natured' Mary Elcho she saw as a 'neglected wife, devoted and tenderly-loved mother, and adored friend'; and the feelings of Balfour and Mary for each other (in words that now sound very Victorian) as 'good sound friendship, with just that touch of romantic regret that it could not have been more, that deepens sex feeling and makes such a relation akin to religious renunciation.' Balfour never had as close or lasting a relationship with any other woman. Did Lady Wemyss forget that, when long afterwards she wrote to him 'although you have only loved me a little, yet I must admit you have loved me long'? Years are perhaps easier to remember and to count than heartbeats.

Elopements call for some pages to themselves. The clatter of hooves, the twitter of gossip, and the miasma of damnation in the air gave them a glamour not often equalled today. Some were spur-of-the-moment infatuations, doomed to fizzle out and be regretted; others were either desperate escapes from a matrimonial trap set by dynastic fortune-hunters, or deeply felt but without the stamina to stand up to pressure from society and family. A few justified themselves by staying the course, sometimes even ending in a happy-ever-after marriage or switch-round of partners.

The loopholes provided by Scottish law sent many couples northwards, heading for Gretna Green, to be 'married across the anvil'. It was the classic – as well as romantic – escapade of under-age Romeos and Juliets whose marriages were blocked in England by parental vetoes. In 1840 the future eighth Marquess of Queensberry longed to marry nineteen-year-old Caroline Clayton, but her father refused his consent. Queensberry turned out to be a philandering, debt-ridden gambler, as unpromising a husband as his immediate descendants, and his prospective father-in-law had the best of reasons to keep him and his daughter apart. But they dashed off to Scotland and were married at Gretna Green. After that Sir Henry Clayton had to accept 'the Gretna Green Marchioness', as she was to enjoy being called, and the ceremony was repeated in London. Five years later the fifth Earl of Jersey's youngest daughter recalled Jane Austen's Lydia Bennet by eloping at Brighton with a dashing captain in the 11th Hussars. They caught each other's eye as they walked about the town and he made his advances by keeping watch on Lady Jersey's house through a 'sea spying glass' and by signalling from a nearby window. Once again the family were horrified, but the couple reached Gretna Green, were married and for good measure repeated the process in a London church.

Parental pressure could drive couples to elope. The Duchess of Gordon was hell-bent on making her daughter a duchess when she insisted on her accepting the fifth Duke of Manchester's proposal, so it was little more than poetic justice when the reluctant wife ran away with one of her footmen. And the seventh Duke of Beaufort's daughter, Lady Rose Somerset, was only seventeen when she too eloped with a soldier. Parents of susceptible girls could not lock up their daughters, but certain obvious risks could be avoided. That of having a young man – even when he was a clergyman – to teach the boys of a family that also included nubile girls became something of a bogey after the fourth Marquess of Londonderry's daughter, Adelaide, ran off with and married her brother's tutor, the Reverend Frederick Law, 'excellent Puseyite' though he was agreed to be.

Occasionally a runaway couple were pursued and landed safely back in the parental or marital nest before irrevocable damage – in the form of matrimony, public scandal, or impregnation – had been done. It was awkward when one of the two suffered a sea-change, as the second Lord Lucan did when he eloped with a married woman and afterwards married but later deserted her. One neatly stage-managed escape was that of Lady Florence Paget, who made a skilful get-away with Lord Hastings the day before she was to be married to somebody else. She set off on a last-minute shopping expedition and drove in her carriage to Marshall and Snelgrove's. There she stepped out, went into the shop by one entrance and walked through to another, where Lord Hastings was waiting for her. Together they went to nearby St George's, Hanover Square, and were married. It was a very different scenario from the fairy-tale adventure of Earl St Maur, the twelfth Duke of Somerset's son who, broken-hearted at being turned down by Lord Cowper's daughter, took his despair for a walk in Hyde Park, where he came across a young (and of course beautiful) kitchen maid who was weeping on one of the benches. He took her home, cared for and educated her, became her lover and the father of two of her children, but then unfortunately died before – very unusually – the Somersets accepted and welcomed her and her children into the family.

Perhaps what might be called 'a talent to elope' ran in the Paget family, for Lady Florence Paget's grandfather, the future first Marquess of Anglesey, was a key figure in one of the century's most celebrated double break-ups, which rang the changes on uncongenial first marriage, elopement, adultery, and divorce, ending up with two satisfactory second marriages. This time the elopement was no frivolous escapade. Henry Paget was a brilliant cavalry officer, son and heir to the Earl of Uxbridge, father of a happy family and the husband of Caroline, daughter of the fourth Earl of Jersey. Lady Charlotte Wellesley, with whom he fell passionately in love and eloped in 1808, was married to Wellington's brother, Henry Wellesley. She felt compelled to go off with Paget but was distraught at leaving her children – for ever, as she was sure it must be – and considered what she was doing to be unpardonably sinful. They went through an inevitable progression of strong mutual attraction, attempts to check this, discussions between Charlotte and her husband, and eventually secret meetings and corresponding. After Paget returned from campaigning in Spain they were drawn irresistibly together once again.

The scene now shifts to the Green Park, London – hardly a secluded meeting-place, it would seem – where Charlotte and Paget managed to walk alone together. Charlotte's footman was in attendance, following discreetly behind his mistress, but he was given instructions to leave them and not come back for an hour or two. Their feelings were stronger than their principles and their scruples, so they decided they must elope. When at last Charlotte's husband noticed her coolness towards him and understood its cause, he helped them by saying that either he or she must leave the house. The following day Charlotte went for her usual walk in the Park, ordered her footman again to leave her, took a hackney-coach and joined Paget in Mayfair lodgings. But she was far from happy. She loved Paget but she had wronged her husband after he had 'been kind to me to the greatest Degree'. Feelings are conditioned by the ethical tenets of the day, and Charlotte's are explained in a letter she wrote to her husband's close friend, Charles Arbuthnot. She could not be persuaded to go back to her unhappy husband and her beloved children:

> degraded and unprincipled as I must appear in the eyes of everybody, believe me I am not lost to all Sense of Honor which would forbid my returning to a husband I have quitted, to children I have abandoned.

She told him how she had struggled against 'this most criminal most atrocious attachment', how she felt unable, in spite of

Wellesley's entreaties, to go back to him after the 'iniquitous act' she had been guilty of with Lord Paget.

Meanwhile Paget was just as wretched. He is said to have hoped to get back to army service in Spain so that he might die in battle and bring to an end both his life and his 'guilty passion'. Drama and tragedy were in the air. Lord Uxbridge threatened to disinherit Paget and he wrote an impassioned plea to Charlotte:

> Dear Madam,
>   Let me on my knees implore you to listen to the prayer of an aged & perhaps dying Father, and to restore my Son to his distracted Family, which for ever will render me your Grateful and Faithful Servant.

Lord Uxbridge's language was cool in comparison with that of the rest of his family. They called Charlotte a 'nefarious damned Hell-hound', a *'maudite sorcière'* and 'the most wicked and profligate whore and liar that ever hell itself could or ever will produce'. It is hard to believe that two years after their elopement the thunder-clouds had all blown away and Charlotte and Paget, now married, were about to become parents of another family of six children.

3

Hearts, Heads, and Hormones

How did people actually feel? That is the most interesting as well as the most elusive aspect of the subject. Although ideas and behaviour change – even the last thirty years have seen a U-turn in these – fundamental emotions must surely remain constant. One problem is that the nineteenth century was such a reticent age; most of those who wrote diaries or intimate letters clamped into cautious silence about their sexual feelings and activities.

The archives of the great families house some honest and revealing accounts, many not yet published. There must be plenty more which would throw light on the subject. Novels and poetry provide some evidence but they cannot be used as primary sources, and as anything else they need (and have had) the whole stage to themselves. Another difficulty is that of arriving at a fair cross-section of evidence. All the material in this book either is or was believed to be true, but even first-hand accounts are subjective and consequently unreliable. And the spread of witnesses cannot help being uneven. Some people talk and write about themselves much more expansively than others. Nobody more so than Byron, of course. But he often wrote to dazzle, shock, or impress, and what he did write has been published and fully discussed elsewhere. So all that can be attempted is as fair and wide a choice of evidence as possible, sparing some sympathy on the way for future inquirers who may look back and try to understand love and marriage as they are today. At least the facts about the private lives of the nineteenth-century country house families were written down, by themselves or their biographers – not poured away in irrecoverable telephone conversations.

It is not easy today to imagine the stream of consciousness that would be triggered off by the mention of sex to the people who are the subject of this book. The men would have reacted very differently from the women, just as men's sexuality was considered to be very different from that – if it was even agreed that such a thing existed – experienced by women. One of the few pioneer investigators of the subject was William Acton, who worked for a time at the Female Venereal Hospital in Paris and in 1870 published a book about prostitution. He warned men of the weakening effects of sexual intercourse and advised intellectual married men in particular not to have sex more often than once every seven days. It was, he said, 'impossible to exaggerate the force' of male sexual desire, but he reported that women '(happily for them) are not very much troubled with sexual feelings of any kind. . . .The best mothers, wives, and managers of households, know little or nothing of sexual indulgence. Love of home, children, and domestic duties, are the only passions they feel.' The usual medical view was that any sexual impulses a woman might have remained dormant until awoken by her husband. Another view, shared by William Cobbett, was that women 'surrendered' each time they had sex. One unusually explicit writer on the subject compared a woman's first experience of sex to the opening of Pandora's box, which let loose a whirlwind of troubles. 'When once a female has tasted the sugar-stick,' he said rather unpleasantly, 'it is not long before she wants another taste.' So it was generally agreed that sexual desires, even in married couples, were to be ridden on a tight rein. Acton recommended achieving this by a pregnancy every other year or so. That meant a very crowded nursery for a woman who had married at eighteen and survived all those pleasureless copulations and agonizing childbirths.

There were heavy odds against men and women understanding their partner's feelings. Nowhere more, probably, than in the refined country house world, where many mothers and daughters as well as married couples found it difficult to discuss such things together. Violent, irrepressible passions, as well as evidence of venereal trouble, prompted questions and occasional explanations. When Lady Stanley's daughter Emmeline, at the age of thirty-five, was at last allowed by her parents to marry, her mother made an oblique reference to her emotional and physical needs. Emmeline and Albert Way had known each other for ten years, and the Stanleys had been against the match because there was madness in his family. It seems that Lady Stanley could not discuss her daughter's feelings with her husband but she could write about them to her daughter-in-law. 'We, women, all know better than any man can,' she wrote, 'how much there is in her character & constitution to make it very desirable she should marry, that is that she should meet with affection & be loved. But I would not *tell* a man, *any* man this for he would only see it in a gross light.' Would a man have disapproved of a young woman with feelings like those that men were known to have? Or welcomed the discovery, perhaps?

Lady Stanley's attitude to men by contrast highlights Caroline Lamb's blatant throwing of herself at Byron, Wellington, and Sir Godfrey Webster. Unbalanced as she always was, she put the blame on her husband. She told Lady Melbourne:

> William himself taught me to regard without horror all the forms & restraints I have laid so much stress on. He called me Prudish, said I was straightlaced – amused himself with instructing me in things I need never have heard or known & the disgust I at first felt to the world's wickedness I till then had never heard of in a very short time gave way to a general laxity of principles which, little by little, unperceived by you all, has been undermining the few virtues I ever possessed.

It sounds a disloyal and not very convincing self-defence to make to her mother-in-law, and it is hard to believe that Caroline had not been an apt and willing pupil.

Byron would certainly have initiated Caroline if William Lamb had not already done so. He burst on London society, it was said, like 'the comet of the year', causing hysterical reactions which cannot have been unlike recent crazes for the Beatles and Elvis Presley. All the women made up to him – so much so that it may well have been Annabella's unusually cool response which first attracted him to her. One of his admirers at that time, the future Lady William Russell, when she was in her eighties still remembered the force of Byron's diabolical charm.

> Lord Byron was Satan incarnate – talent – beauty – genius – wickedness – hypocrisy, vice – the quintessence, mind and body, of the cloven footed. But you looked in his face and listened to his

voice and read his poetry, and his club foot and cloven foot were overlooked.

There was no one like him. The Countess of Rosebery had a sufficiently cool nerve to run away with her brother-in-law, but she was overcome with terror when Byron came near her. Tom Moore told how once when Byron spoke to her in a doorway 'her heart beat so violently that she could hardly answer him'. People were fascinated by him without understanding why; and yet he had his shortcomings as well as his allurements. The Duchess of Devonshire, second wife of the fifth Duke, totted these up in 1812. Byron had, she said, 'a pale, sickly, but handsome countenance, a bad figure, animated and amusing conversation, and, in short, he is really the only topic almost of every conversation – the men jealous of him, the women of each other.'

The excitement and interest were pressurized by being confined within the bounds of a relatively small group of people who had few real personal contacts with non-members of their club. With very few exceptions it was unthinkable that the women should feel any sexual attraction to men from another class. Her breaking of that taboo was one of the reasons they despised George IV's estranged Queen Caroline; it was not, in the circumstances, her infidelity they held against her but the fact that her lover was her Italian courier. Mrs Arbuthnot was one of many who could not believe 'that any women of good conduct will condescend to notice a person who has been proved to have slept for five weeks with her menial servant.'

The insistence on feminine chastity and the greater sexual freedom allowed to the men led to a somewhat lop-sided situation. The great majority – all who could claim to be respectable – of the women had no experience of sex with any man except their husband; while the husbands, usually marrying later, started their wedded lives after adventures with prostitutes or other lower-class women, seldom with a woman from their own class. There must have been many fleeting love affairs between the gentlemen of the house and pretty housemaids, but few of these were recorded. One unusually frank account tells how the writer made love to a servant one morning in a privy before breakfast, and goes on to describe the special thrill such affairs had for him.

One of the charms, to me, of intrigues with servants is the odd, out of the way places and times in which I tail them – the hurried plugging, their intense enjoyment, and then the sensuous pleasure of seeing them at times, almost directly afterwards, at their household duties.

Such unorthodox and outspoken confessions of feelings are hard to find. But one thoughtful young man who attempted to understand his own and other people's sexuality was Viscount Amberley, father-to-be of Bertrand Russell. He noted in his journal in 1864 that he had been reading a book about 'Physical, Sexual & Natural Religion' whose author, a medical man, seemed to 'overturn all the moral theories on the subject of Chastity etc.' and protested against the 'utterly foolish delicacy which prevails on these most important subjects'. Lord Amberley did not merely think and read about sex. He arranged with a London police inspector to take him on a conducted tour of some of the 'low parts' of the town. It was a pioneer venture into mass-observation, only a few years later than Mayhew's in-depth study, and both the subject and the active way he set about his investigation were unusual in a member of his class at that time. Together Amberley and the inspector set off. They called in at 'dance rooms' where sailors and prostitutes spent evenings together, at houses where known thieves were to be found, at a brothel and at a refuge for women who had syphilis. Amberley was then twenty-one and noticed that the prostitutes they met did not accost him. 'They do not want you – they want the sailors,' the inspector explained.

His wife became pregnant immediately after their marriage, and Amberley was again inquiring and uninhibited in noting in his journal details of her labour, the birth, and the trouble she had in breast-feeding. He did all he could to help. 'In the evening before dinner I sucked a little,' he wrote, 'thinking it might do good, but I could not get much. Since I had to apply all my sucking power to get any milk, it is no wonder the infant found it too hard for him.' It is an unusual entry to find in a Victorian diary.

Another exceptionally frank journal was kept by Victoria Sackville-West, the future Lady Sackville and mother of Vita Sackville-West, who in 1890 married her first cousin, Lionel. Was it the mixture of ancient Sackville genes with those of her Spanish gypsy mother that filled her pages with such detailed recordings of their love-making? 'Baby' – the rather curious code-name they had for

Lionel's penis – figures in her account of their honeymoon like some third, ever-present and often insistently importunate character who shadowed them wherever they went. When they arrived at their Paris hotel Baby was 'in chronic condition' and so they had to go straight to bed. When they got back to Knole the idyll hardly changed. 'Every day the same thing, walking and sticking stamps on, reading, playing the piano, making love.' And a few days later: 'What a heavenly husband I have, and how different our love and union is from that of other couples.'

But it did not last. In spite of her husband's need to have a son to inherit Knole, the painful birth of Vita set Victoria firmly against having another child and it also made her – in spite of the 'precautions' they took – an anxious and unco-operative sexual partner. When she was forty-two she somehow obtained a directive from her doctor, advising that there should be no more sex between her and her husband. Lionel launched himself on a succession of affairs with women who belonged to his world and shared his interests in a way Victoria had never managed to do. She for her part attracted many brilliant, often eminent men whose feelings for her seem to have fallen little short of adoration. For years the foreground – in every sense of the word – of her life was taken up by the huge, lovable figure of Sir John Murray Scott – 'Seery', who had inherited the Hertford-Wallace wealth and treasures and was in his turn to give and bequeath so much to Lady Sackville. Vita took her mother's word for it that there had never been physical love between them; it has been suggested that, although loving and demanding love, Victoria lost her desire for sex – perhaps because she had experienced this so intensely with Lionel and now both had gone their separate ways.

So much for sex. What about love? The two have to be treated separately although it is hard to draw a line between them. There were plenty who considered that neither had a place in the lives of well-bred, respectable young ladies. Mary Glynne's father had died and it was her guardian, Lord Braybrooke, who drafted the letters for her and her sister to write, declining offers of marriage from various young men. When Mary insisted on refusing one eligible (but to her, unappealing) peer, her aunt gave her what she felt to be some necessary instruction on the subject.

Women are not like men, they cannot chuse, nor is it creditable

Victoria Sackville-West married her first cousin, Lionel, the future
third Lord Sackville, in 1890. Their only child, Vita, was born two
years later. The portrait is by Carolus Duran.

or lady-like to be what is called in love; I believe that few, very few, well-regulated minds ever have been and romantic attachment is confined to novels and novel-readers, the silly and numerous class of young persons ill-educated at home or brought up in boarding-schools.

Mary Glynne persisted in refusing the suitor she did not fancy, soon married Lord Lyttelton (whom she did), and proceeded to have a large family. And live happily ever after? Unfortunately those two last activities – even in the comparatively sheltered country house world – in the nineteenth century tended to cancel each other out. After having nine children and one miscarriage Mary was exhausted and was given some more advice – wise, this time, by her mother-in-law. 'If you *could* avoid beginning again *quite* immediately, it would be the making of you,' she suggested. But George Lyttelton was loving, virile, and younger than his wife, and a tenth and eleventh child both made their appearance in the Hagley nursery. At this point a serious warning was given – but to whom, one wonders? – that another pregnancy would put Mary's life at risk.

The Lytteltons were both devout. If they were not positively convinced that contraception was sinful, they must have been unskilled in what methods there then were. The suggestion was made that now perhaps they might each have a separate bedroom, but it seems they decided against this, for after a short pause a twelfth child was born and some months later Mary died, remembered and regretted for years by her devoted husband and children. She would doubtless have lived longer if she had followed her aunt's cool advice and had married without being 'what is called in love'. Her story suggests that she did not regret having done just the opposite.

Many parents, probably with the best intentions, pressed their daughters into marriages they did not want. Only the strongest-minded, the most unwilling, and those whose affections were already engaged elsewhere were likely to hold out. The fascinating, already much courted Emily Lamb described one such confrontation in a letter to her brother Frederick in 1803. Lord Kinnaird was being very assiduous but she could not give him any encouragement 'for I never could feign what I did not feel'. But still he would not be deterred, and requested another talk with Emily's mother, Lady

Melbourne, as well as yet one more with Emily. The one with Emily

> began worse than today's with a great many oaths on his part taking heaven & earth to witness that he could love only me. I endeavour'd to compose him and to explain the case, namely that I would love if I could but I could not & that my friendship he should have. . . . I plainly told him that I did not feel myself the least bound, & that I desired he would not feel so either.

Could anyone have handled the interview more sincerely, kindly, and firmly? Emily advised Kinnaird to give up hoping she would ever be his, for she 'never would marry unless it was to a man whom I loved better than all the world besides'. Two years later she married the handsome, rich Earl Cowper and for years during her marriage had a succession of affairs, including the lasting one with Palmerston, whom she eventually married.

Young women were often warned to beware of love, and mothers were advised to be especially careful what books they allowed their daughters to read. Lady Stanley wrote to her daughter-in-law about the novel she had been enjoying and had recommended to her girls. They should be on their guard, their grandmother wrote, against 'the all powerful influence of love, & love at first sight too, has a mischievous effect'. It was the young girls whose heads were turned by such romantic fancies; after the age of thirty or so, whether married or not, women were usually no longer tempted. The clever and attractive Emily Eden was only thirty-two when she wrote in 1829 to another unmarried friend that 'the remains of *youthful* interests' no longer disturbed her. 'Everything else is mended up again,' she went on to say, 'and for the life of me I cannot understand how I ever could have been so sentimental and foolish.' She had been looking at her old 'extract book' and found that what she had felt so deeply only a short time ago now threw her 'into fits of laughter. Calculate from that fact the horrid and complete extinction of sentiment that has taken place.' Today that seems an early age to settle for spinsterhood; at least Emily Eden's despised extract book provided her with copy for her witty and wordly-wise novels, *The Semi-detached House* and *The Semi-attached Couple*.

Opinions varied about love affairs. In the early years of the century Lady Charlotte Bury sorted them neatly into two categories. Lady Oxford's notoriously many 'intrigues' she wrote off as 'melancholy proofs of depravity'. Compassion could be felt for 'long attachments, even when not sanctioned by morality', but on the other hand 'the ephemeral fires of passion, intrigue, interest, and pleasure, are loathsome'. It was certainly a solid statement of one point of view.

There was also disagreement about the possibility of Platonic friendship between a man and a woman. Judgements on such things are almost bound to be subjective, and Byron – not surprisingly – was convinced that such relationships were impossible. And yet his own attachment to Lady Melbourne had cooled off into warm friendship. If she had been a few years younger she would have made a fool of him, Byron said, and he would have 'lost a valuable and most agreeable *friend*'. He remained certain that 'a mistress never is nor can be a friend. While you agree, you are lovers; and, when it is over, anything but friends.' It was on the whole a masculine attitude, though it was understood by Lady Bessborough, whose own experience entitled her to speak as authoritatively on the subject as anyone. She remained devoted to Lord Granville Leveson-Gower, who had been her lover, and to her niece Harriet who became his wife. 'I believe I could find no hour in the four and twenty, waking or *sleeping*,' she wrote to him soon after they became engaged, 'when my thoughts were not in some measure occupied with you.' But she had a clear view of the difference between a man's feelings and a woman's.

I am afraid that tho' a woman may feel pure, tender, devoted friendship for a man, without one other sentiment mingling with her affection, no man knows what friendship for a woman is. They are in love with them, and when that ceases . . . compassion and something like gratitude forms a sort of attachment, which grows fainter and fainter every day. . .

The Souls, as has been seen, found a way to change the pattern. Nearly all the women in the group were married, one of them explained, to a husband 'whom they loved and by whom they had children, but each had her friend who was a friend only'. This frustrating of men's feelings had the effect of increasing their intensity, and found an outlet in passionate letters – sometimes daily, sometimes twice a day – and poems. It was a dangerous dance. Another Soul, Wilfred Blunt, described how it went: 'Each woman shall have her man, but no man shall have his woman'.

Lady Desborough, a central figure in the group, had three planetary adorers orbiting around her at the same time. They corresponded in code, describing their feelings as if they were those of characters in a romantic novel. Perhaps one clue to the whole brilliant, unrepeatable phenomenon is the flavour of poetry and literature it had. One of Ettie Desborough's lovers loved her from the moment he met her until his death in old age. She also inspired passionate devotion in women friends, one of whom wrote to her telling of her own 'great love-friendship' of her life – with a young poet, whom she had never seen. But that, she said – certainly hitting on *le mot juste* – was 'immaterial'.

At this distance both men and women Souls seem almost too brilliant to be true. One of the most interesting and eminent was George Curzon, whose pen-portrait was drawn by the novelist Elinor Glyn. She and Curzon loved each other for years, although this was after the death of his first wife and when he was already middle-aged. 'He has always been loved by women, but he has never allowed any individual woman to have the slightest influence upon his life,' she said. He liked women as other men like fine horses or good wine, 'not as equal souls worthy of being seriously considered or trusted with the scrupulous sense of honour with which he would deal with a man'. It sounds as if Elinor Glyn had been hurt in her affair with Curzon, perhaps as if all women who had affairs with him would also be hurt. 'He is a most passionate physical lover,' her account went on, 'but so fastidious that no woman of the lower class has ever been able to attract him.' He could never love a woman 'with a supreme love'; she would always have to take a back seat in his life, and her best chance of happiness would be to take care never to oppose him. There was no chance of a Platonic relationship between Curzon and a woman friend, said Elinor Glyn; he was so attractive that sex would come into any woman's feelings for him. What a lot of Thames water had flown beneath Westminster Bridge since Emily Eden at thirty-two had been thrown into fits of laughter at the thought that in her youth she had been sentimental and foolish.

Curiously enough, feelings about marriage seem to have been coloured by the law of the land almost as much as by emotional and physical considerations. Aristocratic wives were more fortunate than middle- and lower-class women who, Friedrich Engels said, at worst were slaves, at best a head servant. But they still belonged – body and soul – to their husbands. Lady Stanley told her daughter Rosalind when she married that she must look after her complexion since that was now her husband's property. It was a wifely duty 'to be coquette' for her husband.

Stronger words than those were used. 'Legal prostitution' was a definition of marriage given by Mary Wollstonecraft, whose *Vindication of the Rights of Woman* asked a lot of important questions. But pioneer though she was, Mary Wollstonecraft – at least to begin with – agreed with the majority opinion that sexuality was an evil, for the most part forced upon women by men and justifiable only as a step towards parenthood. Her book reached a huge public at once. The then Lord Palmerston was told by his far from feminist wife that she had been reading it. 'So you must expect me to be very tenacious of my rights and privileges,' she teased.

On emotional grounds, too, marriage had its critics. Sir Francis Burdett saw it as 'the grave of love', and the Princess of Wales in 1810 spoke of her own experience as well as what she saw around her in court society when she declared that few husbands loved their wives. 'And I confess,' she added, 'the moment one is obliged to marry one person, it is enough to render them hateful.' Hers was an extreme, embittered point of view, but there was often a certain sadness in seeing lovely young girls married off before they were experienced enough to make such an important choice. When Lady Caroline Ponsonby became engaged, Lady Elizabeth Foster's son Augustus wrote that he could not imagine her married, as marriage was 'the first death of a woman. They must die twice, for I am sure all their friends, their male ones at least, receive a pang when they change character so completely.'

Girls who signed on for a lifetime with a man they had had little chance of getting to know were heartened by being assured that 'love would come'. And sometimes, improbably enough, it did. When George Lucy, owner of Charlecote, the splendid Elizabethan house with grounds that had been laid out by Capability Brown, proposed to the young Welsh heiress Mary Williams, she was in love with and was loved by another young man. But her father insisted on her accepting George Lucy, and she had been brought up to do as her parents told her. Two years later she met her first love at a ball. He saw that she was now married and rushed away in despair. Mary proceeded to tell her husband – it seems she had not done so before – about her past and present feelings. The conversation reads like a novelette. 'Now you hold my heart and soul,' Mary told George. 'But I must ever love and esteem one who was so dear to me, ere I ever saw you.' George answered in the same key. 'I have no jealous fears. I fully trust you, my dearest Mary,' he said.

One of the most honest accounts of a young wife's feelings soon after marriage comes in a novel, Emily Eden's *The Semi-attached Couple*. It tells how Lady Helen Eskdale married Lord Teviot, who was 'the great *parti* of the year', a Marquess with five country houses, a huge income, dazzling family diamonds, a yacht and 'the good looks of the poorest of younger brothers'. Lord Teviot had the additional advantage, always welcome in the hero of a novel, of having fallen in love with Lady Helen as soon as he set eyes on her. So they were married in sumptuous splendour, but after a while Helen began to ask herself whether she was happy.

She had accepted Lord Teviot on an acquaintance of very weeks, and that carried on solely in a ballroom or at breakfast. She knew that her sisters had married in the same way, and were very happy. No-one, not even her mother, had seemed to doubt for a moment that Lord Teviot's proposal was to be accepted.

But when they were in the country together her doubts began.

He was always quarrelling with her – at least, so she thought; but the truth was, that he was desperately in love, and she was not; that he was a man of strong feelings and exacting habits, and with considerable knowledge of the world; and that she was timid and gentle, unused to any violence of manner or language, and unequal to cope with it. He alarmed her, first with the eagerness with which he poured out his affection, and then by the bitterness of his reproaches because, as he averred, it was not returned.

She tried to satisfy him; but when he had frightened away her playfulness, he had deprived her of her greatest charm, and she herself felt that her manner became daily colder. . . . She wished that he loved her less, or would say less about it.

It is a brilliant exposé of problems which must have shipwrecked many couples of that time and class. How did its spinster author come to be so well-informed about the ways of husbands and wives? Perhaps Melbourne's friends were right in thinking that Emily Eden would have been the right wife for him.

So the experienced-bridegroom-innocent-bride syndrome had its problems, and there was something to be said for a husband too being young and inexperienced. Countess Russell felt that when her son John became engaged at the age of twenty-one to Kate Stanley. 'There is something to me very delightful in his marrying while heart and mind are fresh and innocent and unworldly, and I even add inexperienced – for I am not over-fond of experience,' she added. Was her attitude perhaps coloured by her own marriage, after doubts and a first refusal, to a widowed, forty-eight-year old statesman who already had four stepchildren as well as two daughters of his own?

The society marriage-market had its own laws of demand and supply, and feelings about these bubbled over during the middle years of the century in a delicious and little-known correspondence in *The Times*. It began with a letter to the Editor from 'seven Belgravian mothers' who took the trouble to make it clear that they were 'with one exception, noblewomen'. Their problem was that between them they had twenty-four daughters who were unmarried – 'in running' or 'on hand' were the trendy terms of the time – and so far not one of them had had 'an offer that any one of us mothers could have seriously entertained'. The girls had all been carefully schooled. 'To make them eligible as wives of high rank we spared no pains, no cost, no amount of careful study. They were carefully reared at our country seats in every principle that we, and religious governesses at high salaries, esteemed to be good.' That was the accepted vocational education of their time and class, which might be expected to make 'the first "season" a cautious training in that knowledge of evil which the good must cease to regard with surprise, but must not cease altogether to regret'.

So why was it, the Editor was asked, that after in some cases as many as seven seasons 'our dear girls are still at home'? In offering the market these desirable wives the seven Belgravia mothers were, they said, providing 'a supply of that which ought to be to the nobility of our day, what cotton is to Mnchester, but they had been forced to accept the unpleasant, indelicate, dreadful truth that "marriage in our set is voted a bore – is repudiated" '. They urged that a serious view should be taken of their daughters' plight. 'The "heirs" dance with them, flirt with them, dine with us, shoot our game, drink our claret, but they will not marry.' Why? Because just as Manchester soon found a serviceable substitute for cotton, so the eligible young noblemen were now less interested in Belgravian daughters than in the unmarried and relatively inexpensive charmers whom the letter referred to as 'pretty horse-breakers'. These provided all the joys of marriage – as well as a few others – and were easily accessible in the pleasant purlieus of Brompton and St John's Wood. 'The sin of it all!' the Belgravian mothers' letter ended.

It was answered by another to the Editor, this time from the 'Horsebreakers and Heartbreakers' in question, and it gave Belgravia plenty to think about. It told how one of them long ago when he was contemplating marriage had asked his 'soul's idol' what style of life she expected. Quite the humblest, she answered: 'Just a brougham and pair, a saddle-horse . . . a house in a quiet part of Belgravia, a cottage in the Isle of Wight, an occasional box at the opera.' Other girls listed similar requirements. It was because the daughters of the aristocracy were stupidly conditioned to expect their husbands to spend a fortune on them that so many men were turning instead to the pretty, less demanding horse-breakers.

Sometimes they too were demanding. They play leading parts in Harriette Wilson's gossipy *Memoirs*, which tell how her sister Amy, far gone in pregnancy, was disappointed in her hope of marrying the Duke of Argyll; and how her other sister Sophia was seduced when she was only thirteen by Viscount Deerhurst, the Earl of Coventry's heir, but succeeded in getting Lord Berwick to set her up in a fine London house and eventually to marry her. Phantasy, scandal, and truth are hard to disentangle in the *Memoirs*, whose name-dropping implicated many eminent men of the day – the Prince of Wales, Wellington, the eighth Duke of Devonshire, and Byron among them. But the world they tell of certainly existed, and is worth listening to as the flip-side of the lives described in contemporary diaries, letters, and serious biographies.

Occasionally the serious writers also mention the demi-monde. In 1826 London was very dull, Creevey complained; the 'only thing going on is at Ly. Tankerville's and a few other houses, where ladies of easy virtue meet every night, and as many dandies as the town can supply'. Some of those ladies were very bewitching, none more so (a generation later) than Catherine Walters, the famous 'Skittles', whose adorers included Wilfred Scawen Blunt and the

Marquess of Hartington – who set her up in a Mayfair home with servants, carriage and horses, and £2,000 a year. She was also given the accolade of social acceptance by having her portrait, by Landseer, prominently placed in the Royal Academy exhibition and by numbering the Prince of Wales and Gladstone among gentlemen friends who were glad to take tea with her.

An elegant, charming young woman like Skittles led a very different life from that of the thousands of prostitutes who shocked continental visitors by accosting them in the streets of central London, although they too had their customers from the country house families. Unlike their Parisian counterparts, they were not officially licensed or concentrated in specific areas, but they still had favourite 'beats' on the pavements of what were then known as Langham Place, the Quadrant, the City Road, the Peristyle of the Haymarket Theatre and the purlieus of the Lyceum. All convenient places for men from nearby Mayfair and Belgravia to meet with women from London's often desperately poor, squalid, and diseased underworld. Other meeting-places were in seemingly smart areas like St James's and the Burlington Arcade; 'accommodation houses' were to be found there in the upper floors and back rooms of elegant little millinery and glove shops which men were not embarrassed to be seen visiting. 'Night houses' and other 'houses of ill fame' were in rougher districts where there was less need to gloss over the nature of their trade. Byron was one of those who savoured the spice of excitement that was added to sex by squalor. 'I am buried in an abyss of sensuality,' he wrote to his friend Cam Hobhouse, 'I am given to Harlots, and live in a state of Concubinage. I am at the moment under a course of restoratives by Pearson's prescription for a debility occasioned by too frequent connection.'

Husbands naturally hoped to keep their wives uninformed about any disreputable relationships they had, but occasionally they were unlucky. Joseph Farington wrote in his diary how in 1806 General Clarke, who had married Lady Warwick, died suddenly at a house in Cleveland Street, where 'he was accustomed to visit a young person 2 or 3 times a week before He went home to dress for dinner.' He had been going there for some time but had never told them his name, which they had to discover from letters in his pocket. Farington, like most entertaining diarists, enjoyed recording the foibles of seemingly respectable personalities and he went

Catherine Walters, Lord Hartington's lovely 'Skittles'.

The Peristyle of the Haymarket Theatre was a favourite hunting-ground for prostitutes.

on to say that the General was nearly seventy and 'was in a *very particular situation* when he died.'

The first Earl of Uxbridge was another elderly gentleman who did not manage to keep his family in ignorance of his failings. He too formed an 'unfortunate connection' with an obscure young woman, and his son Charles wrote to his brother Arthur that their father fancied 'that she really loves his *person*'. The old man had taken a lot of persuading that this really could not be so; they eventually succeeded by urging him to imagine that a man of seventy-five whom they all knew could believe that a girl of twenty felt that way about him. 'If you did not laugh at him, should you not be disgusted?' Lord Uxbridge was asked. He was not yet seventy. The family backed up their case by reminding him that he might 'shortly expect to appear before the most awful Tribunal'. At last he was persuaded, and the girl was given an annuity of £300 and saw no more of her elderly admirer.

Virtue had won the day.

4

Dynastic Engineering

The whole structure of aristocratic inheritance was so firmly based on the choice of marriage partners that this called for very careful planning. Often it was the parents, having of course already made their own dynastic moves on the chessboard, who drew up the shortlist of eligibles if they did not actually make the final choice. From a distance their efforts suggest three very different activities: a game of cards played for high stakes by two opposing pairs of partners; an auction-room sale, electric with the suspense of waiting to see which bidder will land what valuable lot; and the cunning luring of a victim into its toils by some hungry insect. Simply and spontaneously falling in love and lightheartedly deciding to get married figure less often than might be expected in the country house archives.

It was one of the many subjects the Queen discussed with Lord Melbourne. He told her that people often forced their daughters into a marriage, and that he 'knew many girls would obey, if their Parents told them it was for their best, and for their happiness'. Sometimes it was the opposite way round, and the parents who said 'No' to a couple of lovers; in several cases they insisted on a moratorium – six months or a year – to see how serious they were. The convention by which a young man asked parents for permission to 'pay his respects' to their daughter put the ball clearly in their court, but outmanoeuvring was sometimes possible. The domineering Countess of Carlisle told her daughter Dorothy that to save her the 'terrible embarrassment of being proposed to' she had refused several young men who had asked if they might 'pay their addresses' to her, but Dorothy was sufficiently independent to insist on interviewing all future applicants herself. It was only when a man was about to propose, Lady Carlisle held, that a girl should ask herself whether she would like to marry him or not; and she also maintained that there should be no friendship or subsequent meetings with a suitor whose proposal had been refused. When Dorothy eventually did become engaged, her mother was so angry at the news that she cursed her and her future husband and children, and for ten months they never met. But the Countess of Carlisle was an exceptional, eccentric woman.

Other parents insisted on obedience more gently, if no less arbitrarily. Mary Williams' conversation with her husband about the man she had loved before their marriage has been described in the last chapter. She had begged her father not to make her marry George Lucy, but he would not listen to her tears and her pleas. And George Lucy was evidently not discouraged. He put a beautiful turquoise ring on her finger and Mary, weeping, ran to tell her mother. Once again Mary's account, written in her old age, is more like fiction than fact. 'My sweet Mary, love will come when you know all of Mr Lucy's good qualities,' her mother comforted her. Old and widowed as she was when she wrote her story, Mary remembered how she had felt. 'I often communed with my heart and strove to forget how I had loved and been loved, and then at last my whole life became as fondly devoted to my husband as if he had been the object of my earliest affection.'

Sometimes parents were so active in marriage planning that it seems that it was they who did the wooing, and they did not always do it well. In 1800 Thomas Estcourt, of Estcourt in Gloucestershire, wanted to marry Miss Sutton of New Park. Did he tell her so? Or write to her? Or, more cautiously, write to her father? No. The first move was made by his own father, who wrote to Miss Sutton's father to tell him how much his son Thomas admired his daughter. Mr Sutton's reply might have been written by Jane Austen's Mr Bennet.

I confess, my Dear Estcourt, you have drawn so flattering a Portrait of my Daughter as almost strikes me dumb, and makes me seriously fear that her simple and modest Virtues will place her at a considerable distance from the high Opinion you entertain of her, and consequently may subject your Son to future disappointment.

That was written in 1799, and evidently the affair survived Mr Estcourt's eulogies, as other letters followed and by January 1800 Thomas was writing to Miss Sutton herself. She was either very cautious and correct, or very much under her mother's thumb, as when Thomas asked her permission to 'address a few lines to her upon a most interesting subject', she agreed but requested that his letter 'should pass through her mother's hands'. It was Mrs Sutton who sent Thomas her daughter's answer – did she help to draft it? Or merely read it through to vet it? – so it was Mrs Sutton to whom Thomas wrote to say how happy he was.

> Ten thousand thanks to you my dear Madam for making me the happiest of mankind, in conveying to me Miss Sutton's permission to hope that the sentiments of my last letter were not displeasing to her. . . . I feel the most exquisite pleasure in the prospect that she allows me to look forward to, that a time may come when it will be my Duty as well as my most earnest wish to study and to gratify every motion of her Heart.

The Estcourts were *petite noblesse*, not the kind of people whose correspondence gets published. It is their ordinariness that makes their letters interesting. Mr Sutton's comments on his future son-in-law's letter would also be worth hearing.

Even in those days of obedient children and authoritarian parents, most loving fathers and mothers allowed a marriage unless they felt there were strong arguments against it. Lord Lyttelton told his sons in plenty of time that he would not object to any reasonable choice of wife they might make, by mentioning this in the affectionate letter he gave to each of them on first going off to boarding-school. After warning them against 'the temptations of growing manhood' he added: 'I shall never refuse my consent to your marrying any one of whom you have a real affection and who is of good character and not wholly unsuitable in rank.' Such things depended, of course, on family circumstances. Lady Caroline Capel had a lot of daughters and a husband who had gambled away so much of their money that to keep together and avoid bankruptcy the family settled in Brussels, where life was cheaper and officers were plentiful, the year before the battle of Waterloo. When one daughter refused an offer from a man who seemed to be an acceptable suitor, her mother explained to the girl's grandmother that it had been her own decision. Parents had a right to veto if a man were really unsuitable, she wrote, 'but I am afraid of *persuasion* because if the thing did not turn out happily I could never forgive myself.'

One young man who was already a Member of Parliament and launched on a distinguished political career reacted with exceptional forbearance when it seemed likely that there would be family objections to the girl of his choice. Lord Derby's archives at Knowsley include an affectionate letter, written to his father in January, 1824, by Edward Stanley, grandson of the twelfth Earl. 'One day this year on coming into the Knutsford Ballroom,' he reminded him, 'you cautioned me that my attentions to Miss Emma Wilbraham had been remarked, and that I ought to be cautious, *if I had no serious intentions.*' He had avoided giving a direct answer at the time, although he had already been well aware of his feelings. Now, however, he was sure, and he was therefore writing to ask for his father's 'sanction'. He assured him that no wife he might choose for his son could have 'more sound religious principles, a better temper, clearer sense, or more unaffected purity and excellence with a warmer and more affectionate heart'.

He had not yet told Miss Wilbraham that he loved her, he said, and did not know whether she suspected this. Her father was soon to be created the first Baron Skelmersdale, but young Stanley knew that his grandfather's prejudices against the Wilbraham family were so 'deep-rooted and violent' that there was no hope of overcoming them. He was devoted to the old man, who was then seventy-two, and the letter shows no sign of any resentment at the happiness of two young people being obstructed by someone who – as he and his father well knew and this chapter will later describe – had himself known what it was to have to wait for years before he could marry the woman of his choice. Today his account of his predicament seems remarkably compliant and patient.

> I would not *insult* a woman I loved by proposing to her to become a member of a family where she would not be received as a daughter, and might be exposed to neglect and almost insult. Without my grandfather's consent it is impossible I should marry and if I thought that consent were to be given, as I fear it would be, if at all, coldly, and more than reluctantly – if I thought that it would break off the terms of attachment and kindness upon

which I have always lived with my grandfather, and always hope to live – dearly as I love Emma Wilbraham, I feel that I could and would bow to his prejudices, and, once convinced of her affection. . .would wait for an event which in the course of nature cannot be very far distant, and when my happiness would not wound the feelings of any one whom I dearly love and respect.

They were both still very young, he said – he was then twenty-five – and he would even welcome the need to wait, as it would give Miss Wilbraham the opportunity 'by a more enlarged acquaintance – of judging of her own heart'. All he asked of his father at present was his permission to write to Mrs Wilbraham, telling her of his feelings and his circumstances. Her daughter was to be quite free to make her own decision. It sounds as if he had no doubts about what that would be. Could he have been quite so dutiful and submissive if there had been a real danger of losing Emma? At all events, his patience was rewarded and the following year the couple were married. It was just as well they did not wait for nature to take its course, as old Lord Derby lived for ten more years.

Sometimes confessions and explanations had to be made. When Lord Granville Leveson-Gower became engaged to Lady Harriet Cavendish after his long and loving attachment to her mother's sister, the Countess of Bessborough, the situation was known and understood y everyone concerned but it still had to be discussed. He wrote to Lady Bessborough that he had spoken to his future father-in-law, the Duke, of his 'former follies, of which he was not ignorant, but which I did not *intend* to persevere in', and that he had also had a 'very open conversation' with Harriet.

Parents found many ways of promoting or discouraging their children's marriages. Boys were sent abroad to travel if they seemed likely to form an undesirable attachment. One piece of dynastic planning described in Joseph Farington's diary worked out well although it sounds dangerous. He tells how William, fourth Earl of Inchiquin, had no son, only two daughters, the elder of whom was deaf and dumb. He sent for his nephew, Lord Thomond, when he was still very young and suggested he should marry the girl. He agreed, they lived happily together, and eventually Thomond inherited his uncle's title. A more ambitious venture was attempted by Frederick, fourth Earl of Bristol, who was also Bishop of Derry.

He wrote to his daughter about his plans for his eldest surviving son, Frederick. If he had any other attachment he would not stand in their way, he said; he would not even cut his allowance. But he had set his heart on a 'beautiful, elegant, important, and interesting object' as the bride for his son. The lady in question was the Comtesse de la Marche, daughter of King Friedrich Wilhelm II of Prussia. He explained the reasons for his choice.

> She would bring into our family £5000 a year, besides a Principality in Germany, an English Dukedom for Frederick or me, which the King of Prussia is determined to obtain in case the marriage takes place, a perpetual relationship with both the Princess of Wales and her children, as also with the Duchess of York and her progeny.

That was not all. There were national as well as personal advantages concerned, and the Prussian King was so keen on the match that the Bishop felt sure he would be ready to double his daughter's dowry. If Frederick was thinking of a love match, 'the examples he has before his eyes in and within his own family ought fully to determine him against. . . so ominous a lottery, so pregnant with blanks, so improbable a success.' Before he made his decision he should carefully 'weigh all we offer to his ambition, his ease, his comfort, his taste, and his pocket'.

The Bishop's sermon was not quite finished there. He drew up a double-entry account of the pros and cons of the match for his son to add up. On the left he put the assets which would come of following his father's advice; on the right what lay ahead for Frederick if he decided to go his own way:

On my side	On his side
£5000 a year down	No fortune
£5000 a year in reversion	Wife and children beggars for want of settlement.
An English Dukedom, which the King pledges to obtain	No connexion.
Royal connexion – Princess of Wales, and Duchess of York	A love match, like all others for four generations before him.

The Bishop's unspiritual machinations were disappointed, however, and two years later Frederick married the daughter of an Irish peer.

It was not every son – or daughter, for that matter – who managed to stand out against parental pressure. The Marquess of Hartington's passion for Skittles has already been mentioned. He longed to marry her and asked for his father's permission. But the seventh Duke of Devonshire refused this, giving as his reason the fact that Skittles had epileptic fits. No doubt he also felt that the young daughter of a Liverpool sea-captain, who was known to have become Lord Fitzwilliam's mistress when she was sixteen, was not the girl to be the next Duchess of Devonshire. As one Marquess of Blandford was to say when a similar decision had to be made, 'Mistress, yes; but future Duchess of Marlborough, *never!*'

Noble parents often reminded their children that 'unequal' marriages seldom worked out well; the pages of Debrett and Burke's Peerage are full of evidence that their advice was usually followed. The seven daughters of the Duke of Abercorn brought him two dukes, one marquess and four earls as sons-in-law, and were said to have been ordered by their mother to marry no one less than an earl. It was certainly in the family tradition: the first Marquess had managed to have the titular rank of an earl's daughter conferred on his first cousin, Miss Hamilton, before she became his second wife so that he should not 'marry beneath his position'. However, even her rank did not make the marriage a happy one, and even its collapse did not make her husband forget the proprieties. When the Marchioness was about to elope, he is said to have sent her a message asking her to take the family coach – so that no one could say she had left her husband's house in a hackney chaise.

Marriage to someone of a different class caused a flutter among the gossips, at least until the middle of the century. The third Earl of Stanhope was exceptional in being delighted when his daughter Lucy became engaged to a commoner, a surgeon who lived near Chevening, the family home. Lucy 'despises Rank and *Aristocracy* as much as I do,' he declared with pride. There were also several successful marriages of widows to their children's tutors. Young Mr Ogilvie, who was tutor to the four sons of the first Duke of Leinster, had been very generously treated by his employer, who paid him well and later set him up in an establishment of his own near Dublin. Farington tells how the Duchess 'conceived a passion' for Ogilvie and visited him in Ireland. After the Duke's death she married him, so making him the legal owner of her fortune and her jointure, and the story ends happily with the birth of two daughters to the couple, and Ogilvie on excellent terms with his brother-in-law the Duke of Richmond and his stepson the Duke of Leinster. Inevitably such experiences sparked off wishful thinking. A widower who was left with a large family of motherless children might be expected – like a single man in possession of a good fortune – to be in want of a wife. When Lord Lyttelton's wife died, his mother-in-law noticed that the children's governess, Miss Annie Smith, was fancying that she might perhaps take their mother's place. She embroidered slippers for Lord Lyttelton and contrived to meet him as he went walking through the park. He suspected nothing, but it was her place and not the late Lady Lyttelton's which was soon taken by someone else at Hagley.

With so many young country lasses busying themselves prettily in the bedrooms and corridors, kitchens and dairies of the great country houses, it is surprising how seldom the sons of the families and their friends actually came to the point of marrying one of them. Occasionally this did happen. 'Poodle' Byng, son of the fifth Viscount Torrington, married his mother's maid who had been his mistress and bore him a daughter. He felt that this was the honourable thing to do, but after that the class barrier clicked into place and he never 'took her into society'. A maid who had a gentleman lover would be tempted to say she was pregnant in the hope that he would marry her, but she would soon find that that did not make her a 'lady'. Lord Stanley wrote to his wife that people were saying that 'Ld Raynham is gone crazy & is to marry a housemaid who persuaded him he had got her with child & he thinks in honour he must marry her.'

A working-class girl was helped on her way if she had already been a gentleman's mistress. By the time the third Earl, later the first Duke, of Cleveland made Elizabeth his second wife in 1813, his children were all grown-up and she was well prepared for her new position by having already been the mistress of the Duke of Bedford and Thomas Coutts the banker. She was the daughter of a market gardener and was roughly spoken although she must have had compensating charms. Creevey wrote her off as a 'brazen-faced Pop' and dismissed the marriage as 'the wickedest thing I ever heard of', perhaps partly because even after her marriage she still received an allowance from the Duke of Bedford. By the time she died in 1861 the scene was beginning to change. New titles were being granted and many old families were being invigorated – both genetically and financially – by partners from further afield; these included Americans, actresses and daughters of wealthy bankers and industrialists. There was still no lack of humbug on the part of noble mammas who wanted the best of both worlds: like Lady Stanley, who congratulated herself on her broadmindeness in not minding that her son Lyulph was 'marrying trade' when he became engaged to the daughter of a steel tycoon.

It was certainly her huge fortune that attracted the twenty-six-year-old ninth Duke of St Albans to Thomas Coutts' widow. She was Harriet Mellon and had been an actress when she married Coutts. After he died she refused St Albans' first proposal, but eventually could not resist the prospect of being a duchess, and when she was fifty they were married. They made a ludicrous pair, and society treated them cruelly, nicknaming them 'Lord Noodle and Queen Dolabella'. Creevey, of course, rose to the occasion. 'The Duke of St Albans is to be married to Mother Coutts,' he wrote; 'a more disgusting, frowsy, hairy old B. could not be found in the Seven Dials.' Lady Holland was indignant at the way the new Duchess was cold-shouldered at parties. 'How can women behave so to one another!' Actress as she had been, she put a brave face on the snubs, and played the part of a happy socialite. It seems that the court wavered in its treatment of her. Creevey tells how she was pointedly excluded from the huge number of guests invited to a ball at the Pavilion; Mrs Arbuthnot, on the other hand, said that it was by receiving the Duchess of St Albans and other 'femmes entretenues' at court that the King 'let down the royal dignity as well as general moral standards'.

The stigma of the stage died hard, and it was only gradually that it became less unacceptable for actresses to marry into the aristocracy. The Queen noted in her journal that Lord Melbourne had spoken of actresses 'marrying out of their sphere; and of its often not answering'. One such marriage which had 'answered' was that of the twelfth Earl of Derby and Miss Eliza Farren, a popular Irish actress whom he had loved for years. His first marriage had been to a duke's daughter and they had three children, but they parted after a few years when the Countess had an affair with her earlier love, the third Duke of Dorset. Lord Derby lived apart from his wife, but to prevent her marrying her lover he refused to divorce her. It was a dog-in-the-manger vengeance, stalemate for both. The Countess lived on her own, tubercular and cut off from her children, who were with their father at Knowsley. It was believed that she never saw them again during the twenty years which followed the separation. All that time Miss Farren was acting, loved by Lord Derby but at a respectable distance. A pamphlet which was published to silence gossip declared that the two of them never met without Eliza's mother being present.

At last Lady Derby died in 1797, and six weeks later her widower remarried. It was a quiet family occasion, in Lord Derby's Grosvenor Square house, and there must have been minor-key undertones, symbolized perhaps by the bridegroom's appearance in mourning. Lord Derby was forty-five, his bride six years younger, his three children grown-up, one daughter already married. This time there was no cold-shouldering by the court or society, and Queen Charlotte gave a reception at St James's Palace in honour of the new Countess, who had been acting until three weeks before the wedding. She was at the height of her career, and of course had regrets at leaving it. Her last appearance was as Lady Teazle in Sheridan's *School for Scandal*, and just before the curtain fell the aptness of her lines made her break down as she spoke them: 'Lady Teazle Licentiate – begs leave to return the Diploma they granted her – as she leaves off Practice and kills characters no longer.' Even when she was unmarried, Lord Derby's relations and friends had treated Miss Farren with affection and respect. The marriage was a very happy one and it brought Lord Derby four more children. Even Creevey was enthusiastic about it. 'I must say I never saw a man or woman live more happily with more grown-up children,' he said when he visited them in 1822; and seven years later when Lady Derby died he said that Knowsley without her was 'like a house with all the fires and candles out'.

American girls who married into the aristocracy were for a time given as chilly a welcome as most of the actresses. Lady Dorothy Nevill's memoirs describe how stately front-doors tended to be closed against 'dollars and impudence'. Slowly, gradually, the bolts were drawn back. The three Caton sisters from Maryland were pioneers; by 1836 two of them were married to the Marquesses of Carmarthen and Wellesley, and a third to Lord Stafford. It could not have been an altogether easy intrusion. Twenty years later Thomas Raikes, another diarist, wrote about them in words that still suggest misgivings – as well as what seemed to many others a characteristically English snobbery: 'It is a singular instance of three sisters, foreigners, and of a nation hitherto little known in our aristocratic circles, allying themselves to such distinguished families in England.' Others were more welcoming, as was Lord Palmerston who prophesied that 'before the century is out these clever and pretty women from New York will pull the strings in half the chancelleries in Europe'. During the second half of the century Lady Randolph Churchill was one of those the Prince of Wales specially admired. He liked American women 'because they are original and bring a little fresh air into society. They are livelier, better educated and less hampered by etiquette,' he said.

American girls on offer in the marriage market also tended to be wealthy, and it was mostly hard-up peers and sons of peers who went in search of transatlantic heiresses. In 1876 an American father whose daughter eloped with the eighth Duke of Manchester found that his noble son-in-law was on the brink of bankruptcy and had to pay his bills; the Earl of Yarmouth also beat a hasty retreat back across the Atlantic with his heiress alongside and creditors in pursuit. It was undignified behaviour. One newspaper published a list of available dukes; another asked a direct question: 'American heiresses, what will you bid?'

Among the best-known marriages of English aristocrats to American brides are those of the Churchill family, none more unwilling and unhappy than that of the ninth Duke of Marlborough to Consuelo Vanderbilt. The Churchills needed money and Mrs Vanderbilt was set on having an English peer – a duke if possible – as her son-in-law. Marlborough and Consuelo both loved and were loved by someone else and were not attracted to each other. Consuelo's account of their story tells how she was virtually imprisoned by her mother, to keep her from the man to whom she considered herself already engaged; and how, soon after their marriage in 1896, Marlborough told her 'tragically' how he had brought himself 'to marry me and to give up the girl he loved'. It was the most money-grubbing, tuft-hunting, wretched marriage that can be imagined, and the only point that can be said in its favour is that at least there was no pretence of affection or disinterestedness on either side. It was hopeless from start to finish.

Consuelo's first meeting with her husband's grandmother, often though it has been told, cannot be left out here. 'Your first duty is to have a child,' said the Dowager Duchess, 'and it must be a son, because it would be intolerable to have that little upstart Winston become Duke.' The marriage did produce children and it brought the Duke an annual income of £20,000 as well as other funds, but the couple had nothing in common and were both relieved when they decided first to live apart and eventually to divorce.

The American marriage market could be comic as well as tragic. After the eighty-year-old fifth Marquess of Donegall lost his second wife he put an advertisement in the *Daily Telegraph*. He addressed it to lawyers and business representatives of heiresses.

An English peer of very old title is desirous of marrying at once a wealthy lady: her age and looks are immaterial, but her character must be irreproachable; she must be a widow or a spinster – not a divorcee. If among your clients you know such a lady, who is willing to purchase the rank of a peeress for twenty-five thousand pounds sterling, paid in cash to her future husband . . . I shall be please if you will communicate with me. The peer will pay handsomely for the introduction when it is arranged.

A fine fish rose to the bait. Twenty-two-year-old Miss Violet Twining accepted the offer and is said to have promised to pay her bridegroom $40,000 a year. The story does not end there. Less than a year later a son was born to the couple, just seven months before his eighty-one-year-old father died. His will was proved at the modest sum of £27.

A son who expected his father to oppose his marriage to an American girl was George Curzon. But when he spoke of his intention of marrying Mary Leiter, Lord Scarsdale surprised him. 'So long as you love her and she loves you, that is all that matters,' he said. 'You are not likely at your age to make a mistake, and she is old enough to know her mind.' Such an enlightened attitude was rare at that time.

There was snobbery from those above as well as towards those below. When the eighth Duke of Argyll's son and heir became engaged to Princess Louise, the Queen's daughter, the Prince of Wales disapproved of her marrying a man who was 'below her in rank'. A generation later, when the Prince of Wales's own daughter, another Princess Louise, was to marry the little-known Scottish Earl of Fife, it was the future Queen Mary (then Princess May of Teck) who considered that for a royal princess to marry a 'subject' was 'rather strange'. Queen Victoria was not worried. 'It is a very brilliant marriage in a worldly point of view, as he is immensely rich,' she purred. As for the Princess's husband being only an earl, the Queen could – and did – wave her magic wand, and on his wedding day in 1889 he was created Duke of Fife.

A foreign princeling scored lower than an English royal in the marriage stakes. The marriage of the fifth Duke of Richmond's daughter, Augusta, to Prince Edward of Saxe-Weimar involved some humiliating forfeits: the news soon got around that they were to have only £2,500 a year, the bride was to go on being called Lady Augusta, and she would not go to court or be recognized by her husband's family. But the report does not sound an objective one, ending as it does with the news that any children were to be 'outcasts without a name'.

In cases of home-grown English princes showing interest in young ladies in their own country, the situation of course was very different. The marriage of any descendant of King George II was by the terms of the Royal Marriage Act of 1772 null and void if it did not receive the sovereign's consent. This in fact was the fate of the two marriages of the Duke of Sussex, King George III's son, who was married first to Lady Augusta Murray and then to the second Earl of Arran's daughter Cecilia. This was another subject discussed by the Queen and Lord Melbourne. He said that her 'disreputable uncles', as the Queen called them, were all very handsome young men; and 'though the Marriage Act may have been a very good thing in many ways, still it sent them like so many wild beasts into society, making love wherever they went and then saying they were very sorry they couldn't marry.'

Early in her own reign there was a reminder of Georgian royal philanderings when in 1842 Prince George of Cambridge, the Queen's first cousin, had a flirtation with Lady Augusta Somerset, the seventh Duke of Beaufort's daughter, and it was said that she was pregnant by him and that her father wanted them to marry. That called for the Queen's consent, which was refused. It was all in fact mere gossip but it throws light on the attitudes of the times. It was said that the Queen forbade all at court to speak to Lady

Augusta and that when Prince George took her to Windsor all the young ladies there obediently looked elsewhere. Greville's diary tells of the flutter the story caused, although there was no basis for it beyond a 'flirtation such as is continually going on without any serious result between half the youths and girls in London'. Greville played an active part in getting the scandal publicly refuted. He went with Lord Adolphus FitzClarence, one of William IV's illegitimate sons, to the office of *The Times* and arranged for a formal contradiction to be published. This was done, but nevertheless Greville considered that 'the appetite for scandal is so general and insatiable that . . . this calumny will affect the Lady more or less as long as She lives.' She had not deserved that, even though she was 'a very ill-behaved girl, ready for anything that her caprice or passions excite her to do'. The usual escape-route for a girl with a damaged reputation was marriage to a foreign husband, and two years later Lady Augusta married Baron Neumann, the Austrian Ambassador.

The dynastic engineers had graver problems than past flirtations to take into account. They might perhaps have been well advised to think more about dangers of inbreeding – marriages between cousins often led to the birth of physically or mentally defective children – and less about differences of nationality, religion, and politics. When Henry Fox, Lady Holland's son, wanted to marry Mademoiselle Natalie Potoka in 1827, his mother urged him not to. 'A foreigner is a guess, & a Catholic foreigner! whose habits & opinions must be so dissonant with those of all your connexions.' There were a few exceptions, she admitted. The eleventh Earl of Pembroke had married the daughter of the Russian Count Woronzov, and his son had married a Sicilian princess quite satisfactorily, but Lady Holland still held that 'any foreign connexion is to be deplored'.

Differences of religion were equally undesirable, and of course foreigners often did have that additional disadvantage. When neither family had strong religious convictions adjustments could be made, and occasionally Anglicans and Roman Catholics crossed the picket-line to another's persuasion. But a devout family like the Cecils could not take such matters lightly. In 1894 Lord Edward Cecil married Violet Maxse, and his family had their reasons for disliking the match. Her father, Admiral Maxse, had been a hero of the Crimean War but he was also an atheist, a radical, and separated from his wife – three very black marks against him. Lady Edward's detachment from Hatfield beliefs and her unwillingness to offend the family by discussing them had the effect of isolating her. She was the only daughter-in-law who for months still addressed her husband's mother as Lady Salisbury; for these and other reasons the marriage failed, and there was the additional problem that to the Cecils matrimony was a sacrament and indissoluble. Lord Edward was the only member of his family whose life as well as his marriage was unsuccessful, and he saw this as an additional cross for his wife to bear. 'To be married to a man you don't care for is bad enough,' he wrote endearingly to her, 'but to an unsuccessful man to boot is poor luck.' There is an unconfirmed suggestion that another family marriage was nipped in the bud by religious differences. Lady Gwendolen, it has been said, might have married the Duke of Norfolk when he was left a widower. But as well as being premier duke he was the lay leader of the country's Roman Catholics, so Lady Gwendolen remained a spinster and the Duke eventually married a cousin of his own religion.

In view of this it is surprising how easily the few Jewish brides who married into the aristocracy were accepted. One of the earliest was a Miss Moses who at the end of the eighteenth century married the sixth Duke of St Albans. Far better known was Frances, the daughter of John Braham, a brilliant and popular opera and oratorio singer, whose marriage to John, the illegitimate son of the sixth Earl Waldegrave, as well as to his brother the seventh Earl will be described in a later chapter. The fact that Frances had a Jewish father seems to have been no problem. Was this because John Braham was converted to Christianity in his youth? Or because Frances was so beautiful and charming and loved by every-one?

An even more important and celebrated Jewish wife was Hannah Rothschild, who married the fifth Earl of Rosebery. She was an immensely wealthy heiress, the only child of Baron Mayer de Rothschild, of the famous banking family. In the 1870s her parents died, leaving Hannah Mentmore Towers, the palatial family home in Bedfordshire that Joseph Paxton had designed, as well as priceless furniture, works of art, and £2,000,000. Four years later she married young Lord Rosebery, who for years had been a close friend of the family and was already heading for a distinguished political career. Hannah was not a beauty, and of course it was said that Rosebery married her for her money, but the evidence is against this. He was very well-off himself, had always admired and been adored by Hannah, and their married life was very devoted and happy. The famous story that as a young man Rosebery had said he had three ambitions – to marry an heiress, to win the Derby, and to be Prime Minister – and that he achieved all three is hardly to be taken seriously. More to the point is a letter that Rosebery wrote to a married woman friend in 1878, when he and Hannah became engaged. 'You do not know my future wife,' he wrote. 'She is very simple, very unspoilt, very clever, very warm-hearted and very shy. This description is for your private eye. I never knew such a beautiful character.' And to his sister, Lady Leconfield, who was very close to him, he wrote: 'My darling Connie, I was engaged to Hannah yesterday. I love her so much that I can never be happy if you do not love her too.'

Rosebery and Hannah had been introduced by Mrs Disraeli and had known each other for ten years, since Hannah was seventeen. She had soon fallen deeply in love with him, but the religious difference held them back from becoming engaged. The main objections to their marriage came from the Jewish community in England, and it was their Press who loudly opposed the engagement. 'We mourn, we deplore this degeneracy, and we pray to God fervently to spare the community a similar grief,' the *Jewish Chronicle* went so far as to declare. Yet Hannah's cousin, Annie, had married Lord Hardwicke's son, and Annie's sister Constance had married the future Lord Battersea – both aristocratic, non-Jewish husbands. In each case the parents had agreed to the marriage and the two wives remained true to their Jewish religion. Religion was important to both Rosebery and Hannah, and there was never a suggestion that either should change, each respecting the faith of the other.

There was great public interest in the Rosebery–Rothschild marriage, and some of the Rothschilds decided not to go to the wedding. Another strong opponent of the match was Rosebery's mother, who had remarried after her first husband's early death and was now Duchess of Cleveland. She was horrified that her son had chosen a Jewish bride, and her welcome to her daughter-in-law was not warm. 'I will receive the future Lady Rosebery with all the kindness and consideration that are her due,' she wrote to her son; but she would not come to the wedding unless it were to be in a

There was controversy about both the Rosebery and St Albans marriages. Hannah Rothschild, the future Countess of Rosebery, is seen standing by the magnificent Rubens chimney-piece at Mentmore, her family home. The caricature is a send-up of the young Duke of St Albans' marriage to Thomas Coutts' wealthy, but middle-aged widow, the actress Harriet Mellon.

church. It was a splendidly planned occasion, starting at 9.45 a.m.
with a civil function before a registrar in the Board Room of the
Guardians in Mount Street, where the bleak official surroundings
were transformed by a mass of flowers and there was a small
gathering of relations, friends, and tenants. Then followed the
ceremony at nearby Christ Church, Down Street, where the bride
was given away by Benjamin Disraeli, now Earl of Beaconsfield,
and Lord Carrington was best man. The Prince of Wales was in the
congregation and he, the Prime Minister, the Duke of Cleveland,
Lady Leconfield, and the bridegroom's brother were witnesses. At
a magnificent wedding-breakfast afterwards the Prince of Wales
proposed the health of the bride and bridegroom, who then left for
a honeymoon at Petworth. The barriers of religion and race could
not have been more publicly and catholically surmounted. Later,
when Rosebery and Hannah arrived home at Dalmeny, they were
given an enthusiastic welcome and it was to a Scottish audience that
he gave a straight and simple statement of Hannah's identity. 'You
have this afternoon conferred a nationality,' he said. 'My wife, as
you know, is a Jewess by race, an Englishwoman by birth, and
to-day, by adoption, you have made her a Scotswoman.' He should
perhaps have mentioned that it was by her religion as well as by her
race that Hannah was Jewish. It was a loyalty as important to him as
it was to her.

Political differences, no less than religious ones, could keep
couples apart, especially when one or other belonged to a family
which played an active part in public life. 'Do Whigs and Tories
ever intermarry?' Lord Grosvenor's young son once asked, and the
question caused great amusement. But he had put his finger on a
real problem. Lady Frederick Cavendish entered in her diary that
the Duke of Argyll's daughter was going to marry Lord Percy, and
she queried: 'Presbyterian and Irvingite, Whig and Tory, I wonder
how it will do.' The Duke of Bedford's plan to marry Lord de la
Warr's daughter gave Lady Holland similar misgivings, as the
bride's family were high Tory and Puseyites. 'These principles will
not do with the domains & departed shades of Woburn,' she said.

Differences in some cases were resolved and all went well, as it
did when the two daughters of the fifth Earl Cowper, a Whig,
married Tory Members of Parliament. Many wives were unpolitical
and content to follow their husband's lead, but parents-in-law could
be less tolerant. Viscount Mahon took an opposite political stand to

both his own and his wife's father, and this drove his father-in-law to forbid his own daughter to enter his house. Political differences cropped up several times in the third Marquess of Salisbury's family; he was Tory Prime Minister when in 1879 his nephew, Eustace Balfour, married the daughter of the Whig eighth Duke of Argyll, and both families were distressed by the political clash. A few years later Lord Salisbury's daughter Maud married the first Earl of Selborne's only son, and this time the Montague–Capulet alliance received the accolade of a *Times* leader, delighting in the link between the foremost Conservative's daughter and the Liberal Lord Chancellor's son. Even so, tact was called for, and when her husband stood as a Liberal candidate Lord Salisbury's daughter diplomatically played no part in his election campaign.

Money was an important consideration when it came to planning a marriage, however amply provided each of the two might be. Already by the beginning of the century it had been through alliances between landed families that the greatest estates of England and Scotland had been got together; it was through what Disraeli called their talent for 'absorbing heiresses' that the Leveson-Gowers were landowners on a scale that hardly any other European family could emulate. The fifteenth Earl of Derby who held various government offices from 1852 onwards noted in his diary the theory that because of their need for money titled families tended to die out sooner than others. To keep up their rank, it was pointed out, they constantly married heiresses. And an heiress had to be 'the last of her race' and so came of a family which was dying out. Lord Derby also thought that titled families tended to thin out because, as he put it, younger sons of peers were not a marrying class.

It was generally accepted that many upper-class couples married for money. Edward Bulwer Lytton criticized the notorious English 'marketing' of unmarried women: 'in good society, the heart is remarkably prudent, and seldom falls violently in love without a sufficient settlement.' A few did, however. George Canning loved and wanted to marry Miss Joan Scott, the Duchess of Portland's sister, but she was very wealthy and he wrote to a friend that he wanted to avoid 'the apparent sordidness and speculation of a proposal to a *great* fortune'. He could not bear the idea of 'being the creature of my wife's' or of being taken to have risen 'on a foundation not of my own laying'. In a year's time, he hoped he would have made his own way in the world, and so it was.

So an engagement was usually followed by solemn financial conversations between the men of the two families and their lawyers. Dowries were discussed, and a girl's father could pay thousands of pounds to his future son-in-law – 'for his own use', one settlement put it. Investments and acres of land were transferred; there were careful calculations of how the property should be apportioned in case of the death of either partner, and how it should be inherited by any children there might be. When all was agreed the bride and bridegroom were called in to sign the settlement. Lady Wilhelmina Stanhope (encountered a few pages earlier as Lord Rosebery's mother who did not welcome his Jewish wife Hannah) wrote about this in her diary. At Chevening, in Kent, the day before her wedding to Viscount Dalmeny in 1843, she was 'fetched down to Papa's room to sign & "deliver my act and deed" '; this was done in the presence of her future husband and his father and brother, as well as her own brother, five lawyers, and a clerk.

The financial planning had begun long before that. A provident father arranged to put aside a 'portion' for his daughter as soon as she was born, and this would be a basis either for her dowry or, if she did not marry, her income in spinsterhood. The size of a girl's dowry decided how free she was to choose her man. When both families were of roughly the same rank, dowries ranged between £10,000 and £30,000; social imbalance between them might cause a daughter of untitled parents to bring a portion of £60,000 when she 'improved her station' by marrying into a noble family. This could be a way out for younger sons, who had no expectations of inheriting, no training for a profession, and were unwilling to demean themselves by having dealings with 'trade'. A young man who could not afford to marry the girl of his choice could always look out for a less socially acceptable heiress. (Wealthy girls in Trollope's novels describe themselves as 'weighted'.) 'I shall never marry, unless I am ruined,' Byron bluntly put it, and it was in fact his huge debts which eventually drove him to what Hobhouse called his 'matrimonial scheme'.

Parents hesitated to speak quite so plainly, but they could not deny that they were relieved when a son chose a girl who had 'means'. There is a hint of a previous confrontation on the subject in the letter that Lord Duncannon received in 1805 from his father the Earl of Bessborough.

I never meant to control you in any match you wished to make, neither did I want you to marry a very great fortune. I only represented to you it was necessary that the lady should have some fortune, otherwise you would have great difficulties in your living, and I should hope in the choice you have now made, there will be that which will remove some incumbrances off my estate & enable me to add to your income enough to make you comfortable though not in affluent circumstances.

In this case it was not only financial problems that the marriage was hoped to solve. Duncannon was a notorious philanderer and breaker of hearts; perhaps now at last he would settle down? His grandmother, old Lady Georgiana Spencer, when she wrote to congratulate him could not resist adding that she hoped that his engagement would 'put an end to a certain degree of careless but dangerous attentions to young women which, I fear, has been justly imputed to you'.

Marrying for money or 'for an establishment' still called for a certain delicatesse, and some matches were engineered too blatantly and shamelessly for even that worldly society. Emily Eden described an extreme case in 1830, when she wrote to a friend about Lord Edward Thynne's engagement.

I think if Edward had been thirty-three instead of twenty-three, had *wearied* of the world, as the Scotch say, and been disappointed in love several times, as all people are by that time, it would not have been unnatural that he should have married for an establishment; but a boy of that age has no right to be so calculating. . . . I heard from a great friend of the family that it is the sick plain sister Lord Edward marries; that he did not pretend to care about her; supposed that if he saw her once before their marriage it would be enough – and so on, which was disgusting.

No one could disagree with that, but where did the dividing-line come between the acceptable and the disgusting in fortune-hunting? When her cousin married a man who was only a 'second son', Charlotte Canning felt that it was not wrong to hope that the elder brother would not have an heir, so that her cousin might eventually inherit. Canning's reluctance to depend on his wife's fortune was very rare; even rarer was the idea that marriage of a very wealthy to a very poor individual would serve a purpose in helping to even things up. The accepted view was that a *beau parti* was worth its price. As Lady Holland said about Lady Charlotte Ashley's fiancé, 'he is well spoken of, but is not rich enough to have a lovely wife out of a great house, & have a hunting establishment besides.'

Being an heiress could also have its disadvantages. When Angela Burdett inherited Thomas Coutts' fortune she found herself suddenly the possessor of unsuspected charms, and ardently wooed. Fortunately she kept her head, but in spite of her resolve to spend her fortune on charities, one of her admirers went on courting her for eighteen years. Daisy Maynard's fortune, a vast inheritance of over £30,000 a year, was also a mixed blessing as it prompted Disraeli to suggest to the Queen that, although then only sixteen, she would be a charming bride for the haemophiliac Prince Leopold. So Lord Brooke, Daisy's future husband, was forbidden for two years to tell Daisy that he loved her, and the Queen was greatly displeased when after summoning Daisy to Windsor and approving of her as a royal bride the engagement came to nothing. The Prince had told Daisy that his affections were engaged elsewhere, and she for her part was glad to be free.

Occasionally a glittering dowry was the means of bringing together a couple who were well suited and proceeded to marry and live happily ever after. One such marriage was that of Viscount Cranborne, eldest son of the first Marquess of Salisbury, to the heiress Miss Frances Gascoyne in 1821. Inevitably it was said that he was marrying her for her money, and some sharp words were spoken. Princess Lieven, the Russian Ambassador's wife, had nothing favourable to say about Frances. 'She is lucky enough to fancy she is beautiful, and unlucky enough not to be. She is not without intelligence, but entirely without charm.' It is one of those portraits that tells as much about the painter as about her subject.

Miss Gascoyne was very young when she first met Lord Cranborne, and soon afterwards his mother and her father had a serious talk. Lady Salisbury said that she and her husband wanted to see their son, who was then twenty-nine, 'settled in life'. He had had some earlier 'attachments' and Frances had also had other suitors. Her father felt that she was still too young, and he also mentioned 'the extreme shortness of the acquaintance'. Lady Salisbury was

thinking ahead, she said. Would Mr Gascoyne allow Lord Cranborne to try to make himself agreeable to Frances, and if he
succeeded perhaps her father would consent to the match? It would
be a great honour, Mr Gascoyne acknowledged.

The curtain rises next on Gorhambury, not far from Lord
Cranborne's home at Hatfield, where he and Miss Gascoyne were
both guests of Lord Verulam. Their host decided that they
appeared 'to suit one another exactly. They make love quite as they
ought.' Lord Cranborne's debts were not much more than £4,000,
so the engagement could be announced and a start made on drawing
up the marriage settlement. As he did this the Gascoyne family's
agent added an unusual and interesting aside:

> Men in high ranks of life have of late shown such a turn for
> licentiousness that too much care cannot be taken to guard
> against it. I never knew a clause providing against a divorce for
> misconduct in the husband. . . . If such an unpleasant event
> should happen it is only right that the husband's life interest in
> the wife's estate should thenceforth cease, and she to have it for
> life.

The Gascoynes' agent need not have worried; licentiousness was
not a Cecil failing. The marriage settlement arranged that Lord
Cranborne should add his wife's surname to his own and that their
descendants should be called Gascoyne-Cecil. At the wedding in
1821 the Duke of Wellington gave away the bride, and throughout
her life they remained very close friends. It was another of the
Duke's women friends, Mrs Arbuthnot, who wrote in her diary
about Frances at the time of her marriage. Her description is kinder
than Princess Lieven's. She was, she said, 'a very pretty girl who
has £12,000 a year. They say he has married her for her money.'
More to the point is what Frances's husband said about their
marriage after his wife died, in 1839:

> In her I have lost a loving friend. During the nineteen years that
> we have been married, we have hardly had a difference. She set
> me an example of the performance of every duty, and it is to her
> education that I owe the excellent disposition of my children.

Two more personal histories must be added to complete the

account of the link-up between money and marriage. The first is that of Arthur Balfour. He loved and was loved by many women but he never married, probably because of May Lyttleton's early death. When he was forty it was the reverse of fortune-hunting that made him think perhaps he ought to marry. Was it perhaps his duty – because of his inheritance? But 'What have I got to offer anyone – nothing but ashes!' he said.

The other story is happier and shows that in a mercenary age and class some couples did marry only for love and in the face of what, to them at least, seemed an alarming shortage of funds. It could still by no means be described as love on the dole, but when in 1889 Lord Robert Cecil married Lady Eleanor Lambton her brothers were worried that for a long time the couple would have only £1400 a year to live on. Lady Salisbury shared their anxiety; Nelly would prove a fast and expensive wife, she feared. In fact they lived happily on Lord Robert's earnings as a barrister, added to his wife's small income and the £1,000 a year that each married Cecil son was given by his father. The Prime Minister had been right when he disagreed with his wife's forebodings. Having already enjoyed the good things that money can buy, their daughter-in-law would be more likely to be ready to do without them, he said.

So the dynastic engineers yielded in the face of really strong feelings, and gave their blessing to couples who snapped their fingers at fat bank balances. As Emily Eden put it: 'After twenty-one, young people may surely choose for themselves whether they will be rich or poor.'

5

Stairs to Marriage

The rituals and antics which led to marriage seem today hardly less strange and spectacular than the pre-mating display of peacocks or grebes. The great country houses provided some of the habitats, the annual London season the others. Evening after evening the carriages clattered through the quiet streets of Mayfair, Belgravia, and Kensington to draw up and deliver their passengers at front doors, deferentially opened by flunkeys in livery, of fine houses which blazed with the warmth and light of wax candles – and later, thanks to the marvels of technology, of gas too. It was a full programme. Rosalind Stanley's diary for a couple of weeks during the 1863 season mentions a ball at her mother's house in Dover Street, with English and Danish royals among the guests, the Princess of Wales' first reception at St James's Palace, and a week later an 'odious ball' at Lady Stanhope's. One evening there were three balls and she went to them all.

It was paradise for some, hell for others, a curious mixture of gaiety, romance, and fortune-hunting with undertones of cool calculation and bleak despair. Everyone knew that the purpose of the London season was to give the 'right' young people an opportunity of meeting and getting to know each other. But it was very expensive, as clothes and jewels and carriages were needed – sometimes a town house had to be rented too – and parents with a lot of daughters had problems about paying for these things year after year. They had to work out carefully how many balls and parties they could afford to give; one girl who did not have many partners at a ball had the impression that it was the young ladies who gave parties who were most often asked to dance. The seamy side of the season was realistically described by Tennyson in 'Aylmer's Field':

> Whatever eldest-born of rank or wealth
> Might lie within their compass, him they lured
> Into their net made pleasant by the baits
> Of gold and beauty, wooing him to woo.

Behind all the frivolity and light-heartedness, lives and dynasties were at stake and anxious mothers gave careful thought to important details. Old Lady Stanley advised her son's many-daughtered wife that she had found that there was more opportunity at balls for conversation and for making acquaintance; quadrilles did not give enough time for that.

There were not many who did not accept and take for granted the humiliating parts played in this comedy by the girls, at least those who held fewest social, financial, and physical trumps in their hands. Lady Melbourne's son, George Lamb, described their plight in verse. A young married woman looks back on the tribulations she has survived and tells how she

> chang'd a Misses trammel'd life
> For all the glorious licence of a Wife;
> And every candid female here allows
> How hard a Misses life, who seeks a spouse.
> At Operas, plays and routs we never fail,
> Put up, alas! to everlasting sale.
> First in Hyde Park, sent by Maternal care,
> At Noon we walk, and seem to take the air.
> Or Bond Street's gay resort, for game we try
> And call at many a shop and seem to buy,
> While, like a Dealer, the good Matron shews
> Our shapes, and paces, to the chapmen Beaux,
> Well skill'd th'unfitting suitor to dispatch,
> And to allure the Eligible Match.
> At night again, on us all pleasures pall;
> Bid for by inch of candle at a ball –
> And e'en when fashion's toilsome revels cease,
> For us no pause, no liberty, no peace –
> Then when the Matrons speak of suppers small,
> 'A few choice friends beside ourselves – that's all,'

Two aspects of the social round: Rotten Row on a summer day in 1880 (*above*). In a carriage or on horseback, walking or sitting the beau monde gathered there to see and to be seen; and an early photograph (with names added over thirty years later) of a house party at Goodwood in 1866 (*below*).

Duke of Richmond. Rt. Hon. Henry Chaplin. Late Lord Henry Gordon-Lennox. Marchioness of Blandford. Earl of Sandwich. Lord Algernon Gordon-Lennox. Sir Fredk. Johnstone. Late Earl Annesley. Hon. W. Carrington.

The late Earl of Bradford. H.M. The King. Countess of Lucan. H.M. Queen Alexandra. Duchess of Buccleuch. Lady Constance Howard. Lady Caroline Gordon-Lennox.

This language in plain truth they mean to hold
'A girl by private contract to be sold.'

Even the men were threatened by the system and by the manipulations of matriarchal strategists. In his early twenties Lord Hugh Grosvenor, the future Duke of Westminster, was considered 'England's most eligible bachelor' and he was both aware of the dangers and confident that he could escape them.

He wrote indignantly to his mother from Munich in 1847.

I had heard before I left England that you were anxious that I should stay abroad over next season as you thought I could not escape being bagged by some horrid old dowager. I do not believe this, as you cannot think me such a weak fool as to be hooked and made to do anything I should not wish to do.

Few of the girls could take such an independent line. Once again their predicament inspired some witty verses, this time by Lord Robert Cecil, telling the story of his own engagement in 1888.

'Life is all very pleasant for you,'
    Said fair Chloe one night at a ball,
'You men, you have plenty to do,
    We poor women have nothing at all.'

I urged her to paint or to play
    To write or to knit or to sew,
To visit the poor and to pray,
    To each and to all she said, 'No'.

At last I exclaimed in despair,
    'If you really are anxious to be
Of some use, and for none of these care,
    You must marry! Why not marry me?'

There is plenty of evidence of how couples courted and became engaged. (It was only after the wedding reception that they fall silent.) A spot selection might as well begin with the story of the Hon. William Lyttelton and Lady Sarah Spencer in 1812, which had been a difficult year for them both. Sarah, still unmarried at twenty-five, was being courted by a man who did not attract her, and she was relieved when he spared her what would have been an unpleasant decision by ceasing his attentions. William Lyttelton had recently proposed to a girl who had turned him down. Then it was suggested to him that Sarah would be just the wife for him. After their uncertainties both were bowled over by their happiness. William's admiration of Sarah was wholehearted. As soon as she agreed to marry him he felt he was a more religious man, he said, and hoped he was already a better one. She for her part wrote of her 'slippery, dangerous, blinding happiness'.

Then there was William Lamb's courting of the fascinating, flighty, unstable Lady Caroline Ponsonby. Unhappily though it turned out, it was both fervent and romantic. They had known each other for years, and Caroline was little more than a child in the Devonshire House nest of legitimate and bastard children when William decided that she was the girl for him. But he was only the second son of a recently created Irish viscount – his almost certain illegitimacy has already been mentioned – and this made him an inadequate match for Caroline, daughter of the Earl of Bessborough and granddaughter of Earl Spencer. Then William's elder brother, Peniston, died and William became Lord Melbourne's heir. This transformed his prospects and in 1805 he wrote to Caroline:

I have loved you for four years, loved you deeply, dearly, faithfully, – so faithfully that my love has withstood my firm determination to conquer it when honour forbade my declaring myself – has withstood all that absence, variety of objects, my own endeavours to seek and like others, or to occupy my mind with fix'd attention to my profession, could do to shake it.

Caroline for her part declared that she adored William. Had she forgotten another childhood love, to whom the news of her engagement came as a tragic blow? The fifth Duke of Devonshire's eldest son told Caroline that he had always thought of her as his future wife and that all his hopes of happiness were linked with her. She was the great love of his life. Endlessly sought after, of course, he never married and was known as the Bachelor Duke.

The cool, correct manoeuvres of a young man, set on choosing and landing his bride, are described from start to finish in the unpublished diary of Lady Constance Primrose, daughter of Lord Dalmeny. The first shot was fired in May, 1867, when an anonymous bouquet was delivered to her. 'Very interesting and exciting,' she noted. Who could have sent it? The only clue was the cut-off corner of an invitation-card to a ball given by her family, on which her name was written above the printed address. So the sender must be one of their guests. After that, for a fortnight the diary says, no more, although the name of 'Mr Wyndham' had appeared regularly for some time in its listings of visitors to the house. It seems that Lady Constance did not confide all her feelings to her diary, for Mr Wyndham's next recorded move was a letter to her mother, requesting that he might call and speak to her. The letter came on 4 July, and the meeting was fixed for the next morning at eleven o'clock. There was evidently no doubt about the reason for his visit, or about Lady Constance's attitude. 'I was twenty-five hours in suspense, and that it was what made yesterday seem so long,' she wrote. Her mention of her suspense is the nearest she gets to describing her feelings; the rest of her entry is unbrokenly low-key. She goes straight on to say that it 'is all settled now as far as it can be'. Not a word about any conversation they might have had together, no description of her suitor, no confessions of how she felt about him. He was a captain in the Life Guards and had to be on duty the next day, so he had to wait to go to Petworth and ask for the approval of his father, Lord Leconfield. Until then the engagement has to be a close secret, although he did come back that same evening and dine with them.

Old Lord Leconfield was an eccentric recluse, who might be expcted to raise difficulties. He had never come to terms with the anomaly of his position as the eldest of Lord Egremont's illegitimate offspring. He managed a short note, confirming his approval of his son's engagement. A scrap of paper in the Petworth archives, without date or address, must have been brought back after Wyndham's visit to Petworth. It reads:

My dear Young Lady,
    I am greatly pleased in what I have learnt from Henry, and shall be happy to welcome you as a Daughter.
                        sincerely yours
                        Leconfield

Back in London, Wyndham went at once to the house of Constance's stepfather in St James's Square. (Her own father had died in 1851, and three years later her mother married the Duke of Cleveland.) Again the diary is deadpan and down-to-earth, concerned with how they should set about telling people their news. They went off together on some initial visits, and these moved her to record that everyone liked her future husband. But she still wrote and thought of him as 'Mr Wyndham', and they still had to stick to the rules. When they arrived back at the house together in a hansom, he 'left me at the door, as he is not allowed to come in while Mama is away'.

Two days later Mr Wyndham was Henry at last. Perhaps they were helped to get on more intimate terms by the custom, mentioned in many diaries and letters, of leaving engaged couples on their own. Early in June they went off together to visit relations; 'Henry and I were shut into the back room together,' Constance told her diary. By then the news was out, and congratulations and wedding present began to arrive. The serious matter of 'trousseau labours' also started, with visits to Madame Descon and Madame Elise. Constance saw a wedding-dress she liked, but it cost £250. Was that too much? She and her mother eventually decided on it, and when her stepfather heard of their misgivings about the expense he said it must be a present from him. Even after that anxiety had been smoothed away, there seems to have been not much joy in the hours spent deciding which patterns should be used for 'those horrible undergarments' and planning dresses for the bridesmaids. 'I think my trousseau will effectually check any taste I have to dress,' Constance sighed.

Together they went out to dinner, paid visits, and spent an evening at the opera, where they were chaperoned by Constance's two brothers. She dined with Henry at the House of Commons – he was the Member for West Sussex – and went with him to Garrard's to see the diamonds he was giving her. They were still left on their own at parties; at one given by her mother, Constance was irritated by this. 'Henry and I were avoided as though we were infectious, which makes one feel foolish.' There were also practical matters to arrange. One busy day's appointments included interviews with the bishop who was going to marry them as well as with a maid, a tailor, and a cook. It was settled that Coates, a house on the Petworth estate that had been earmarked for Henry when he decided to marry, would be theirs a few months after the wedding, and that they would live there until Lord Leconfield died (as in fact he did,

two years later) and they moved into Petworth House. On 15 July
they were married. It was less than two months since the mysterious bouquet of spring flowers from an anonymous admirer had
been delivered at the house in St James's Square.

Country houses and London ballrooms were not, of course, the
only places where people fell in love. One day the fifth Duke of
Newcastle's heir Lord Lincoln was out walking in Nice when his
eye was caught by a beautiful girl and he determined to find out
who she was. On the whole what he discovered was welcome. His
father the Duke had big financial worries at the time, and the girl
who had caught his son's eye was Miss Henrietta Hope, illegitimate, but the heiress to her father Mr Henry Hope's huge fortune.
London buzzed with interest. Lord Stanley wrote the news to his
wife, far away in the country.

> Lord Lincoln is to marry Miss Hope the daughter of ugly little
> Henry Hope with the big house in Piccadilly. She is illegitimate
> but pretty. . . . She will have all Hope's fortune, 50,000 a
> year. . . . It is a great thing for the Dukedom of Newcastle & will
> put it on its legs again.

Lord Stanley explained that Mr Hope was already paying his future
son-in-law's debts, and 'starts him fresh on the Turf, which
however he promises to abjure'. Unfortunately not even a pretty
heiress could straighten the Newcastle finances. Lord Lincoln
succeeded his father in 1864 but six years later he faced bankruptcy. Everything had to be sold, including the celebrated Hope
diamond which always brought bad luck to its owners.

Only a year before his son met Miss Hope, the Duke had made
every effort to stop a less acceptable marriage in his family. His
daughter Susan and Lord Adolphus Vane, the third Marquess of
Londonderry's son, had fallen in love; but the Duke knew that
Lord Adolphus was threatened with insanity and so forbade the
marriage and told Lady Londonderry that he would never allow it.
'Of course, Lord Adolphus will feel that as a Gentleman he must
not think of correspondence,' he wrote to her. The Duke made his
daughter write to her lover refusing his proposal, but they met
secretly and on the day she came of age they went to a London
church and were married. The Duke had been right, however.
Lord Adolphus went mad, his wife was terrified and took to opium,

and both lived wretchedly and died early.

Another match that had been strongly opposed must have been fresh in the memories of the Londonderrys. Charles Stewart, the future third Marquess, was forty and widowed, Ambassador to Austria, and a celebrated lady's man when in 1818 he met the eighteen-year-old heiress, Lady Frances Vane-Tempest. Until she came of age she was a ward in chancery, and the aunt who was her guardian was resolutely against the marriage because of Frances's youth, her suitor's amorous reputation, the suggestion of madness in his family, and her suspicion that he was after the girl's fortune. But her attitude made Frances all the more resolved to accept him. A chancery action dragged on for three months, during which a governess had to be present at all meetings between the couple. There was no lack of people to tell Frances about Charles's many affairs, but she was not put off and in 1819 the marriage took place and Frances, still not yet twenty, happily took on the duties and the dignity of an ambassador's wife.

The father of Lord Robert Cecil, whose verse description of his engagement has just been quoted, set out on his own married life in the face of heavy gunfire from his parents. He too was a Lord Robert Cecil and he was the future third Marquess of Salisbury and Prime Minister. The second Marquess was vehemently against his son's engagement to Miss Georgina Alderson, even though his own wife had come from outside his class and Lord Robert's wife was to bring much happiness to her husband and new vitality to the family just as she had done. Lord Salisbury told his son that if he married Miss Alderson he would be hard-up – Lord Cranborne, his older brother, was then still alive so he did not expect to succeed his father – and that he would be cold-shouldered by society. Lord Robert agreed to test his feelings by not seeing Miss Alderson for six months but he was not impressed by his father's arguments and told him so. 'The persons who will cut me because I marry Miss Alderson are precisely the persons of whose society I am so anxious to be quit,' he said, with careful attention to his grammar. When the six months were up his feelings were unchanged, and in 1857 there was a quiet wedding with no family celebrations, and they started life on £500 a year in unfashionable Fitzroy Square. Lord Salisbury eventually relented; he died in 1868, three years after his invalid heir, and was succeeded by Lord Robert.

Another couple who survived the ordeal of separation were John

Russell, Viscount Amberley, and Kate, daughter of Lord Stanley of Alderley. She had been bored by her partners at London balls and parties and found her brother's intellectual friends better company – but unfortunately all very ugly. Then she met Lord Amberley, who satisfied both requirements. They were excellently suited and seem to have been allowed unusual freedom for those times. 'Kate and I had a very interesting walk in the evening after it was dark,' Amberley wrote in his journal in July 1863; 'she is wonderfully intellectual.' Had he too been bored by the partners he had met during the London season? But he was only twenty, and both mothers thought him too young. 'This evening Mama spoke to me about Kate Stanley, which of course I did not at all like,' he wrote in February 1864. 'It seems I am to be "prudent" not to get "involved" &c. I am so "very young" that I cannot be trusted to judge for myself.'

Meanwhile he and Kate had more talks, sometimes disagreeing on important matters, as they did about divorce. However, she told him 'in a few quiet words . . . that nobody satisfied her ideal as I' did', and she added 'other most comforting assurances which deeply touched me'. Two days later they again met alone and had 'one fervent embrace; one long loving kiss which was worth hours of conversation'. It had to last them a long time. A week or so afterwards, after a 'long & tediously irritating conversation with Mama' it was agreed that Amberley and Kate should not meet or correspond for six months, and that they would give notice of any change in their feelings. Amberley took it very badly and was scolded by his mother for his 'unsocial, morose, unsympathetic habits'; but Kate determined to be cheerful, by way of training for her future life. It would be essential for Amberley, she wrote to her mother, to have a cheerful companion.

Lady Stanley wrote kindly to Amberley and sent him photographs of Kate. When Kate's sister Rosalind became engaged to George Howard (later ninth Earl of Carlisle) – both were younger than Amberley and Kate – Amberley wrote to Lady Stanley, saying that he did not feel worthy 'of the love of a being so perfect as Kate is', and she replied with a 'most kind & tender' letter. At last the six months came to an end. Amberley asked if he might now come to Alderley, and on 17 September 1864 he arrived. He was greeted by Lady Stanley who seized him by the hand and led him into her own room, where he found Kate, by herself. They 'embraced fervently

Two couples who faced up to pre-marital separation: Viscount Amberley and his wife, Kate, in the study at Ravenscroft; and the Duke of Wellington's wife, Kitty, sketching. Short-sighted, she did not recognize people at parties or when their carriages passed in the street.

and had a few words together' and after that there were no more obstacles. Two months later they were married amid rejoicings from both families.

The amount of freedom allowed to unmarried daughters varied. After Percy Wyndham and Madeline Campbell had fallen in love, Percy wanted to send Madeline a gold cross. But her mother had her reasons for not allowing this. 'You must not think me unkind, but only very old-fashioned,' she wrote, 'when I tell you it has been my rule never to allow my daughters to accept presents except from very near relations.' Two months after they became engaged she wrote to Lord Leconfield, Percy's father, about Madeline's lack of dowry. Lady Campbell explained that she had been left a widow ten years before, and had had a struggle to bring up her large family. When she died, each of her girls would have £50 a year and that was all. 'So you must be content with Madeline's good qualities as her portion.'

In those times of high mortality risks, even for young people, many engagements were broken by the death of one of the *promessi sposi*. In 1871 Arthur Balfour spent a lot of time with May Lyttelton, riding in Rotten Row with her, taking her to concerts, waltzing with her at London balls, meeting her in both their homes. Then suddenly and unpredictably May fell in love with Rutherford Graham, also brilliant, wealthy, sought-after, and devoted to her. Lord Lyttelton forbade the marriage because Graham had two serious faults: he was a Presbyterian and a flirt. (Which was the worse?) So twice May had to refuse him, and her father sent Rutherford Graham off to prove his mettle by doing a year's hard work overseas. But on his way to America he died suddenly of diphtheria. May was particularly unlucky as her first love had also died, a few years before. Once again she was heartbroken, but by the end of 1874 she and Balfour were again deeply attached – all his life he belived that May had accepted his proposal – when she was taken ill at Hagley, the Lytteltons' country home. It was typhoid fever, and in March 1875 she died. This time it was Balfour who was brokenhearted. 'I was to have made her my wife,' he told her brother, and he asked him to put a ring that had belonged to Balfour's mother in May's coffin. He never married, and none of his women friends ever took her place in his affections.

Few wooings were more rigorous and testing than George Curzon's of the beautiful American heiress Mary Leiter. It began with a bang. Curzon afterwards said that he loved Mary at first sight, never more than at the moment he saw her making her splendid entrance at the Duchess of Westminster's magnificent ball in 1890. He was by no means her only admirer on that occasion. The Prince of Wales went up to her at once and opened the ball by dancing the first quadrille with her. Mary was soon in love with Curzon, although it was three years before he proposed and she accepted – still secretly, almost accidentally. Curzon's work, writing, and travel were his top priorities. In 1893, after eighteen months' separation, they met in Paris. 'I had entered the hotel without the slightest anticipation that this would be the issue,' Curzon wrote; Mary told him how she had waited nearly three years since their first meeting, rejecting countless suitors, waiting always for him. He still had dangerous travels in Asia ahead of him before they could marry. Mary declared that if he died she would remain single and enter a convent.

So they became engaged, but not a word was to be said to anyone for two more years. Meekly and lovingly Mary agreed. She went back to America and went on rejecting enamoured young men. He said to her: 'Give me a girl who knows a woman's place and does not yearn for trousers.' She said to him: 'I well know, dear, that now as always you must do as you will.' The consequence was that on the anniversary of their engagement they met again, still sure of their feelings. One more meeting, and Curzon set off on another dangerous trip. This time there were long silences when he did not write. At last Mary received an encouraging letter. 'The time of waiting is drawing to a close,' he wrote, 'and you will find me loving enough when me meet.' And she did. Patient Grizelda was rewarded at last.

Another lovely girl who caught the connoisseur's eye of the Prince of Wales has left a step-by-step account of her courtship. Lord Sackville's daughter, Victoria, had made a brilliant impression in Washington D.C. and during her London season, and had numerous adorers. In 1889 she met her first cousin, Lionel Sackville-West, and the two were at once attracted to each other. The rise and fall of their love have already been described. Lord Sackville's family were all his illegitimate children by the Spanish gypsy dancer, Pepita, so Lionel was heir to the barony and to Knole, and it was even said that Victoria married him so as to keep these. But her diary certainly suggests infatuation, if not love, although her grandson warns that she was not the most accurate of writers. It was in the King's Bedroom at Knole, gleaming with Restoration embossed silver furniture, that the words burst out of Lionel: 'God help me, Vicky, I love you so!' Three months later and in the same room he proposed again and was accepted. She wrote the Sackville family motto, *JOUR DE MA VIE*, in her diary that day. 'For love?' she also asked herself. 'I really don't know. They say that women change their minds so often. Men also. . . .' Lionel's mood was anything but doubting; he could hardly bear not to see her, he told her.

All was not plain sailing, however. The family disapproved because they were first cousins, and she was five years older and a Roman Catholic. Lionel asked Cardinal Manning whether he could arrange a dispensation, but he could not. Victoria was distressed when she was told that she would be eternally damned if her children were Protestants. But not even that deterred her, and they were married in the chapel at Knole.

One or two people made some disastrous mistakes. Among the silliest – it is really the only word that fits – was that of one of the most brilliant and attractive of men, a soldier who would never have led his army into an ambush like the one in which he surrendered his personal happiness. Kitty Pakenham was in her early twenties and pretty when she and the Hon. Arthur Wellesley (as he then was) met in Ireland in 1792. A year later he proposed. Kitty's father had recently died, and her brother thought that army pay would not be enough for them to live on, so she refused him. Wellesley wrote that if anything happened to change that opinion his offer still stood; 'my mind will still remain the same', he promised. Eight years passed, during which young Wellesley was by no means unmoved by the many young women who were attracted to him. A fellow-officer told how Colonel Wellesley – promotion came quickly – was known for his 'very susceptible heart, particularly towards, I am sorry to say, married ladies'. But he had not forgotten Kitty. Back at last in England in 1805, Sir Arthur Wellesley – he was now both a Knight of the Bath and no longer short of money – resisted the temptations of his many alluring admirers and repeated his request for the hand of his first love.

It was a touching but lunatic action, and Kitty insisted that he must not feel tied by a promise made so long ago. 'I am very much changed,' she wrote, and it seems it was true. 'She is now very thin and withered (I believe pining in his absence helped to make her more so),' went another description. It was eleven years since they had seen each other, and Wellesley's charms had increased during that time as much as poor Kitty's had dwindled. But he refused to be warned and wrote again proposing marriage. As for what he had been told of how changed she was, he retorted that he did not care. It was her mind he was in love with, and that could not alter. But it could and did. At the wedding in Ireland in 1806 he was confronted with an unattractive bride aged thirty-two. He had to admit the truth to his clergyman brother who was marrying them. 'She has grown ugly, by Jove!' he whispered. Their disastrous marriage will be described alongside others that came to grief.

A magnificent or exotic setting could be as misleading to the passions as long years of absence. The wordly-wise Lady Holland warned her son that couples who became engaged on their travels often felt differently when they met on home ground. Sydney Smith, she told him, said that 'marriages settled up in a country house ought to be considered as null & void when the parties meet in society.' Sometimes an unpropitious start turned out well, however. One amorous suitor, on his way to propose to the Duke of Beaufort's daughter, broke his journey at Castle Howard for a few nights; this gave him second thoughts, and he proposed instead to his host's daughter, Lady Georgina Howard, and was accepted. As Greville described it, 'There never was a less romantic attachment or a more businesslike engagement; nor was there ever a more fortunate choice or a happier union.' Almost exactly the opposite of that story occurred when Lord John Russell, the future Prime Minister, asked Miss Elizabeth Rawdon to marry him. His brother had had the same idea. 'You are too late, Johnny,' said Miss Rawdon. 'I have just accepted William.' The contrast does not stop there. Perhaps Johnny would have suited her better. Her marriage to William could hardly have been more wretched.

The initiative did not always come from the men. Lady Charlotte Bury's diary tells how one 'impudent, forward girl' shamelessly pursued Lord Hartington, the fifth Duke of Devonshire's heir, while he for his part declared that he did not intend to have anything to do with her. She also tells how another girl was sent a *carte blanche* by a ducal lover, who told her to write on it whatever she wanted in return for receiving 'his professions of admiration'.

She wrote one word – 'Duchess' – and returned the card. But that was the last she heard from her duke.

There were certain conventions to be observed – often third parties to involve – in the process of courting. Sometimes a formal application had to be made before any wooing could get under way. When in 1813 Byron decided that Annabella Milbanke was the only woman who offered him 'a prospect of rational happiness', he asked her aunt, Lady Melbourne (who was also at least one of his most intimate women friends), to find out how the land lay. Why did everything have to be so tentative and indirect? Byron later told Annabella that he had wanted to know if he could be permitted 'to cultivate your acquaintance on the chance (a slender one I allow) of improving it into friendship and ultimately to a still kinder sentiment'. This had been, Byron said, 'the *first direct or indirect* approach ever made on my part to a permanent union with any woman & in all probability it will be the last'. Annabella gave Lady Melbourne a statement of what she looked for in a husband, and this was forwarded to Byron. Lady Melbourne acted as both confidante and go-between, and it was not her fault that the story did not have a happy ending.

Annabella had recently played a part in a very different scenario. She was wealthy and clever – Byron nicknamed her the Princess of Parallelograms – but she was not beautiful, and she was still unmarried after four London seasons when she handled one of the coolest rejections of the day. General Edward Pakenham, Kitty's brother, asked Annabella to marry him, but she turned him down because they had different 'principles' and because of the Pakenham tendency to insanity. There was not much passion on either side. The General said: 'I am grateful for your friendship – be assured you shall never repent it.' Annabella answered: 'I have perfect confidence in you.' And they then 'talked as if nothing of this nature had passed between us'. That same day Annabella weighed up the pros and cons of another suitor. Lord Jocelyn had recently broken off his engagement to the Duke of Richmond's daughter because she too had madness in her family. Ugly, bandy-legged, lanky and gawky, his charms could certainly not compare with those of the irresistible Lord Byron – 'mad, bad and dangerous to know'. Those were far more enticing characteristics.

These were all frivolous affairs compared with the serious courtships, leading as they deserved to lasting and happy marriages, of the two Glynne sisters. George Lyttelton had loved Mary Glynne since he was eighteen, and he was hoping to marry her when her sister Catherine became engaged to William Gladstone. Mary was not a girl to be hurried into an important decision; she preferred to meet Lyttelton accidentally, she said, in the Park or elsewhere, rather than on 'settled' occasions which were too 'marked', before she had actually made up her mind to accept him. When at last she did, there was a famous occasion when Gladstone met Lyttelton on his way downstairs, took hold of him, and 'pulled him down on to his knees so that together they might give thanks to Almighty God'.

Nothing could have been more different from the later, lightning-quick engagement of Lord Randolph Churchill and the lovely American, Jennie Jerome. They met in the romantic setting of a ball given on the guardship *Ariadne* in honour of the Tsarevitch and Tsarevna in Cowes Week 1873. It is interesting that both so soon sensed that they would marry. Jenny cajoled her mother into inviting Randolph to dinner the following evening, and after that each guessed what lay ahead. Randolph told a friend how much he admired the Jerome sisters. 'If I can, I mean to make the dark one my wife,' he said. And Jenny told her sister, who did not find Randolph likeable, that she had 'the strangest feeling that he's going to ask me to marry him' and that she was going to accept. A few days later that is exactly what happened.

During the six weeks between then and their formal engagement they came up against some awkward obstacles. Mrs Jerome objected to the suddenness, and considered her daughter worthy of better 'prospects' than those of a younger son who was unlikely to succeed to the dukedom of Marlborough. Her husband wrote from New York that he had grave misgivings because the British aristocracy were inbred and overbred; it is sad that he did not live to see how little decadence there was in Randolph and Jennie's son Winston. His parents' marriage was 'a love match if ever there was one,' Winston said, 'with very little money on either side.' Randolph, then twenty-three, lived on his allowance from his father and asked the Duke to increase this so that he could ask for Jennie's hand. He said that he felt sure that as his wife she would 'encourage me to exertions and to doing something towards making a name for myself'.

Jerome had been wealthy but had recently been nearly ruined.

Even so, he would manage to allow Jennie £2,000 a year. He was convinced that Randolph loved her. 'You are no heiress,' he wrote, 'and it must have taken heaps of love to overcome an Englishman's prejudice against "those horrid Americans".' He was right about that. 'Under any circumstances, an American connection is not one that we would like,' the Duke told his son. His attitude nearly made the Jeromes forbid the match. Jennie's mother wrote to Randolph that she and her husband loved their daughter too much to permit her to marry any man 'without the cordial consent of his family'. And she insisted that if the Duke did give his consent there must be a long engagement so that they could have time to get to know each other much better. When Mr Jerome heard of the Duke's objections, he cabled 'Consent withdrawn'. But gradually all objections were overcome, and it was agreed that, if they still wanted to, they could marry in a year's time.

It was an important year for them both. Randolph was elected to Parliament, and Jennie prepared herself for her future position by reading – on Randolph's recommendation – Disraeli's speeches and books about British politics as well as Gibbon and Horace. There were long, complicated financial discussions between Randolph, both fathers, and their lawyers. Randolph felt he was not offering Jennie much – only his title, a house in London, a pair of fine horses. The Duke and Duchess did not go to the wedding, which took place in Paris on 15 April 1874. The year's delay that had been stipulated was not yet up, and the wedding celebrations were simpler than might have been expected. A few people remembered this with raised eyebrows when Winston was born seven months later, but his brother also was a seven-months' baby. And Randolph and Jennie soon had knottier problems to face.

These glimpses of couples coming together in their various ways must end with a touch of romance and poetry. Where better to find these than in the heart of that brilliant but often tragic group, the Souls? The love story of Alfred Lyttelton and Laura Tennant began in 1884 when they were placed next to each other at a dinner-party. He was then convinced that he must have 'a leathery heart' as by the age of twenty-five he had never been in love; Laura, the fourth of the five fascinating Tennant girls, had had a great many admirers and she too was unhappy at having had to say 'No' so often. Her younger sister Margot, who was to marry Herbert Asquith, described the scene which brought them finally together. It was

January 1885, and Laura had asked Margot what dress she should wear. Margot advised her white muslin – miles of white muslin must have been worn by Victorian young girls – and told her that Mr Lyttelton was strumming on the piano. 'Go and entertain him,' she said. Her description brings us right into the room with them. Margot afterwards described how

she tied her blue ribbon in her hair, and thrust her diamonds into her fichu with lightning rapidity; and with her eyes very big, and her whole being very small and shy, she went into our sitting-room . . . and shut the door, leaning against it. Alfred was playing – he turned round and gazed at the little white figure so near him, so delicious in her dainty muslin next to his great rough travelling clothes – he was going to London that night. He began to break the conspicuous silence by saying something about not many leaving Glen without telling her they loved her, but it all broke down; in a minute his great figure was bending over her, and she was in his arms.

What could be more different from the calculating fortune-hunters and snobbish tuft-hunters? The scene sparkles with music and muslin, Laura's whiteness and shyness contrasting with Lyttelton's bigness and his rough clothes. Would anything ever have happened if Laura, hard to please and shy though she was, had not taken the initiative by remembering those diamonds in her fichu and by provokingly shutting the door and leaning so fetchingly against it? Laura's figure is a Whistler painting, a *fin-de-siècle* vignette to close this chapter on the many different stairs – broad, narrow, ceremonial, or barricaded – which led onwards and upwards to the *piano nobile* of marriage.

6

Weddings and Honeymoons

Even weddings which date from the years before photography are well documented. There are plenty of descriptions of what happened, from rituals which still have their recognizable echoes today to others which now seem altogether strange and outlandish. Ceremonies and celebrations ranged from the simple and rural to the most magnificent of occasions in Westminster Abbey. Exclusively non-religious marriages in registrars' offices did not occur until the Marriage Act of 1836, but both before and after that many weddings took place in private houses. Byron and Annabella were married in the drawing-room of her mother's country home, and the only other people there were her parents, her governess, the two officiating clergymen, and Byron's friend Cam Hobhouse. A touch of splendour was given to a similar occasion in the 'Great Saloon' of the bride's father's house when Viscount Cranborne (later the second Marquess of Salisbury) married Frances Gascoyne in 1821; the bride was given away by the Duke of Wellington, then at the peak of his glory so soon after Waterloo. But private, home-based weddings were not to everyone's taste. The Duke of Bedford explained to his son William in 1817 why he advised him to be married in church. 'Those sort of private marriages which take place in houses never appear to me to carry with them the sanctity and solemnity of the marriage vow,' he wrote.

Sometimes there was good reason for a low-key wedding. Parents often decided not to be present if they did not approve of their child's choice. Or a death in the family could cancel ceremonial arrangements, as it did in 1846 when the Dowager Marchioness of Westminster was taken fatally ill a week before her granddaughter

Elizabeth was to be married with great pomp and circumstance in York Minster, and instead the couple were quietly married in London, with no one present except the two families. Pressure of work was another reason for minimizing the ceremony. The widowed and dissipated Lord Ellenborough was twice the age of his seventeen-year-old bride, and although he found time to woo her passionately and to write her ardent love-poems – and was also soon to find time to divorce her by Act of Parliament – he was so anxious to get back to his political work that his marriage and honeymoon were rushed through at top speed.

Country weddings of course attracted less attention than those in London, but there is a good description of Lady Dorothy Nevill's in 1848. It took place at Wickmere Church in Norfolk, and the wedding-party set off in their carriages at half-past two after sitting down to a festive luncheon. The bride went with her mother in a fine coach-and-four, passing under a welcoming arch of evergreens and flowers at the park gates and another at the entrance to the churchyard. From there to the church the path they walked on was strewn with flowers, and there were crowds both inside and outside. More than a hundred schoolchildren were there, all with 'favours', as well as tenants and 'the poor' of the three local villages. The ancient velvet hangings from the Nevill private chapel had been brought out to decorate the church, which was so crowded that some of the congregation were standing on chairs to get a glimpse of the bride. Did they weep too when they saw that she, according to the eye-witness account, 'wept and went on weeping'? After the service there was a wedding breakfast, with two or three speeches. At long last, after coffee at half-past eight in the evening the bride went off for her honeymoon taking her dog, her cat, and other pets – including 'one or two reptiles'. There is one omission in the detailed description of her going away. She forgets to mention whether, as well as her pets, she also found room in the carriage for her husband. . . .

One of the most notable weddings of the century had an even more distinguished setting than Westminster Abbey. In 1852 Lady Constance Leveson-Gower was only seventeen when she married the ultra-eligible Earl Grosvenor, the future first Marquess and Duke of Westminster. They were first cousins, the bride's father and the bridegroom's mother being brother and sister, which may have some bearing on the fact that the first child of their marriage was epileptic and died when he was only thirty. Constance was a

The Déjeuner for 150 guests in the picture-gallery of Stafford House after Earl Grosvenor's marriage in 1852.

favourite of the Queen, who felt a personal interest in the match; and it was at her wish that the wedding took place in the Chapel Royal, opposite St James's Palace. The Queen herself had been married there and had not been to a wedding in the Chapel – it was usually only for royal couples – since her own.

So from start to finish the celebrations had all the flourish and panache of royalty. Three days before the wedding Constance and her mother, the Duchess of Sutherland, visited the Queen, who presented Constance with a handsome carbuncle brooch. 'Dear girl, I wish her all possible happiness,' the Queen wrote in her journal, and she added her personal accolade: 'It is such a nice marriage.' The next day's *Times* included a detailed description under the cross-head *Marriages in High Life*. This told how the Queen, the Prince Consort, and the Duchess of Kent arrived privately by the garden entrance to the Chapel and entered from the ante-room into the royal closet which faced the altar. A few minutes before one o'clock the bridegroom and his best man, Lord Anson, took their places in front of the Bishop of London and Dr Wesley. Then the bride arrived with her parents and was received by her eight bridesmaids, four of them her future sisters-in-law. 'All these ladies,' the *Times* recorded, 'were beautifully attired in white glacé silk dresses, with jackets to correspond, and white lace bonnets. The bride wore a dress of rich white satin flounced with guipure lace. A wreath of roses, myrtle and orange blossoms and a veil of guipure lace completed the costume.' There were loud cheers from the crowd outside as the couple drove 'in the noble Earl's chariot' the few hundred yards to Stafford House, where in the picture gallery a 'magnificent déjeuner' was awaiting the guests. At half-past three the Earl and Countess set off in a travelling carriage and four, preceded by outriders, for the Duke of Sutherland's house at Cliveden, above the Thames near Maidenhead.

Equally grand was the wedding a generation later, in 1881, of Lord Brooke, the future fifth Earl of Warwick, to Miss Daisy Maynard. It was in fact a love match, although the love did not survive for long and Daisy's money was very welcome to her bridegroom and his family. Editorial comment in *The World* put things bluntly when it welcomed the marriage because it meant that Warwick Castle could now 'be restored by its noble owner, without continuing the appeal to the general public for the necessary funds'. Once again the congregation, in the Abbey this time, included

Lord Brooke's marriage to the heiress, Miss Daisy Maynard, in
Westminster Abbey in 1881.

royals as well as numbers of tenants, brought up in special trains from the country. Crowds lined the road to see the bride as she passed. She had twelve bridesmaids, and there was a touch of pageantry in the bride and bridegroom's departure from the west door of the Abbey in the ancient family state coach which rumbled them away to the reception.

The Duke of Wellington and Disraeli headed the list of great men of their day who were in demand to add glamour to a wedding by being present, witnessing it, giving away the bride, or proposing the toast to the bride and bridegroom at the reception. In 1850, two years before he died, Wellington wrote to the Marchioness of Salisbury that he then had '3 young Ladies to give away in Marriage'. Two were sisters who were to be married together. Wellington joined the wedding party at eleven in the vestry room at St George's, and when the service was over and the parish register duly signed they all went off to what he called 'a sort of luncheon breakfast' at the Brunswick Hotel, a few steps away in Hanover Square. 'I was in my usual bride-giving dress,' he wrote, 'and I believe that the mob took me for one of the bridegrooms.' (That was a joke, of course, as he was then eighty.) It seems he attracted less attention at the other wedding he described to Lady Salisbury. Although dressed as usual for the occasion, he did not think he was taken for the bridegroom that time, as he 'rode to Church alone, and returned from it on horseback alone; and went from my house through the Parks and returned home by the same road on horseback'. A good way to appreciate the almost rural quiet of London in those days when the old Duke could clip-clop peacefully and anonymously from Apsley House to Mayfair or Westminster is to make that same short journey today.

What the *Times* called 'Marriages in High Life' could also be simple, intimate occasions, and these of course were often preferred for second marriages, when usually at least one of the couple had been widowed. In 1870, two years after he had resigned from the position of Secretary of State for Foreign Affairs, and two years too after the second Marquess of Salisbury had died, the fifteenth Earl of Derby married the Dowager Marchioness, whose letters from Wellington have just been quoted. The marriage brought both of them great happiness, although Lord Derby's entry about it in his diary could hardly be more factual and deadpan. At eleven on the wedding morning he and his best man (who was Lady Salisbury's brother) set out from his house on the north side of St James's Square and walked to the Chapel Royal, five minutes away. Some friends were already waiting there and at 11.15 Lady Salisbury arrived and they were married, the Dean of Windsor reading the service. The bride was given away by her eldest brother, Lord De la Warr, and the couple were cheered by the crowd outside as they drove back to St James's Square to see Lord Derby's old mother. Then they went on to the De la Warr house in Grosvenor Street, where the bride's family were waiting and she changed her dress. By 12.40 they were on the way to the country, and there they were greeted by peals of church bells in their honour. The day ended quietly. 'We walked in the park and sat by the lakes in the afternoon,' Lord Derby remembered.

There was nothing young about that wedding, but it was not only middle-aged couples who wanted to escape the flamboyance of a smart society occasion. In 1887, three years after the death of young Lord Grosvenor (the delicate eldest son of the couple whose marriage in 1852 so delighted the Queen), Grosvenor's widow, Sibell, married George Wyndham, nephew of the second Baron Leconfield and a central member of the Souls. Wyndham wrote to his mother that the wedding, in the private family chapel at Eaton Hall, was perfect; it was 'so unlike what I feared would have to be submitted to, no crowd of smart and idle people, no false sentiment, no *train*, it was so artistically hitchless that driving through the little crowd of servants to the pealing of the bells I felt it must be an opera of some sort or stage play.'

Wedding presents and clothes of the past are now as interesting as the hour-by-hour happenings of the day. Before the quiet ceremony that George Wyndham has just been heard describing, the congratulations poured in. 'One large sack still unanswered,' he reported some time after their engagement was announced. The bride also had to get to work on her wardrobe. A good description of this comes from Jane Welsh Carlyle, who did not belong to the great country house world and had never seen a *trousseau* before 1851, when Lord Stanley's daughter, Blanche, at last decided to marry the seventh Earl of Airlie. She was astounded by what she saw.

Good heavens, how is any one woman to use up all those gowns & cloaks & fine clothes of every denomination? And the profusion

123

of coronets! every stocking, every pockethandkerchief, every-thing had a coronet on it!. . . Poor Blanche doesn't seem to know, amidst the excitement & rapture of the trousseau whether she loves the *man* or not; – she hopes well enough for practical purposes.

Another bride was to have all too little time to wear the elegant clothes that were bought for her marriage, because her premonition that she would die giving birth to their first child proved to be a true one. She was Laura, whose husband Alfred has recently been watched falling in love with her as she stood in her white muslin and diamonds, leaning against the sitting-room door. In 1885 she went to Paris to buy clothes, and ordered her wedding-dress from Worth. She humorously suggested that clothes had a symbolism, a suggestion of status. Back in London before the wedding, she wrote: 'I have tried on four gowns and feel hopelessly married, because one is supposed to have a little something not *jeune fille* about one's future gowns. . . – the dignity-giving flounce! and the wifely widening skirts, and the little 'no more proposal' tucker. Can you see all the subtle changes?'

The piles of coroneted clothes and the array of lavish presents were the conventional trimmings of the *dolce vita* of the last century, taken for granted alongside the poverty and deprivation they all knew – with varying degrees of acceptance or indignation – surrounded them. Then as now, friends and family all contributed their presents, and those who were late about it had their memories jogged by the display of other gifts received. This happened to the Duke of Wellington when he visited one of those brides he wrote about in 1850. Spread out for all to see lay 'all the finery to which I imagine I must make some addition'; so off he set on horseback and rode about all morning to find a gift.

Occasionally there was a surprise. Lord Leconfield asked his nephew, George Wyndham, what he would like. A book, he answered, 'any standard work, histories in particular, to start a library'. Back in London after their wedding, they found Uncle Henry's present waiting for them. 'A complete library', Wyndham described it, at least a hundred volumes, all elegantly bound. On these occasions brides were given splendid family jewels, and presents could also include such things as a carriage, a house, or an estate.

George Wyndham, a brilliant member of the Souls, married Sibell, Lady Grosvenor three years after her first husband died. The portrait of her by Edward Clifford was painted in 1887, the year she married George Wyndham.

This description of wedding customs might as well end with a comic scene, described by Lady Holland, who had an eye for such things. In 1824 she wrote to her son, Henry Fox, telling him how 'the silly Bishop Pelham' had officiated at Lord de Dunstanville's wedding. 'The little he had to do he did ill throughout,' she said; the high spot of the occasion came when the bishop should have declared the couple to be man and wife. His concentration slipped for a moment. 'You are now God and Man,' he solemnly informed them.

So much for weddings. How did things go afterwards? That is much harder to discover. Lady Constance Wyndham entered every detail of her engagement in her diary, but as soon as they reached Uppark, where they went for their honeymoon, 'I find it quite impossible to write up my journal from the time we arrived here', she was not the only one to say. After that her diary loses its sparkle and gossip, and before long is weighed down with endless details of births, illnesses, and daily doings of a succession of little Wynd-hams.

There were heavy odds against a happy honeymoon in times when most brides were very young uninformed virgins, no doubt frightened and bewildered by the prospect of sex. What was it that happened after the wedding? Who would tell them about the mysteries of marriage? Although hardly encouraging, it was kind and helpful of Mabell Airlie to write in 1885 to Ettie Grenfell, telling her unpoetically and honestly about her own experience. 'One's honeymoon is chiefly passed in feeling dreadfully ill,' she wrote. 'I, who never feel ill as a rule, did nothing but faint . . . .I was nearly frightened to death and suffered *tortures*!'

It would be an emotional as well as a physical ordeal. The mixed feelings of a young girl leaving her home and family behind were described by Kate Amberley. 'It is an awful moment driving off from the door of one's old home, a choking dizzy sensation, but one is soon consoled, & the joy one has been dreaming of is all realized.' Society weddings were often greeted by cheering crowds in the streets and villages, and there were magnificent family mansions – sometimes a lot of them – to visit and gradually get to know. Bridal couples were given enthusiastic welcomes at railway stations. Randolph and Jennie Churchill were met at Woodstock as they stepped off the train by cheering villagers and tenants, and some of the men unhitched the horses from the carriage, pulling it up to the

Park gates and along the drive overlooking Capability Brown's lake and the monument to Randolph's great ancestor the first Duke, up to the front-door of the Palace. When Sir George Sitwell and Lady Ida paid their first married visit to Renishaw, it was the crew of the Scarborough lifeboat who unharnessed their horses and towed them to the house.

Quiet though their wedding and the start of their honeymoon had been, there was a great welcome at Knowsley for Lord Derby after his marriage to the Dowager Lady Salisbury in 1870. Perhaps it was just as well that this time the bride was not a young girl, but a woman with years of experience of public occasions. A carpet was laid on the platform at the station, which was festooned in their honour, and they were greeted by a salute of fog-signals. At the bottom of the hill below the house, a team of men again took over from the horses. In front of the house tenants and other locals were waiting, with 'every possible demonstration of pleasure and good-will', as Lord Derby noted in his diary. He thanked them from the carriage, but 'there was such curiosity to see her that we were almost mobbed, and her dress torn; but it was all done in kindness.' The crowd stayed till it was dark, and many pints of beer were drunk. 'The police and volunteers alone saved us from serious inconvenience,' the eminent bridegroom wrote.

The American brides who were given these tumultuous receptions were not used to such things. When in 1895 George Curzon took his young bride to Kedleston after their Washington wedding, a special train with one engine and one coach took them to Derby, where Curzon's father, the fourth Baron Scarsdale, and his sister met them. Mary was then escorted on her father-in-law's arm through ranks of city fathers, and the four of them drove in two barouches through crowded, beflagged streets, to the pealing of church bells. Thirty-five thousand people lined the two and a half miles to the gates of Kedleston, where an escort of forty tenants on horseback was waiting to escort them up the drive. At the house she was met by George's three brothers and five of his sisters. And there was more to come. Over five hundred tenants turned up to welcome her with a formal address, inscribed on parchment, which was recited as well as being presented to her on a silver tray. There was music from a band, and much photographing.

Even English brides found it daunting to meet and adjust to a new, often large family. Lord Salisbury's daughter Maud, when she stayed after her marriage with her father-in-law the Earl of Selborne, said that it was 'rather a bore getting into a new family, worse than new stays on the whole'. However, she found them all very friendly and felt sure she would soon 'shake down with them'.

A honeymoon on the move was unconventional and unusual. After their joint wedding – to George Lyttelton and William Gladstone – Mary and Catherine Glynne spent only a few days apart with their husbands before coming together on their way through the Scottish Highlands to the Gladstone family home in Kincardineshire. The four made their way through wild, mountainous country, the girls riding ponies, the husbands alongside on foot. Each bride had been used to attentive escorts and was disconcerted to find that her husband often had a book in his pocket – often a Greek or Latin author she was unable to share – and at odd moments would neglect her by bringing it out and concentrating on its charms rather than hers. William and Catherine shared a deep interest in religion, and read the Bible together every day. Evenings were the time for billiards and chess as well as singing and talk.

Unhappy honeymoons, like bad news in the Press, tend to make livelier reading. Few were more disastrous or more willingly described by the bridegroom than Byron's. His determination to wreck what he called his 'treacle-moon' is clear from the start. As he and Annabella drove to her father's Yorkshire house, he was enraged by the sound of joyful church bells pealing for them. And there was no ambiguity about his feelings for his wife. Did she mean to sleep in the same bed with him, he asked? For his part, he hated sleeping with any woman, but she might do as she pleased. He told how he woke his wife during the night with his loud outburst: 'Good God, I am surely in hell!' His feelings and motives are often hard to disentangle, and although the message is clear it is puzzling that the first and last of the lines written after their wedding are in Byron's writing while the two middle ones are in Annabella's. As they are headed 'Bout rimés Nonsense', they should not be taken too seriously, but all the same they have their tale to tell:

> My wife's a vixen spoilt by her Mamma
> Oh how I pity her poor hen-pecked Papa
> The Lord defend us from a Honey Moon
> Our cares commence our comforts end so soon.

7

For Better for Worse

The image as well as the reality of marriage in the nineteenth-century aristocracy is hard to pin down. So many different circumstances and ideas blew it this way and that. A good starting-point perhaps is the religious ideal, often aimed at even if seldom achieved. Lord Hugh Cecil, who never married, insisted that the letter of the Christian law of marriage must be meticulously followed but he also pointed out that that was not enough. He was a close friend of Winston Churchill, was best man at his wedding, and wrote to him that 'Christian marriage is for Christians . . . . And the marriage vow must be kept altogether – you cannot merely abstain from adultery and leave loving, cherishing etc. etc. to go by the board.' It was a helpful guideline for any couple, whatever their walk of life. The world of the great country houses had many material advantages to make the 'loving, cherishing etc. etc.' easier than it was (and is) for less privileged spouses. Above all, they had plenty of space. George Gissing, the novelist, drew attention to the value of this in that 'it allows husband and wife to keep a great deal apart without any show of mutual unkindness, a condition essential to happiness in marriage'.

On the other hand there were long hours of unavoidable socializing, delightful to some but odious to others. During the London season, formal and stately dinner-parties had to be given by couples who belonged to the top families, all the more often if the husband had a political career, as so many did. That meant accepting invitations to other great houses – Devonshire House, Lansdowne House, Holland House, Apsley House, Norfolk House, and others. Families with royal contacts were summoned to the Palace and attended levées and drawing rooms there. Parties were made up for

the Derby and Ascot, and there were other *al fresco* junketings –
'breakfasts' and 'déjeuners' in gardens, with dinner served in
cathedral-like marquees.

Listening-in to contemporary ideas will help to fill in the gaps. A
happy marriage must be 'the height of human felicity', Lady
Charlotte Bury thought, but she was afraid it was seldom achieved.
The first quality to look for in one's companion – that surely was a
very cool word to choose – would be 'good temper, the second good
sense'. Rather surprisingly, Byron could occasionally be as unde-
manding. 'I wish I were married,' he wrote in 1814 to Lady
Melbourne. 'I don't care about beauty nor *subsequent* virtue' – even
Byron felt entitled to expect a chaste bride – 'nor much about
fortune . . . but I should like – let me see – liveliness – gentleness –
cleanliness – & something of comeliness – & *my own* first born – was
ever man more moderate?' A year later, not long before his
marriage, he told Lady Melbourne he had never met a woman he
'*esteemed*' so much as Annabella, although no passion of his lasted
more than three weeks. 'As to Love, that is done in a week,
(provided the Lady has a reasonable share) besides marriage goes
on better with esteem & confidence than romance.' He found
Annabella pretty enough to be loved by her husband without being
so 'glaringly beautiful as to attract too many rivals'.

Byron's words seldom tallied with his life. Lady Holland's
description of a happy marriage is more convincing. After five
years, she said, the future twenty-third Baron de Ros and his wife,
the fourth Duke of Richmond's daughter, were happy in a down-
to-earth way. 'He is become gardener, carpenter, mechanic, boat-
man, fisherman: in short, always occupied, & consequently always
happy. Five children & much love; it is a beau ideal realised of
happiness.' Lady Holland may have had reasons for sending this
blueprint of married joy to her son, Henry Fox. In 1824 his parents
vetoed his engagement to Miss Villiers because they considered her
not sufficiently well off. Henry was sent abroad, still swearing he
would have no one else – although he did marry another girl, in
Florence in 1832. The Hollands were criticized for their intransi-
gence, particularly in the light of their own story. Lady Holland
had been married at fifteen to Sir Godfrey Webster, who divorced
her when she fell in love with Lord Holland and went off with him,
abandoning her husband and daughter. The Hollands' marriage
was too late to prevent the illegitimacy of their first son, Charles, so

Lord and Lady Holland with Dr Allen and W. Dogett in the Library
at Holland House. A mezzotint by S.W. Reynolds, after the painting by C.R. Leslie.

Dinner at Haddo House, the Earl of Aberdeen's home, in 1884. The
Roseberys and the Gladstones – he is at his hostess's right – can be
seen among the guests. A painting by A.E. Emslie.

it was Henry who succeeded his father and needed a wealthy wife. Charles, free of such considerations, found a bride who was both royal and illegitimate when in 1824 he married Lady Mary Fitz-Clarence, William IVs daughter by Mrs Jordan. As for Lady Holland, the stigma of her divorce for many years kept society ladies from visiting her, although her salon at Holland House attracted the most brilliant political and literary men of the day. Quite apart from her divorce, her own marriage was not everyone's 'beau ideal', as she bossed and snubbed Lord Holland with a sharpness that women in particular found intolerable. It was even said that her husband never had a place in a Whig cabinet because it was feared that the reins would soon be in Lady Holland's hands.

Caroline Lamb's instability and her husband's tormented patience are famous, but their marriage also had its happy moments although these have been rubbed out of the picture by the turbulence that followed them. There is an account of them soon after their wedding when Caroline, already pregnant, followed William everywhere like a devoted dog. At a house party they were never apart, and sat in the same chair reading the same book. She jotted down their daily routine on another visit; they got up at ten, or after that if they had had a late night, had breakfast, talked a little, and then read together. William went for a walk while Caroline finished dressing, took a drive, or walked with the others before going upstairs again. They read Hume or Shakespeare till the dressing bell, and then had a scramble to be ready in time for dinner. What could be more harmonious and contented? No foreboding of the disasters that lay ahead – one child stillborn and another seriously handicapped, Caroline's increasing eccentricity, her affair with Byron, their separation, her early death, William's success and Prime Ministership, and the scandals and lawsuits caused by his intimacies with younger married women.

If only Lord Melbourne (as William became in 1828) had had a supportive wife like his sister, Lady Palmerston, whose brilliant Saturday evening parties were dazzling affairs, bringing together people from a wide range of opinions and backgrounds. A recent biography of Palmerston describes their splendid appearance as they welcomed their guests. Lady Palmerston, then in her mid-fifties but still handsome and elegant in sparkling diamonds, stood at the top of the great staircase beside her husband who greeted everyone warmly, only afterwards admitting that he had no idea who many of them were. Lady Palmerston was the widow of the fifth Earl Cowper who had been a Fellow of the Royal Society, and herself came of a distinguished Whig family. So she was confident and at her ease as a statesman's wife.

It was far harder to an outsider like Mary Curzon, coming from the altogether different background of Washington D.C. During the 1895 General Election, when her father footed the whole bill for Curzon's campaign, she charmed his Southport constituents in spite of the horrifying impression they made on her. Although devoted to Curzon, she was lonely and wretched during the first years of their marriage. He felt that women should have nothing to do with politics and never talked to her about his work. 'He sits and sits at those Foreign Office boxes until I could scream!' she exploded. And yet she was determined not to stand in the way of his career or make demands that might keep him from the House. Her own ill-health worried her as a possible limitation to her ability to help Curzon. An English politician's wife, she explained to her father, 'must always be ready to be a kind of smiling hand-shaking machine'. It is all the more remarkable how valiantly she rose to the occasion when the Queen appointed Curzon Viceroy of India in 1898, also creating him a peer. Mary found herself the second lady of the Empire and played her part to perfection, always warm and gracious on long tours and in crowded assemblies. At last her wish to be a help to her husband had been granted. 'We might as well be Monarchs,' she said. Her personal contribution to Curzon's success was recognized. Years after her death, when he remarried, he requested that his second wife be permitted to wear the order that had been conferred on Mary. But that was not allowed. Mary had been honoured for her own outstanding services to India, not because she was Lord Curzon's wife.

His term of office as Viceroy included the literally crowning occasion of the 1903 Coronation Durbar, but at any time it was a heavily taxing job and it is no coincidence that both Lady Curzon and her predecessor, Lady Canning, who in 1858 became the first Vicereine, both died young. Unlike the Curzons, the Cannings had no children and Charlotte Canning for years had been a 'working wife' as Lady of the Bedchamber to the Queen. Travelling with her to Scotland, Germany, and elsewhere – often on the new royal steam-yacht – had accustomed her to being parted from her husband and in 1845, after many happy years, he fell seriously in love with another woman. It has been suggested – although not confirmed – that it was to shake him free of this liaison that his name was suggested as Governor-General of India. Charlotte did not want to go, but felt it was her duty to be 'ready to follow like a dog'. Worse things than Durbars occur in India; little more than a year after they got there the Mutiny broke out. It was a nightmare time, contrasting luridly with Charlotte's peaceful life in England. The Queen wrote admiringly to her: 'What a comfort for Lord Canning to have such a wife as he has in you, – calm, and pious & *full* of trust in *Him* who will not forsake those who call on Him.' Charlotte may have called on Him more often than the Queen realized, for Canning was not being at all nice to her. Young Johnny Stanley, his aide-de-camp, adored Charlotte and raged at the way he saw her treated. He told his mother that Lady Canning was 'constantly thinking only of him & how to please him & he is as sulky as possible & last night at dinner he snubbed her dreadfully for nothing & her poor face looked so pained, she tried to laugh it off but it was a very agonised laugh.'

Public acceptance with a good grace of a husband's snubs and sulks must always be one of the less well-known ordeals that fall to the lot of a woman in the public eye. 'Clemency Canning' aimed at being a forbearing Governor-General and Viceroy, but was often not a clement husband. But their story ends happily before it ends sadly. Perhaps Canning's mood changed with his fortune; at all events he was much praised, in 1859 was created an earl, and then became loving to his wife once again. Their six-year stint in India was due to end in 1862 and then they would go home to England. Johnny asked his mother to write and tell Lady Canning 'how much I have worshipped her, for I cannot well say so to her face'. But Charlotte never saw England again. After eight days' illness, during which Canning was constantly at her bedside, she died of jungle fever in November 1861. Canning was heartbroken and he too soon died. He was succeeded as Viceroy by Lord Elgin, whose wife welcomed the appointment less than he did. It is again the Stanley family's letters that mention this. Lord Stanley wrote to his wife that Lady Elgin was in despair, not knowing whether to leave her husband or her children. He seems to have seen the problem from the husband's angle. 'He bears this with philosophy,' he wrote '& I don't think cares much about it either way.'

Of all the leading statesmen of the century, few had a happier married life than Gladstone. As a young man he had been solemn, devout and earnest, and his wife and – when they came – his children brought out the warmth and fun in him. One of his friends noticed how marriage had improved him and put it down to the good choice he had made. Gladstone was, he said, an instance of superior men selecting superior women, which was 'generally considered an impossibility'. He did not make Curzon's mistake of not discussing his work with his wife. She could choose, he told her early on, either to be told no political secrets or to be told them all without ever mentioning what she had heard. She chose the second option, which of course brought them much closer together. Even so she did not altogether escape the loneliness that had distressed Mary Curzon a few years earlier. But Gladstone had the empathy to sense this. The claims of public life would increasingly make him something of a recluse, he admitted; he did not want her to be lonely.

Catherine described their life to her sister, Mary Lyttelton, away in the country with her husband in attendance. William had gone off, she wrote, at eight, 'just having swallowed his dinner. I now seldom get any sort of talk and even at breakfast he is reading the newspaper.' Sometimes he worked a fourteen-hour day. Catherine Gladstone devoted her husbandless hours to good works for the sick, the hungry, the old, and 'fallen women'.

Later, particularly of course when she was mistress of No. 10 Downing Street, she was ever-present and active in Gladstone's public life, and was criticized for influencing him more than his colleagues as well as for persuading him to stay on when he and many others thought he should retire. A biography of Catherine includes an eye-witness account of a characteristic appearance by both at a political meeting in Marylebone. Gladstone entered,

followed by a simply-dressed woman who busies herself in warding off the hands of enthusiasts eager to touch him. This is Mrs Gladstone, with the soft face, high-coloured like a girl's, and tremulous mouth, intent on one thing only in this life – her husband. They step up to the platform. . . . A dozen willing hands would aid him but it is hers which grasp his ankles to steady him lest in his eagerness he should slip. She begs a seat immediately behind him.

Not many wives were as all-present and ever-supporting as Catherine Gladstone, but many did do all they could to help, bolstering up diffident husbands, canvassing at election times, and devotedly turning up to hear speeches and debates in the House of Commons, where accommodation for lady visitors was cramped and uncomfortable until the new Gallery was built after the 1834 fire. Some wives overdid their support. It was said that the fifth Earl of Rosebery's marriage, exceptionally happy although it was, was 'founded on admiration and warm affection on the one side, admiration and adoring devotion on the other'. He had had an affectionless childhood and needed the warmth that his wife lavished on him as well as the goodwill she brought by being a gracious hostess at their three homes in England and Scotland. Lady Rosebery's country house background was the somewhat exotic, off-beat one of Mentmore and the Rothschilds, and she was haunted by fears of doing or saying the wrong thing on some important public occasion. She shared with Catherine Gladstone the forgivable failing of being too whole-heartedly dedicated to her husband's career, but theirs remained a remarkable marriage, outstanding at that time for its bridging of the racial and religious gaps. Rosebery was a devout, death-fearing man to whom the Bible, the communion service, and daily prayers were all-important; his wife remained true to her orthodox Jewish faith, which he too respected.

The difference of religion was not a problem until after Hannah's early death from typhoid fever in 1890. He explained this in a letter to the Queen.

> At the moment of death the difference of creed makes itself felt, and another religion steps in to claim the corpse. It was inevitable, and I do not complain; and my wife's family have been more than kind. But none the less it is exquisitely painful.

His grief was never altogether to leave him. He always spent the anniversary of his wife's death alone in his study; he never used any but black-edged writing-paper, and without her backing his ambitions evaporated. His nights were divided between dreams of his dead wife and hours of dreaded insomnia.

Lord Randolph Churchill was one politician whose wife notably made up for her husband's weaknesses. It was not merely Jennie's

George Curzon and his American bride, Mary Leiter, on their first visit to Kedleston after their marriage in 1895.

'A love match if ever there was one', said Winston Churchill of his parents. Lord Randolph Churchill married the beautiful Jennie Jerome – another American wife.

wealth and her charm and beauty which opened all doors to them. Her transatlantic freshness made her question the conventions accepted by English society, and she helped Randolph with his speeches and stiffened his self-confidence at a time when he already had syphilis and his ability was patently on the ebb. She went with him to political meetings all over the country, canvassing and campaigning energetically and brilliantly. Their friends agreed that, without Jennie, Randolph would have achieved much less, probably never becoming Chancellor of the Exchequer and Leader of the House of Commons. He for his part had opened up a brilliant world to her, introducing her to talented, distinguished people among whom she was soon an admired and sparkling figure. Yet it was a miserable marriage, love match though their son declared it to have been. They were pulled apart by Jennie's beauty and charm, by the admiration that the Prince of Wales and many others had for her, as well as by Randolph's debilitating syphilis. So many men were in love with Jennie, and yet her husband was offhand with her. and travelled abroad without her for months at a time, leaving her among the admirers and lovers he knew she had. Her biographer tells that it was only when his jealousy became unbearable that Randolph lost control, as he did with both the Prince of Wales and the Prince's twenty-three-year-old son, ordering the Prince out of his house and threatening to thrash his son because on several occasions their feelings for Jennie were all too apparent. Lord Rosebery urged Jennie to prevent Randolph making any more public appearances now that he was, as he put it, dying 'by inches in public'. Divorce would have destroyed Randolph's career, and Jennie stood by him for this reason and because she realized how much he needed her. She stayed with him even after he was quite insane, although that wrecked her important relationship with Count Charles Kinsky, who was twenty-five years younger than Jennie and broke with her a short time before Randolph died at last, in 1895.

Jennie's achievements were not only those of a tortured marriage and a brilliant social life. She was one of the pioneer wives who undertook public work of her own, helping to found the Ladies' Grand Council of the Primrose League as well as working for an association which sent medical supplies to women in India. It was for her own efforts that in 1885 she was invited to luncheon with the Queen at Windsor, where the Insignia of the Order of the Crown of

India was conferred on her. Gradually recognition was coming for the work done by women, quite apart from what they did to promote their husband's careers. One early step forward was taken by Charlotte Canning when she insisted on describing herself in the 1851 census by the royal appointment she had held for the past eight years. 'Peeress & Lady of the Bedchamber', her entry reads, alongside her husband's as 'Peer and Privy Councillor'.

Court appointments were the only careers open to the daughters and wives of the aristocracy. They were part-time jobs, offered personally by the Queen, generally to young women she knew and liked, sometimes also because they happened to be badly off or widowed or for some other reasons in need of not over-demanding employment. The appointment lasted sometimes for a year, sometimes for a long time. They seem to have been usually successful – apart from the notorious case of Lady Flora Hastings – and they often provided useful experience, giving a young woman confidence to face the publicity and formalities of public life. 'As I have had the pleasure of knowing you ever since *we were* Children, I should be very happy if this would suit you,' the Queen wrote to Charlotte Canning when she invited her to be her Lady of the Bedchamber. The Queen was then twenty-three and had been married for two years. Charlotte was delighted to accept her offer.

What did the position involve? And how much did it interfere with a husband's claims on his wife's time and energy? Before Christmas, 1842, Charlotte wrote from Windsor Castle to her mother that Canning had just paid her a four-day visit there, and she supposed he would be asked again at Christmas. Windsor Castle at Christmas would be an attractive proposition for some husbands; but others – other wives too – might prefer to spend it in their own homes. The Queen knew both Cannings well – Canning was regularly invited to stay, and went shooting with the Prince Consort – and when Charlotte was in her early thirties and still had no children she offered them the Stud House at Hampton Court as their country home. They must feel quite free to say 'No', she said, and this they eventually did, partly because of the expense it would involve, 'certainly 5£ a week', Charlotte wrote. Did her duties with the Queen shake the foundations of her marriage? Or did they on the other hand make up for the shortcomings of her relationship with her husband? There may be a clue in the fact that when in 1851 the Queen suggested that Charlotte's sister Louisa might also become a Lady of the Bedchamber, Louisa declined the honour because, she said, her husband was unwilling for her to be so often away from him and her home in Ireland.

There were other royal positions to be filled. The Duchess of Northumberland was governess to the Princess Victoria, as she then was, from 1835 to 1837, and the Duchess of Sutherland was four times Mistress of the Robes as well as a close friend. When Lord Lyttelton died in 1837, his widow of course lost the family home at Hagley, where she and her children had lived and which would now go to her eldest son. She was not well off and was happy to accept the Queen's offer to be a Lady of the Bedchamber at first, and later governess to the royal children. The family link was continued when in 1863 Lady Lyttelton's granddaughter Lucy became one of the Queen's Maids of Honour.

The job-market for aristocratic wives and daughters was a hit-or-miss set-up which must have wasted much promising potential. Although many able wives supported the leading statesmen who were their husbands, there must have been plenty of others who never had a chance to show their mettle. Granville Harcourt, Frances Waldegrave's third husband, was furious when at one of Lady Palmerston's parties he heard Lord Granville tell Frances: 'You ought to be a Prime Minister's wife, if you had been Lord John's you would have kept the Whig party together.' Another husband who suffered from giving his wife no outlet for her political enthusiasm was Eustace Balfour, who married Lady Frances Campbell, the Duke of Argyll's daughter. Her passion for politics and her devotion to Eustace's politician brother, Arthur Balfour – in whom she found all that was lacking in her husband – strained their marriage and helped to drive Eustace to drink.

There were other cases of a wife's abilities being cramped by marriage. It was only after her husband's death that Lady Stanley of Alderley became a strong pioneer in the movement for women's education; during his lifetime she was content to follow his lead and would not let her name be publicly connected with the work because he would have disapproved. Her daughter Rosalind's marriage had something of the same pattern, as it was only after the birth of her eleven children and her separation from her husband, George Howard, ninth Earl of Carlisle, that she threw herself into social and political work so intransigently that she eventually antagonized her own sons as well as other members of her family.

It certainly seems that the shipwreck of their marriages hit women harder than the men. Disraeli noticed this. 'There is in unhappy marriages,' he wrote, 'a power of misery which surpasses all the sorrows of the world. The entire soul of a woman reposes upon conjugal attachment.' Was he perhaps overstating things a little? There were, after all, some remarkable women – Lady Randolph Churchill, for instance, as well as the Countess of Warwick and Frances Waldegrave – who were strong enough to survive and thrive without a husband's support. Those who were less independent fall into three groups: either they sank into wretchedness and recriminations, or sublimated their feelings and devoted themselves to good works, or they took the logical step of finding somebody else.

Spouses had petty annoyances to put up with, as well as large-scale marital disasters. Lady Elizabeth Grosvenor had to spend long, tedious months with her parents-in-law at Eaton Hall, and she made good use of her boredom by giving, in letters to her mother, amusing vignettes of the humorous second Earl Grosvenor and his solemn, squashing wife.

> Lord Grosvenor is at present able to indulge in the full flow of his little pleasantries and high spirits, as Lady Grosvenor has got a sore throat and so is very much absorbed in taking water-gruel and salt petre in her own room, and he talks away incessantly and in high glee *unchecked* all dinner time, which is a great treat to him and to us.

Welcome though it was to have Lady Grosvenor banished from the dining-room, other strains on a marriage were even harder to bear than a bossy, unamused partner. Sometimes there was nothing for it but to part company. After only one year of marriage Lord Anglesey sent his wife away – we are not told where she was sent – for 'being repeatedly drunk & shying plates at his head'. For those who did not care what people thought, keeping a separate ménage was a solution. The eighth Marquess of Queensberry, whose family provides examples of almost every variety of sexual and marital offence, did this when he brought his family to London from their home in Scotland. He seldom saw them, and carried on with his promiscuous life in his bachelor quarters in St James's Street as if they were still three hundred miles away.

One woman, brilliant and beautiful and fascinating as she was, was aware that she lacked the ability to 'attach' a man's affections. Caroline Norton had not loved her husband, although she never seems to have expected that that would doom their marriage from its start. At the time it crashed, in 1836, she analysed its shortcomings in a letter to Lord Melbourne, with whom she had a much warmer relationship.

> I do not *attach* people . . . . I did what I could for my husband. I was of great service, of great comfort to him. I nursed him devotedly at a time when many young married women would have shewn great displeasure & resentment. I thought I *owed* him to *replace* that love which is *in*voluntary, by all the cheerful effort which can so easily be made voluntarily. No man ever admired me *more*, loved me *less*. I have been eight years his legal mistress & nothing more – no kindness – no tenderness, no *clinging* to the companion of younger days, no sentiment for the Mother of his children. He thought me beautiful and full of talent but I did not *attach* him.

Her punishment for her failed marriage and for giving her husband reason to be suspicious of her affection for Melbourne was monstrously out of proportion to her offence. There was no proof of anything more than indiscretion against her, but society ostracized her for years and her children were taken away from her, torturing her with anxiety that they were not being well looked after. (A boy of eight did in fact die.)

It was the same basic mistake of marrying without love that wrecked the Duke of Wellington's marriage and cut him off too from his children. He was another brilliant, sought-after person who was cruelly punished for a stupid marriage. 'Would you have believed that anybody could have been such a *d----d* fool? I was not the least in love with her,' he told Mrs Arbuthnot. Things had gone wrong from the start. After a week of honeymoon they went their separate ways, Kitty to her Irish home, Wellington back to army service in England. Harriette Wilson claimed that he had been one of her lovers, but he said he did not see her after his marriage. He was certainly not short of other feminine admirers. Kitty was soon pregnant, but complained that Wellington was unloving and uncaring; her adoration annoyed him and sparked off irritation which made her all the more nervous and awkward. It was clear that she was not the right wife for him. He needed someone who would be a warm, welcoming hostess, but poor Kitty was shy and gauche; she bored his friends, he said, and so they did not come to the house. She spoiled their two sons, criticized other women, and ran up big debts. Whether because she was over-generous and gave large sums away or because Wellington did not allow her enough, they certainly had arguments about money. On one occasion he accused her of 'misappropriation' of her housekeeping money; he never forgot having said that.

Meanwhile he was surrounded by clever, elegant women of the world who shared his political interests. How could he help comparing them with Kitty, who dressed badly and because she was shortsighted did not recognize people at parties or when their carriages passed in the London streets? In 1821 she was forty-seven but looked older, with greying curls and a colourless complexion. To try to please Wellington she dyed her hair, but it was too late. Their ideas and their ways of life were too different, and they parted company, Kitty taking Stratfield Saye as her base while Wellington stayed in town at Apsley House. She must have felt ill-treated as well as a failure. It was at that time that she asked Wellington to increase her allowance from £500 to £670, and met with a refusal.

Theirs was one of those relationships which are all the more torturing because they lack the indifference which can anaesthetize resentment and exasperation. In their agonized ways they loved each other. After Kitty's death Wellington said that she was 'his only bride beyond the grave', and Kitty in spite of everything always loved her husband. 'With all my heart and soul I have loved him straight from the first time I knew him (I was not then fifteen).' As she lay dying and holding Wellington's hand she felt for an armlet she had given him years before and found that he was still wearing it. 'She found it, as she would have found it any time these twenty years, had she cared to look for it,' he said.

It is easy to forget that the great country houses were not the only setting for their owners' loves and marriages. Surprisingly many couples spent their first years together either in a rented furnished house in London or, if they needed to economize, as resident guests – and therefore with still a suggestion of the parent-child relationship – in one of the family homes. When the head of the family died there was of course something of a general post, with his widow moving out of the house that had been hers for years, and the heir entering on his succession, probably with his own wife and family. It was a help that the houses were so big. William and Caroline Lamb were given the whole first floor of the Melbourne town house in Whitehall, with their own entrance and independent 'establishment'. Others, like Randolph and Jennie Churchill, were less lucky; after their marriage in 1874 they had to live more carefully than their smart, wealthy friends. Although the Duke of Marlborough gave them a thirty-seven-year lease on a fine house in Charles Street, Mayfair, they decided that to begin with they could not afford to furnish more than two bedrooms and a downstairs sitting-room which they would also use as a dining-room.

Even well-to-do couples were often expected to go on long visits to their parents. Lord Grosvenor's wife has already been heard describing her ill-matched parents-in-law at Eaton Hall. She also wrote to her mother of the rare treat it was for her and her husband to be 'quite alone and doing what *we* like'. There were so many other dreary days that had to be spent with her mother-in-law, going with her in the carriage to call on equally boring neighbours and elderly friends, during the long evenings embroidering and reading with her. Or worse still, listening to 'Mr Aychbourn reading aloud "The Last of the Mohicans" or "Rokeby" in so lachrymose a manner' that even the dog howled. She also had to put up with the 'twaddling and incessant chatter' of her mother-in-law's visitors. Her husband had a much easier time of it, as he had leisure and work which took him away from the house. Their own experience might have helped them to make things easier for their son, Henry Lupus, Earl Grosvenor (the future first Duke of Westminster) and his wife. But the second Marquess of Westminster, as he then was, nagged them endlessly about what he felt was their extravagant way of life. The young couple had three princely households to run, and certainly had an income of over £8,000 a year – a large fortune in those days – but it was not enough for the social life they led; four years after their marriage they had to ask for a rise. After a first refusal and some more lecturing about the need to economize, the Marquess eventually came to the rescue. Yet both families were among the wealthiest in the land and a vast inheritance lay ahead of the couple who found it so hard to make ends meet.

A few – fewer than might be expected – did take an independent stand and decided against living with parents because they were not willing to accept their way of life and their constant company. Viscount Amberley and his wife Kate were invited to stay with Kate's parents in the Stanley home in Dover Street when they were in town, but they decided that neither of them would like it and they would not be as quiet or independent as if they were on their own. So they made do with 'lodgings' in Grosvenor Street – a sitting-room and small dining-room on the ground floor, and bedrooms upstairs. Kate felt that it was her father's dislike of their being in lodgings that made him invite them to Dover Street.

Growing up in an ancestral home among inherited furniture and works of art, however splendid they may be, is a very different experience from making a deliberate choice of where to live and what possessions to have around. Perhaps this helped couples to accept the prevailing custom of taking rented London houses which were full of other people's belongings. Some rented houses were unfurnished, but this did not always give a wife the freedom she wanted to arrange her own first home. When George and Mary Curzon married in 1895 and moved into a large rented house in Carlton House Terrace, Mary was horrified to find that George had taken it upon himself to arrange the decoration and furniture and even to engage all the servants. Accustomed as she was to transatlantic standards of comfort, she found the house intolerable, with its smelly lavatories and disobliging staff. It was also too expensive for them, so after a few months they moved, this time renting Arthur Balfour's house. It is a clue to their relationship at that time that once again it was Curzon who decided how the place should be decorated and furnished, even though it was Mary's father who paid the bills.

8

Second Marriages

Most second marriages, even at the end of the century, followed the death of one of the original couple – for the simple reason that divorce was such a rare and expensive affair. A respectful interval of at least one year was considered proper. The frequency and danger of childbirth put wives especially at risk, so that replacements for them often had to be found. Even in aristocratic families where a widower's children had nannies and governesses to look after them, they needed to be mothered no less than their father needed to be wived. Bereaved widowers often forced themselves to become suitors and lovers once again.

It was a daunting task, all the more so if the earlier marriage had been a happy one. In 1857 Lord Lyttelton was forty, not at all well off, and the father of twelve children when his wife died, loved but overcropped. He faced up to his predicament: there was nothing for it, he must marry again. He wrote to his brother that it was 'hard to look forward to perhaps thirty or forty years without some real hope in prospect', even though 'a poor substitute for the past it needs must be.' So what kind of woman would be suitable? A young girl would not do, he decided, as twelve children were more than enough and he did not want a second brood. If she were a widow she must not have children of her own, 'which is always incon-venient'; and some money would also be welcome. His choice was a widow, Louisa Marchioness of Waterford, and in 1861 he made an oblique approach by writing to her sister to enquire whether she might be open to an offer of marriage from him. He put his cards candidly on the table. He had not seen Lady Waterford more than once in the last twenty years, he wrote, and she might well think that he was attracted more by her money than by herself. 'Indeed I *could* not marry any one without any fortune,' he admitted. It was not a flattering proposal and it came to nothing, but in 1869, after he had been on his own for twelve years, Lord Lyttelton did find an excellent second wife, Sybella Mildmay. Even though also a widow and already thirty-seven, she did present her husband with three more children. The youngest boy of the first family, Alfred – who has been seen in another context falling in love with, marrying, and mourning the white-muslined Laura Tennant – was twelve when he acquired a stepmother. 'Never did any newcomer into a large family,' he wrote afterwards, 'identify herself more completely with her surroundings or more unreservedly lavish her resources in making us happy.'

Some such offers were unacceptable. Lord Lyttelton's sister Caroline was about the same age when a similar opportunity came her way. She had been in love with a man who had married someone else, and she must have known that it was her last chance of marriage and a family when a proposal was made to her by Lord Dartmouth. Twenty years older than she was, he had recently lost his second wife when he turned to Caroline. 'There are six little children hoping to call you Mamma,' he said. Not altogether surprisingly, she settled for spinsterhood.

One of the happiest and most remarkable marriages of an old man to a young girl was that of the famous Thomas Coke of Holkham, who at the age of eighty-five had at last accepted the earldom of Leicester as a reward for his agricultural work. He had previously refused the title. Only fifteen years before that, in 1822, he married the eighteen-year-old Lady Anne Keppel, a friend of one of his daughters – as well as the daughter of one of his own friends – whom he had agreed to look after while she was on a visit to London. His first marriage had been in 1775, nearly half a century earlier, and for over twenty years he had been a widower. It was in fact Lady Anne who took the initiative; she fell passionately in love with Coke and determined to marry him. Once again it was a happy marriage and five more children were born, with a fifty-year gap between the births of Coke's eldest and youngest offspring. Coke died when he was ninety and his wife not yet forty. Far from grudging her her youth and a second husband, he had deliberately encouraged her affection for another of his own friends, a widower whom she did eventually marry. He was glad to know that someone he liked and trusted would look after her during what might be a very long widowhood. On one occasion he met his wife and his friend as they came in from riding together. 'I hope you will have many happy rides together,' the excellent old fellow was heard to say.

When widowed fathers married young women and proceeded to have second families there was inevitably a jumbling-up of the generations, children and grandchildren of about the same age growing up together as if they shared the same parents. This happened in the second Marquess of Salisbury's family after his first wife died. In 1847, after an eight-year pause, he married again and had five more children. Lady Mary Sackville-West was twenty-three, but in spite of the age-difference and the fact that her sister married the ninth Duke of Bedford, her family considered that hers was the 'best' – what did they mean by that? – of their three girls' marriages. So is there any truth in the story that Lord Salisbury was refused the first time he proposed to Lady Mary? And that the second time he was overhead telling her that he would not live more than five years – he was then fifty-six – and she would then be a rich widow? Fortunately he broke his word and they had twenty-one good years together, as well as five children, before he died. It was two years later that his widow married her late husband's friend and colleague the fifteenth Earl of Derby.

Their wedding-day, honeymoon, and welcome at Knowsley have already been described. Married life went equally calmly and happily for them both. There had been recent upheavals in each of their lives: Lord Derby's diary tells of his sympathy for Lady Salisbury, who in two years had lost her husband, both her parents, and her sister. Her home, too, of course. On her husband's death this went to the third Marquess, her husband's eldest surviving son by his first marriage, who moved into Hatfield with his wife and children. Lord Derby's life had also undergone what he called a 'great change' during the past year, when his own father had died and he too had succeeded. He was forty-four when he married, and had held cabinet office in several governments, the last being that of Secretary of State for Foreign Affairs from 1866 to 1868.

The day the newspapers announced his engagement he was greeted in the House of Lords, his diary tells, with many congratulations – 'Not the least cordial being that of Salisbury, which under the circumstances I am glad of.' But how would Lady Salisbury's own children feel about their mother remarrying? (Lord

Salisbury was, after all, only her stepson.) That same day he was reassured.

> Much pleased also at Mary Cecil's manner, with her mother and me, we dining *en trio*. It is impossible that any girl should like, or should not be affected by, the remarriage of her mother; but it was impossible to show the feeling less than M. did. I shall remember it to her credit.

Lord Derby did more than that. His diary entry for the following day tells that he walked with Lady Salisbury in Kensington Gardens, and it adds: 'Bought for Mary a ball-dress. Cost £15.'

Lord Derby's diary changed key after his engagement. 'Blank day', 'Alone', 'Nothing happened', earlier entries had read. But now it told of drives, walks and visits together, letters written, and a shopping outing to choose a dressing-case. 'I do not know how long it is since my days have passed in so completely, but pleasantly, idle a fashion,' he wrote on one occasion. Soon after that came an outing that meant a lot to them both. They went by train to Hatfield and had lunch in the Vineyard there. That was where, fifteen years earlier – Lord Derby still remembered the day – they had had an important talk; and now they had luncheon together 'nearly on the spot where in July 1855 we had held a conversation which led to a close friendship between us, never since interrupted'.

In that relatively warless century not many young husbands died before their wives. (The tables were to be tragically turned during the first twenty years of the next.) But Lord Grosvenor, the delicate and epileptic son of the first Duke of Westminster, died only ten years after his marriage, having been devotedly nursed by his ravishingly beautiful, multiply adored wife Sibell. Because she was ethereal and very young, while he was clumsy and immensely rich, it was assumed that theirs was a loveless, arranged match, but their ten years together do not suggest this. When she was left a widow with three young children it was certain that she would marry again. At least eighty suitors – many of them, including George Curzon, brilliant fellow-members of the Souls – were in love with her. An *embarras de richesse*, in every sense. Her father-in-law the Duke was so fond of Sibell that he was determined she would not marry the wrong man, and when she decided on George Wyndham he vetted him carefully to be sure that he was likely to make her

149

happy. The Westminsters are a good example of generation-interweaving. Constance, the first Duke's wife, died in 1880, four years before her epileptic son, and two years later her husband married again. This time his bride was thirty-two years his junior, younger even than three of her own stepchildren, who were already married and parents themselves. The youngest of the Duke's first family were only a few years older than the four who were born of his second marriage.

Margot Tennant's marriage in 1894 to Herbert Asquith, then Home Secretary and later to be Liberal Prime Minister, was spotlit by public interest. He was a widower, and there were plenty of sardonic comments. 'Really, to lose your wife, be made Home Secretary, and marry the woman you love in three years is too much luck for one man,' said their friend Evan Charteris. The Queen, however, considered Margot 'most unfit for a Cabinet Minister's wife', and many people agreed with her. Lord Rosebery went so far as to warn Asquith against the match. (Both she and her marriage were the subjects of E.F. Benson's best-selling novel, *Dodo*.) Margot, unconventional, brilliant, elegant, and fascinating, ceased to play her star part among the Souls after she married Asquith. She recognized the problem, common to many second marriages, of having to reconcile the probably very different groups of friends each has made. For someone of her temperament, she said, this meant keeping friends she had already made and converting her husband into caring for them. Ettie Grenfell, another Soul, assessed Margot's marriage. 'She is not the very least in love with him and faces it, but I do thoroughly believe it will all go well.'

Earlier in the century the difficulty of divorce as well as the conventions of the time led to many couples loving each other – and often also living together – for years before the death of a first partner set them free to marry. By then there was often opposition from the children of the first marriage as well as from society. One of the best known of these was the marriage in 1809 of the fifth Duke of Devonshire to Lady Elizabeth Foster, who during his first marriage had been the Duke's mistress, mother of two of his children, and also 'dearest Bess' and loving friend to Georgiana, his Duchess. It is a sign of the times that although the Devonshire House illegitimates were brought up easily and happily alongside their legitimate playmates, Burke's Peerage does not acknowledge their existence. It mentions that in 1809 the Duke married the widowed Lady Elizabeth Foster, and then goes on to say that 'that lady had no issue'. (Her two Foster sons are of course mentioned in their father's family.)

Society took much the same line. After all those years of tolerant and affectionate family acceptance, things changed when there was a chance of Lady Elizabeth marrying the Duke. As their mother's illness brought her death nearer, her son, Lord Hartington, and the rest of the family dreaded this more and more; although in this case there could not have been the usual fear of another marriage bringing the possibility of more children to share the inheritance. One of the few who tolerated the marriage, when it eventually came, was the dead Duchess's sister, Lady Bessborough; she did what she could to lessen the antagonism between the Spencers (her own family and that of the Duke's first wife), and to oppose the suggestion that her niece Harriet should leave her father's houses now that they had a new mistress.

The confrontation was distressing for everyone concerned. Lady Elizabeth offered to refrain from using her new title – out of respect, she said, for old Lady Spencer, the dead Duchess's mother, and because the Duke advised it. But the younger members of the family called her some terrible names. 'That wily woman' and 'this mistress of yr. papa's', Caroline Lamb called her in letters to Lord Hartington, her old admirer; and he, a week before his father's marriage, referred to his future stepmother as 'that crocodile'. Even after the Duke's death two years later, his son (now the sixth Duke of Devonshire, of course) complained about her. Bess, now the Dowager Duchess, expected a lot from him financially, he said, both for herself and for the children she had had by his father.

A similar set-up was much more smoothly handled by his successor the eighth Duke, who for thirty years had an affair with the German-born, good-looking Duchess of Manchester. When at last the Duke of Manchester died, his widow married her lover in 1892 soon after he succeeded to the dukedom, and became known as the 'Double Duchess'. A prettier name than 'that crocodile'.

Years before that, another long extramarital relationship had come into harbour in 1839 when, two years after her husband's death, Lady Cowper married Palmerston. Although they had been together for so long, she had her doubts about taking that step. She was already fifty when her husband died; would it not be ludicrous and undignified to marry again at her age? Lady Cowper was Lord Melbourne's sister, so of course her second marriage was one of the things the Queen and he discussed. Lord Palmerston had always wanted to marry Lady Cowper, Melbourne explained. But were people ever happy, the Queen asked, when they married so late in life, after they were already set in their habits? A good question: Palmerston, by then fifty-five and Foreign Secretary, was known to be flirtatious and to live beyond his means. It would be a great change for him, Lord Melbourne admitted to the Queen, as he had been 'accustomed to run about everywhere'. Lady Cowper was anxious to have the Queen's approval, he said, and to be assured that she did not think it 'foolish' to marry at her age. The Queen graciously complied, although she guessed that Prince Albert – her own wedding was only a few months ahead – would be amused by so seasoned a bridal pair. She gave him the news in a letter written a few months before their wedding.

> They are, both of them, above fifty, and I think that they are quite right so to act, because Palmerston, since the death of his sisters, is quite alone in the world, and *Lady C.* is a very clever woman, and *much* attached to him; still, I feel sure it will make you smile.

He was not the only one to smile. Lady Cowper's family foresaw gossip, and they also thought it a come-down for her to marry a mere viscount – his was only an Irish peerage too – after having been the wife of an earl. His £12,000 a year was also less than she had been used to. But the warmth of their affection melted away the doubts. Lady Holland wrote that it would be 'the union of the best-tempered persons in the world. *Never* did I see a man more in love & devoted; so there is every prospect of happiness for them, as her family on both sides are friendly & kind upon the subject.' Their prospect of happiness was probably much surer than that of many young engaged couples, precisely because they certainly did know each other. They each let their London home, and together took a fine house in Carlton Gardens where – and later at their Piccadilly home – Lady Palmerston's parties were a great help to her husband. She was still attractive, and his fancy too could still be caught by a handsome woman. One story goes that when she was over sixty Lady Palmerston went out of her way to avoid travelling

Frances Waldegrave, who was not 'really married' until after her fourth wedding.

William Lamb's sister, Emily, married Lord Cowper in 1805 when she was eighteen and for years Palmerston was her lover. In 1839, two years after Lord Cowper's death, they married.

unaccompanied in her coach with the notorious womanizer, 'Poodle' Byng, so as not to make Palmerston jealous. He for his part gratefully remembered each wedding anniversary and one year celebrated it by writing her a love-poem.

When there could be doubts and disapproval about a second marriage, how could a woman be four times a wife and still respected and admired? John Braham, the Jewish singer who was one of the most popular tenors of his day, has already been mentioned, as has his brilliant and beautiful daughter whose many suitors included the Duke of Newcastle and the heir to the Duke of St Albans. Frances' two extraordinary first marriages can only be summarized here. On her eighteenth birthday she agreed, mainly from compassion, to marry John, the illegitimate son of the sixth Earl Waldegrave. He was a drunkard, epileptic, and always in debt, but he was passionately in love with Frances, and after their marriage in 1839 she lived in a *ménage à trois* with him and his legitimate brother George until John became insane and died a year later. Frances had mothered and nursed John Waldegrave, who had never been able to consummate their marriage. Predictably she and George became fond of each other. The Marriage Act of 1835 forbade a widow to marry her deceased husband's brother, but John's illegitimacy and unconsummated marriage were taken into consideration, and in 1840 Frances married George (by then the seventh Earl Waldegrave) in Edinburgh.

Once again Frances had a problem husband. George had been implicated in a hurly-burly in which a policeman had been injured, and he was heavily fined and sentenced to six months in prison. Frances, always a devoted wife, insisted on joining him, and contemporary accounts tell of their enjoyable social life together there, the dinner parties they gave, and the crowd of friends who flocked to them. After his release George too became semi-imbecile and needed nursing, and he died of cirrhosis in 1846 on the sixth anniversary of their wedding. Frances, now the Dowager Countess, was wealthy and still only twenty-six. Of course she would marry again, in spite of her first two discouraging experiences. She was still troubled by doubts about the validity of her second marriage, and it has been suggested that that may have been a reason she accepted as her third husband George Harcourt, eldest son of the Archbishop of York. Perhaps the archiepiscopal connection would cancel out the old question-mark?

Even so, how could an attractive and intelligent woman accept three such impossible husbands? Harcourt, sixty-one, widowed and grumpy, could hardly have been less appealing. Three years after their marriage, Frances's future fourth husband enters the story. Chichester Fortescue, Liberal Member of Parliament and two years younger than Frances, who was then twenty-nine, fell deeply in love with her. He broke off the affair he was then involved in and surprised all who knew him by chastely loving Frances for eleven years until he eventually became her fourth husband. It is one of Frances's previous critics, Lady Cremorne, who has left a compassionate description of the joyless marriage to Harcourt. She pitied Frances, she said, 'such a loving nature as hers, no children and such a husband – such a want of fireside happiness – such perpetual brilliancy and admiration *abroad*, such a *manque* at home'. That was in 1860, when Harcourt was seventy-five, Frances not yet forty. Again she cared for her husband devotedly, and when he died in 1861 his will expressed the appreciation of his wife that had often been missing in his lifetime. Then he had bullied her, forbidding her to help pay her father's debts – with money that had, of course, been hers – and insisting that he had married beneath him. But he left everything to Lady Waldegrave, as she was still called, and left a note advising her 'earnestly to unite herself again with someone who may deserve to enjoy the blessing of her society during the many years of her probable survival after my life'.

In her third widowhood Frances was still admired and courted in society. By no one more ardently than the faithful Chichester Fortescue, who told a friend about his devotion – 'how desperately I loved her – how for her sake I had not known what a woman was for eleven years – that I had intended not to speak out to her until she took off her widow's cap'. Her friends urged her to marry him, but the wisest advice came from her old nurse, who told her not to marry Fortescue unless she loved him. 'You have never really been married yet,' she said, 'you never yet really married for yourself. I want to see you *really married* at last.' Years before, when she was a girl, Frances had been promised by a gypsy fortune-teller that she would have wealth, rank, fame, and four husbands, but the last would be the only one she loved. And so it was. Fortescue described his devotion in a thirteen-page letter to Frances, and in 1863 they were married at Old Brompton Church, the scene of her first wedding nearly twenty years before.

They had sixteen happy years together before Frances died. Fortescue held various government offices and in 1874 was created Baron Carlingford. From 1868 to 1870 he was Chief Secretary for Ireland, and an anecdote from those years gives an attractive picture of Frances. Soon after arriving in Dublin she was seen entering the Chief Secretary's official box at the theatre there. She looked elegant and beautiful, and a voice called out to her from the gallery: 'And would your ladyship be after informing us,' it enquired, 'which of your husbands do ye like the best?' She looked straight up to the gallery, and her answer was clearly heard by everyone. 'The Irishman, of course,' she called, and the whole theatre rang with applause at her answer.

9

Let no Man put asunder

Variations in sexual conventions and behaviour were both cause and effect of some important changes in the law. For the first half of the nineteenth century a legal divorce was obtainable in England only by a husband who had both an unfaithful wife and enough money to get an Act of Parliament passed. Scottish law was more permissive; for nearly three hundred years divorce there had been available to both men and women, and was much less costly. A speech in the House of Lords pleaded for divorce in England to be granted on similar grounds to both sexes, but it was opposed by the Lord Chancellor of the day. 'The adultery of the wife,' he argued 'might be the means of palming spurious offspring upon the husband, while the adultery of the husband could have no such effect.' Unfair it might be, but it was strong pleading, specially where ancient inheritance was at stake.

The Bible, of course, pronounced firmly against divorce: whom God hath joined together let no man put asunder. Was it that teaching, combined with the ancient threat to visit the sins of the fathers upon the children, that inspired Lady Airlie when her daughter married a man whose parents had separated? For years she addressed her letters to her daughter in her maiden name, to avoid using the one her parents-in-law had polluted.

Where there was no doubt about a wife's adultery and the need for this to continue, divorce had to be accepted. When Henry Paget, the future first Earl of Anglesey, and Henry Wellesley's wife Charlotte fell deeply in love, they were both tortured by remorse but found it impossible to carry on with their separate lives. Charlotte was distraught at leaving her children, but she had to go to Paget, and divorce was the only tolerable answer for all four partners. Or a duel? Charlotte's step-brother made a desperate attempt to save her from scandal and sin, and challenged Paget, who deliberately 'aimed off'. Nothing would induce him, he said, to 'add to the injuries' he had already inflicted on Charlotte's family by firing on her brother.

The law forced them all into endless falsity – even perjury – in ways which are now neither interesting nor easy to disentangle. The divorce had to be regularized by the Church, and the two couples had to be seen to return and openly live together with their original partners. Charlotte was pregnant with Paget's child when this requirement brought her back to live for several months with her husband and two of her children. Even those who accepted the workings of the law as it then stood were amazed. Charlotte's brother-in-law, the future Duke of Wellington, could not understand how Charlotte could be allowed 'to live & *perform* with a Man, from whom she has been divorced by the Church; & I conclude that poor Henry will again be dragged through the Mire, & will marry this blooming Virgin again as soon as she will have been delivered of the consequences of her little amusement.'

There was no question of that. On the grounds of Charlotte's adultery Wellesley brought an action for 'Criminal Conversation' against Paget, with damages of over £20,000, and his private Bill in the House of Lords in 1810 brought about the dissolution of the marriage. But English law did not allow Caroline Paget, who was of course equally wronged by her husband's adultery, a chance to sue for divorce. Fortunately the law of Scotland provided an escape-route, so Paget and Charlotte rented a house in Perthshire and lived together there. They still had problems: it had to be proved that there was no connivance, but it was well known that Caroline would marry the Duke of Argyll when her marriage had been dissolved. So this involved them in perjury, as did the law's refusal to allow marriage between a divorced husband and the woman with whom his adultery was proved. An easy way out of this quandary was for Paget to be seen by witnesses in bed with some other woman, but that was more than Charlotte could concede. Eventually a solution was found, and the witnesses said they had seen Paget in bed with a woman whom they had not had a chance of identifying. At last the decree was made absolute, and Paget and Charlotte married – first in Scotland, and afterwards in England. The following month the Duke of Argyll and Caroline became husband and wife.

Innocent employment for Foreign Princes

— Harley — St. } *vide evidence on the* Swartzenburgh *affair* Lady Ellenborough

The Ellenborough divorce case received record Press coverage. This newspaper cartoon shows Prince Schwarzenberg lacing up Jane Digby's stays, illustrating part of the evidence given in court by a witness.

How much more simply the same conclusion would be reached today. Gradually ideas were changed by public interest in such cases and by increasingly outspoken comments in the Press and in Parliament. Another much-discussed marriage which played an important part in drawing attention to the law's unfairness to women was that of Lord Ellenborough to Jane Digby. She was beautiful, talented, and much younger-than her husband, who was absorbed in his political career and neglected her grossly. So she fell in love with a young diplomat, Prince Schwarzenberg, and had a flamboyantly open affair with him, eventually giving birth to his child. Lord Ellenborough agreed to a divorce, and it was the verbatim account in the *Times* of the House of Lords debate – the closely printed, narrow columns take up most of the first two pages in the issue of 1 April 1830 – that attracted so much attention to the shortcomings of the law as it stood. The marriage was finally dissolved by Act of Parliament, and Jane's case was persuasively pleaded in the House of Commons by Joseph Hume, M.P.

> In this country a woman is punished severely for faults which in the husband are overlooked. For a single slip she is banished from society. And yet. . . can anyone overlook the gross neglect on Lord Ellenborough's part that has led to the unhappy events of the past couple of years?. . . What is a young lady to do who is neglected by her husband? Is she to stop at home all day?

Mr Hume overstated Jane's case; it was certainly not a question of a 'single slip'. But his main argument was valid and needed to be aired in public. Whether trivial details given in evidence by the Ellenborough's groom, coachman, butler, and maidservant deserved front-page coverage in the *Times* is doubtful, but anyway that concerned nobody except the Editor. A leading article that day asserted that Lord Ellenborough's right to divorce followed on proof of his wife's adultery, so long as there had been no collusion or connivance with his wife, no gross negligence of her morals or comforts, no gross profligacy. It ended by calling for 'the fullest, the most fearless, and above all, the most impartial investigation of this extraordinary case'.

As often happens, it was the description of all the intrigue and details of adultery that attracted so much interest. The next case that helped to bring about the reform of the divorce law was that of

160

Lord Melbourne and Caroline Norton, whose unjust treatment made her take up the cudgels to canvass public opinion and lobby for legislation which did eventually – although too late to be of any help to her – improve the legal status of women. When in 1836 Caroline's husband, George Norton, brought an action for damages against Lord Melbourne, who was then Prime Minister, the court returned a strong verdict against Norton, but Caroline was left without her children and without any allowance from her husband. As Norton's wife, Caroline was not entitled to be represented by counsel in the case, could be forbidden by her husband to see their children, and had no right to any property of her own. Her clothes, her jewels, even what she earned from her writing could all be impounded by Norton. Moreover, because after leaving her husband she had on one occasion returned to him, she was debarred from divorcing him on grounds of cruelty. Legal separation by mutual consent was a possibility, but this would cause difficulties if either afterwards attempted to obtain a divorce from the ecclesiastical court.

So the innocent although undeniably indiscreet Caroline lost everything – her children, her home, her friendship with Lord Melbourne, her possessions, and of course her reputation. Not till 1839 was she again received at court – evidence of no longer being the object of royal disapproval. From 1836 to 1841 she struggled bravely to get her children back and to change the law which had parted her from them. She urged her case in a pamphlet and by tireless lobbying, but the Infant Custody Bill was opposed and rejected before at last being passed by both Houses in 1839.

Throughout her campaign the Press attacked Caroline, but she was helpless because a married woman was not entitled to sue except through her husband. The only way she could fight the good fight was by urging her case in pamphlets. *English Laws for Women in the Nineteenth Century* was one; another, on the subject of Lord Cranworth's Divorce Bill, *A Letter to the Queen*. At last the Matrimonial Causes Act of 1857 redressed many of the old injustices. After that a deserted wife could keep any money she earned without her husband having any legal claim on it; the court could order an allowance to be paid for her maintenance; a married woman could inherit or make a bequest as freely as a single woman; and a wife who was separated from her husband was entitled to have recourse to the law in a civil proceeding.

One of the most remarkable contradictions of Caroline Norton's tormented life is that in spite of all the injustice and crusading she did not for a second believe in the equality of the sexes. There is no doubting what she said about that.

> I believe in the natural superiority of the man as I do in the existence of God. The natural position of a woman is inferiority to a man, that is a thing of God's appointing, not of man's devising.

How extraordinary that sounds today! It needs to be remembered, as does the vigorous opposition there was to the movement for reforming the divorce law. Six thousand clergymen petitioned against the 1857 Bill, and both Gladstone and Bishop Wilberforce were among those who fought it with all their conviction. Even when the law had changed, the social stigma of divorce was still there, and many society women decided to keep clear of this by staying safely inside the confines of a dead marriage. The Queen backed them up by inviting unfaithful husbands to court functions while until 1887 she never included any wife, however wronged, who had petitioned for divorce. She was also strongly against details of Divorce Court cases being aired in the Press. In 1859 she wrote to ask the Lord Chancellor what could be done to prevent this. The cases were sure to increase, the Queen said, as the new law became more known, and they were given so much coverage

> and are of so scandalous a character that it makes it almost impossible for a paper to be trusted in the hands of a young lady or boy. None of the worst French novels from which careful parents would try to protect their children can be as bad as what is daily brought and laid upon the breakfast-table of every educated family in England, and its effect must be most pernicious to the public morals of the country.

Not all her subjects agreed with the Queen. Not surprisingly, it was a 'Freethinker' with a failed marriage, the eighth Marquess of Queensberry, who made out one of the strongest cases against indissoluble and holy matrimony. His wife held other views and gave him no grounds for divorce. 'Marriage ought to be, and is, a human institution; not a divine one,' he asserted, calling for further reform of the divorce law. Marriage in his opinion should be based on 'a law of man and not bolstered up with the unnecessary falsehood that any Supreme Being has bound two unfortunate people together for life, however unsuitable they may turn out to be to one another'. Queensberry's wild and threatening behaviour – not any change in her principles – did at last make his wife agree to divorce him in 1886, twenty years after their marriage.

By the last decades of the century divorce had become more usual, less unacceptable. The Queen had been right to fear Press coverage of matrimonial disputes. Not even her own family escaped being mentioned. In 1870 the Prince of Wales was called to give evidence in a divorce case which followed the birth of Violet Mordaunt, future wife of the fifth Marquess of Bath. Violet's mother had told her husband, a close friend of the Prince, that he was not the father of her child; she also said that the Prince was one of a number of lovers with whom she had 'done wrong'. And worse was to come. In 1879 the Prince, together with the fourth Earl of Lonsdale and Lord Londesborough, was named as a co-respondent in a divorce petition filed by the husband of the actress Lily Langtry. Lady Brooke, another great love of the Prince of Wales, also crusaded for the reform of the divorce law. What was needed, she said, was 'to overcome our thoroughly English tendency to observe the letter of the law while letting the spirit take care of itself'. In her youth the marriage laws had been even more stringent, so they were ignored on the tacit understanding that people sought their happiness where they could find it. Royals in particular, she said, had a very slim chance of being allowed to marry for love.

Separation was an easier option than divorce, providing escape from the wrong partner without risking the trammels of the law or the snubs of society. But there were still certain conventions which had to be obeyed. Back in 1821, five years after separating from Annabella – 'that virtuous monster Miss Milbanke', as he called his ex-wife – Byron was deeply embroiled, in Italy, with the Contessa Guiccioli. He felt that because it was for him that she had parted from her (elderly) husband, he had to accept certain obligations, and he described these in a letter to Augusta in 1821.

You know when a woman is separated from her husband for her *Amant*, he his bound both by honour (and inclination at least I am), to live with her all his days; as long as there is no misconduct.

By this he must have meant infidelity on her part. Byron wrote that he was 'more attached to her than I thought it possible to be after three years – (except one & who was she can you guess?)'.

William Lamb and Caroline, whose escapades early on in her marriage had brought as much publicity as any divorce case, were another couple for whom separation proved the only workable arrangement. It was the lull after the storm; gone were the days when she threatened to leave William and go to Byron, provoking him to retort: 'Go and be damned.' In 1821 they separated on terms which were generous to Caroline, who lived at Brocket, the Lamb family home, until her death. William visited her there and wrote to her affectionately. Her emotional instability made her impossible to live with, oscillating as she did between her old infatuation with Byron, incomprehension that he could ever have stopped loving her, and the affection she still had for William and for her childhood love, the Duke of Devonshire. It was emotional as well as social insecurity that had made her ask for his help in fending off the separation from William, at least for a time.

Separation would be 'destruction' to her, she said. For twenty years she had been 'not only tollerated [sic], but loved with such devotion that when I have offered & begged to go away I have been detain'd'. William himself did not want the separation, she said, and was miserable. Could the Duke do what he could to urge for things to be made easy for her? What she needed was some money, a house, and not to be treated like a madwoman. If the separation had to come, it would be better if it could be after she had 'gone out a little, & in some measure restored myself to the good will of a few friends & relations'.

There is a parallel between Melbourne's and Wellington's relationships with their wives. Each had once loved his wife, then found her impossible to live with, separated but did not divorce, and never remarried after being widowed. Each was an affectionate, attractive man who needed women in his life and formed close and lasting attachments to other men's wives who appreciated and reciprocated his devotion. The comforts and complications of some of these will be seen in the next chapter.

10

Outsiders

There remain three groups of 'outsiders' – whether victims, rebels, or contented mavericks – who for one reason or another did not fit into the pattern of accepted stereotypes. It was a conventional, intolerant, often priggish century, quick to disapprove and to give a hard time to all whose ideas or lives were disturbing by being different. But outsiders from the world of the great country houses at least had the advantage of social confidence – and usually wealth as well – to help them take their independent stand. They had the chance, quite beyond outsiders of the middle and poorer classes, of panache and colour in their lives. Most of them could still be welcomed in Mayfair drawing-rooms. Or they could travel.

But even at country house level, spinsterhood was a daunting prospect which all but the toughest girls hoped to avoid. Lady Charlotte Bury, as she so often did, took the majority view. 'Every woman should make it her business, as a duty she owes herself, to find a husband; for no other interest in life is ever stable, abiding, or sufficient to the happiness of a woman.' Her diary tells of a letter from a friend, 'poor Miss – ', who gives a wretched view of the lives of 'us *old maids*'.

I believe *in early* life it is woman's end and aim, and perhaps does not cease to be so until sorrowful disappointment tells her that the fondly-cherished hope, nursed for years, may in an instant be blighted, and the confiding heart thrown back on itself to feel all its bitterness.

Her words have a desperately authentic ring to them. Young girls saw the possibility differently. A pleasant hour and a half was spent

165

one afternoon by Rosalind and Kate Stanley, talking by the fireside about what they would do if they were 'left two old maids together, and we settled we would live a very happy and cheerful life'. They would have a cottage at Alderley, they decided, and 'make it very lovely and snug'. They would enjoy the life very much, they thought, 'though of course there would be some regrets'. But Rosalind was only seventeen then, and they must both have been fairly confident of the loving young husbands who in fact soon did come their way.

Daughters were conditioned from nursery days to see marriage as their future lot. 'Of what else have young ladies to think, but husbands? Of what else do their dear mammas think?' Thackeray asked as he let that archetypal outsider and non-spinster, Becky Sharp, loose on the matrimonial stakes. Rosalind and Kate Stanley were younger and much more innocent than Becky when they pored over the map of England, pinpointing stately homes and daydreaming about which one would be theirs. Did their older sister, Maud, ever play that game with them? She was the only one of the Stanley girls who did not marry. Because she was ugly? Because she had loved a man whom her mother considered 'not good enough'? Or because Lady Stanley wanted an unmarried daughter to keep her company and run errands for her? Maud seems to have made the best of it, throwing herself into good works, pioneering girls' clubs, and – later – giving literary parties at her house in Smith Square. There had been plain, pathetic unmarried daughters in the previous generation of Stanleys; two of Maud's seven aunts, Rianette and Louisa, lived disconsolate single lives in attendance on their dominating mother, and another sister had a narrow escape, marrying late but happily, just in time to have one child as well as several miscarriages.

Even that adventurous spinster, Lady Hester Stanhope, is believed to have been catapulted on her romantic travels by disappointment in love. 'I have been *going* to be married fifty times in my life, said to have been married half as often, and run away with once.' She certainly fell in love with Lord Granville Leveson-Gower in 1804, and believed that he was fond of her and that he jilted her. When he was posted to St Petersburg as Ambassador there were recriminations as well as talk of Lady Hester's taking some (but not enough) poison. She did take the always counter-productive step of ceasing to bother about her appearance. Lord

Granville's mother wrote to him that she had seen Lady Hester for the first time, imagining her to be 'very pretty, in Place of which she look'd like a middle aged married Woman with a dingey Complexion, no Rouge, a broad Face, and an unbecoming fur cap'.

On the rebound from her various abortive love-affairs she set off on her travels. In 1810 she met her brother's friend, Michael Bruce, who was much younger than she was; she became his mistress and at last had a happy and reciprocated relationship. She wrote to Bruce's father, explaining that she had no intention of marrying his son. 'I never had or ever will *have further claims* upon your son than any woman he might have picked up in the streets.' She did not give a rap for what society might think, although she had lived at its sparkling centre in London in the home of her uncle the Prime Minister, William Pitt.

So far from wishing to be received in society, I shall most scrupulously avoid ever setting eyes upon a modest woman. . . . I will never give an opportunity to those fine ladies who have married for a title, a house, and fine diamonds, having previously made up their minds to be *faithless wives* to *sneer* at me.

And she ended,

You must not imagine, Sir, because my conduct has been imprudent that my heart is either devoid of sentiments of real delicacy or honor.

It was a spirited manifesto. She and Bruce travelled together to Constantinople, Egypt, and Palmyra before, as she had always expected, in 1813 he left her. In the dress worn by Turkish men, visited by travellers as one of the sights of the Levant, self-absorbed and mystical, what could be a further cry from the classic image of the timid, virginal, home-loving English spinster?

Florence Nightingale was no less untypical. It takes a strenuous jerk of the imagination today to appreciate what it meant in the 1850s for a young unmarried woman from the English *petite noblesse* to launch herself upon the man's world of hospitals and the Army. Lady Charlotte Canning was herself something of a pioneer in engaging Miss Nightingale as Superintendent of the Institution for the Care of Sick Gentlewomen – 'Gentlewomen', the very word is like a bell – and in herself being chairman of its committee. She was reproached for offering her the job without first asking her parents' permission. Florence's mother was baffled by her beautiful daughter who showed no interest in society parties or admiring young men. 'We are ducks who have hatched a wild swan,' she told Mrs Gaskell. When her wild swan went to teach at a Ragged School in Westminster and wanted to visit families in the slums, her mother protested that young ladies did not walk on their own in London. A footman must go with her.

Her vocation – to relieve pain and misery – was certainly not the escape into good works of an unattractive girl. From her début she was a great social success. She was invited to Chatsworth with her mother and sister, and to dinner with Lord Palmerston at Broadlands, where she met the brilliant Richard Monckton Milnes, the future Lord Houghton, who fell in love with her and asked her to marry him. Although he was, she said, 'the man I adored', his was one of the offers she refused. Throughout her life Florence Nightingale inspired an almost religious devotion in both men and women, and the mainspring of her own vocation was also religious. She felt herself called by God. In 1849 she wrote in her diary: 'Today I am 30 – the age Christ began his mission. Now no more childish things. No more love. No more marriage. Now Lord let me think only of Thy Will.'

Those words suggest that it is a mistake to see Florence Nightingale as a Sister of Mercy who would have been happy in some well-scrubbed convent. She had known love and thoughts of marriage. Were they really no more than 'childish things' when she said goodbye to them on her thirtieth birthday? She was deeply disgusted with the lives led by upper-class women, absorbed as they were in social frivolities or at best in narrow family interests. 'Women don't consider themselves as human beings at all,' she complained; 'there is absolutely no God, no country, no duty to them at all, except family.' Even unmarried women who had no children were felt to have nothing better to do with their time than devote it to their mothers. Two years after that important thirtieth-birthday milestone, Florence was still a schoolgirl to her mother, who felt entitled to read her daughter's letters and supervise the invitations she received. And that was at a time when her intimate friends included Sidney Herbert and his wife Elizabeth, George Eliot, Elizabeth Barrett Browning, Palmerston, and Lord Shaftesbury.

Was her sister right, she wondered, when she had said 'as a reproach, that I was "more like a man". Indeed I began to think it was true.' But the men in her life did not think so. Arthur Hugh Clough loved her passionately, and even after he married another woman he gave Florence all his time, happy to 'do the work of a cab horse' for her, fetching and carrying, writing letters and tying up her parcels. Her feelings were ambivalent but intense. 'Sidney Herbert and I were together exactly like two men – exactly like him and Gladstone,' she wrote. 'And as for Clough, oh Jonathan, my brother Jonathan, my love for thee was very great, PASSING THE LOVE OF WOMEN.' She felt that she had been three times widowed – when she lost Sidney Herbert, when she lost Clough, and most of all (surprise surprise) when she lost her aunt. 'We were like two lovers,' she said. It was she who had been her 'nearest and dearest'. Tangled feelings, baffling analysis both then and now. But there is no doubting their strength and warmth.

So much for spinsters. What about bachelors? Their image of course is a happier, freer one and at the end of the century it reached a kind of apotheosis in the celebrated Bachelors' Club at 8 Hamilton Place, one of the fine *palazzi* where the then quiet stream of Park Lane flowed into the Grand Canal of Piccadilly. The Bachelors' Club – how unimaginable a Spinsters' Club would be! – accepted only celibate members, although after marriage they could be re-elected on payment of a £25 fine. Ladies were invited as guests, and the Club was the scene of famous dinners given by Curzon and other members of the Souls.

Bachelors could be vulnerable too, at least to feminine eyes. At the other end of the century young Georgiana Capel felt very sorry for them. In Brussels with her family at the time of Waterloo, she was a tender-hearted girl who was to see many dashing young officers wounded and invalided. 'Papa's illness makes me more than ever pity *Batchelors*,' she wrote; 'for after all, what is so kind, so useful as a woman, and what miserable helpless wretches men are without them, if they require any sort of comfort or attendance.'

One such miserable helpless wretch was Viscount Tavistock, the future eighth Duke of Bedford, a delicate, eccentric recluse who told his father that he did not expect to marry or to live at Woburn. Could his inheritance go to someone else, he asked? It could not, and meanwhile he was of course an enticingly *beau parti*, prompting the pretender to the Spanish throne, Don Carlos, to write to the

Duke proposing a match between his pretty young niece, the Princess Isabella Bourbon, and Lord Tavistock. The offer was politely declined by Tavistock's mother. He knew that marriage was beyond him and in 1841 wrote to his father to explain this. He had a feeling almost of horror at the thought of 'uniting a young girl full of life to a semi-corpse. I feel the machinery is nearly worn out.' He was then only thirty. He lived partly in a small house in Kensington where he went by the name of Mr Johnson and kept a mistress whom he cared for devotedly even when she became insane. Ill-health and melancholy were the blights that came to him along with the treasures of his family inheritance; when he succeeded, aged fifty-three, he was still ailing, depressive, and unmarried. All he could do, he decided, was to have a close contact with his cousin and heir presumptive, Hastings Russell, who went to live at Woburn and took over its administration. Why should he marry, he asked? Could he have a better son than Hastings?

Every century and society has its *Salon des Refusés* who have been disappointed in love, and reactions to such disasters change from age to age. By the time Queen Victoria and Lord Melbourne had all those quizzical conversations about the ways of the world, Melbourne's affections and his amour-propre had had some rough buffetings. As a young man he had been more sensitive, he told the Queen. 'I do believe if I had been refused I should have died of it; it would have killed me; I was so very vain.' But those who think they will die of a broken heart often survive. Of the noble heartbreaks described here, some healed surprisingly quickly; others were bravely patched and mended, and went on to be broken, patched, and mended again, sometimes many times. Many of the women and some of the men settled for celibacy.

The affection of Hartington, the fifth Duke of Devonshire's son, for his cousin Caroline Ponsonby, who was to marry William Lamb, has already been mentioned. Her feeling for him may well have been the most stable of all her loves. 'You once loved me as I always shall you,' she wrote to him; 'dearest of wild young women', he called her, and 'God bless you dearest'. They sent each other hundreds of loving letters. 'Devilshire' and 'my heart of hearts', Caroline punned on his name; she begged him to 'write to me, as I cannot live if I do not hear from you. . . .That you love me I feel sure, dearly & deeply though you now & then see my faults.' Probably she gave the greatest proof of her trust and affection for him not long before her death, when it was to no one but the Duke of Devonshire that she could bear to entrust the presents that Byron had given her, his letters, the poems he had written to her, everything, with the request that he would burn them all.

A few unfortunate people were, unlike Caroline, simply unattractive to the opposite sex. Lord John Russell, the future Prime Minister, was one of these. A short, unimpressive-looking man, he found women easy to love but difficult to please. He was drawn to the wife of a Genoese nobleman, but that did not help him in his search for a wife. Lady Holland wrote sympathetically about Lord John's predicament in 1828. He wanted to marry Lady Hardy's young daughter, but she had turned him down, she said. It was a pity he had 'the rage to marry upon him, as he is so frequently repulsed'. It would be so much better if he were, as he would be in Italy, 'content to be Prelato or Monsignore of the family, as he is a delightful person in all relations but those of lover or husband; at least so I should think, & so do the young ladies.' At long last, when he was forty-two, he found and married a widow who within two years presented him with two daughters and then died. What happened to him afterwards will be told in a 'close-up' description of his second marriage.

Why was it that so many who figured in the *Salon des Refusés* eventually consoled themselves by marrying a relation of their earlier love? Sometimes of course they had dynastic motives, but not always. Sir Harry Verney was a widower when he fell in love with Florence Nightingale and asked her to marry him; a year after her refusal he married her forty-year-old sister. It seems that Florence generated passionate admiration in those around her, and when this could find no lasting purchase on her it landed on another of the group. Another of her devotees, the poet Clough, eventually married the daughter of Florence's aunt. Both Clough and the aunt were unlimitedly devoted to Florence, and five years after his marriage Clough was spending all his time in London with Florence while his wife and children were left to get on with their lives without him.

One faithful, unrequited lover of a married woman met with unusual sympathy and tolerance from her husband. T.J. Sanderson loved Kate Amberley for years, and Amberley appreciated Kate's attitude as much as he pitied her poor *inamorato*. He noted in his diary in 1871 that Sanderson had always loved Kate though of course never said a word that was not proper. He has no unchaste relations with women. I allow him (and have, ever since 1866) to touch, caress and even kiss Kate. Kate now thinks this should stop. I feel so sorry for him that I don't want to stop it altogether. Her kindness never goes too far.

It is a strange *pas de trois* from all three points of view. The Amberleys had a very loving marriage, but even during their short lives together a permitted lover for Kate occurred again. Robert Spalding, the children's brilliant tutor, was consumptive, and both Amberleys felt that he should not marry and have children. But they also considered that it was hard for him to go without sex, so they both agreed that he should be allowed to sleep with Kate. Bertrand Russell, the Amberleys' son, thought that his parents were 'very foolish about medical matters' and even suggested that more knowledge and care might have prevented their early deaths. The Spalding story indicated at least that they did not know that tuberculosis was infectious, and that they must have had confidence in whatever contraceptive methods they used.

Arthur Balfour, one of the brilliant central personalities of the Souls, played a leading part in three other heartbreaks. Years after her marriage, Gladstone's daughter Mary asked a mutual friend to tell Balfour that she had once been in love with him. Another friend was amazed at this. How could any woman admit to a man that she had loved him without being loved in return? But Mary Drew (as she then was) was glad to have done this. It would have been a great waste, she felt, to have given her love without Balfour knowing it. It has already been told how Balfour had loved May Lyttelton, Mary's cousin, and never got over her early death. When May's brother Alfred Lyttelton became engaged to Laura Tennant, the ever-devoted Mary wrote that she had hoped that Laura would marry Balfour, as she was 'the one person who might have come nearer to what May was'. That was something Mary knew she would never be. Laura too must have felt the affinity with Balfour. She died, as she had expected, giving birth to her first child, and she left a special bequest to Balfour as well as one to his wife if he ever married. If she died then, she would never see Balfour's wife, she wrote, but she had so often imagined her 'that I feel in the spirit we are in some measure related by some mystic tie'. Both Balfour and Alfred Lyttelton found spiritual consolation in their bereave-

Arthur James Balfour in 1877, from a drawing by George Richmond.

ments. Balfour tried to get in touch with May by psychic experiments, and Lyttelton shared Laura's belief that they would find each other again in a future life.

As well as the loners and the losers, there was a third important group of 'outsiders'. The Platonic friendship or *amitié amoureuse* seems to have been something of a speciality of the nineteenth-century aristocracy. Such things are always difficult to pinpoint or define. Wilfred Blunt got the balance right when he described Balfour's long and loving relationship with Mary Elcho as 'a little more than friendship, a little less than love'. In their case it was probably not so little more than the first, and very little less than the second. Walter Savage Landor also assessed it well. 'There is a middle state between love and friendship more delightful than either, but more difficult to remain in.' At its best it was a sensitively balanced two-step which was central to the lives of both partners without offending anyone else.

Was it perhaps characteristically English, suited to reserved and rather (but not altogether) cool temperaments? At least in the case of the three most remarkable relationships described here, the men were exceptionally attractive and brilliant public figures, and had already suffered something of a battering in their personal lives; while the women were much younger, also attractive and intelligent. There was certainly always some sexual attraction on both sides; the presence in the background of a permissive husband could be a chief factor in keeping the relationship within its Platonic bounds.

It is impossible even for those concerned to be certain where the dividing-line lies. Byron was in his amorous heyday during his close friendship, which had begun by being sexual, with Lady Melbourne. He told her unreservedly about his most intimate passions and plans. 'I do love that woman (*filially* or *fraternally*) better than any being on earth,' he told her niece Annabella, who was to be his future wife. But in another mood he could speak very differently. After the break-up of Byron's marriage, Annabella's mother wrote to her husband that Byron had

> told his wife that in 1813 he had *absolute criminal* Connection with an *old lady*, at the same time as with her Daughter in Law – that *She* absolutely *proposed it to him* – and that he said 'She [was] *so old* he hardly knew how to go about it.'

The 'old lady' was Lady Melbourne, and the daughter-in-law was Caroline Lamb. But Byron's entertainment value often tops his veracity; the anecdote tells more about how he might talk about such things than about his actual feelings.

Lord Melbourne's relationship with Caroline Norton is one of the most interesting examples of those relationships between a man and a woman which, whatever the mix of sexual and Platonic affection may have been, cannot be classed as love-affairs. They met soon after his indiscreet affair, when he was Chief Secretary for Ireland, with Lady Brandon was still the tittle-tattle of the day. Melbourne was fifty-one and Caroline twenty-two when in 1831 she asked his help in furthering George Norton's career, and Melbourne, then Home Secretary, complied by making a magistracy available to Norton at a welcome salary of £1,000 a year. Caroline came of a Whig family and her political sympathies were aligned with Melbourne's, not with those of her Tory M.P. husband. It was as natural for her to enjoy a ringside view of the inner political scene and the intricacies of cabinet placings as it was for this to trigger off Norton's jealousy. In 1836 Melbourne was Prime Minister when Caroline's marriage crashed and George Norton charged Melbourne with adultery. The jury unanimously acquitted him, and both then and on his death-bed Melbourne solemnly declared that Caroline had not 'sinned' with him or 'in any way abused her husband's confidence'. The following year Norton himself said that he had never believed Caroline guilty of what he called 'the last offence' and asked her to go back to him.

Once again Melbourne had been at least unwise in being seen so often in the company of another man's wife. Sharp public interest had been aroused, and of course it was Caroline's reputation – not Melbourne's or Norton's – that was tarnished. She was particularly bitter at Melbourne's refusal to see her once Norton's attack had begun. Her sense of having been betrayed by him comes across in the letters she wrote at that time. She pointed out to Melbourne the unevenness of their relationship: he was everything to her while to him she had been no more than 'the amusement of his idle hours'. Her life, she told him had been

divided (in *my* eyes) into the *days I saw you* & the *days I did not* – *nothing* else seemed of importance but you; your opinions, even your *fancies* (for you *have* had them) have been laws to me. . . . I

175

was not two & twenty when you first visited me & I thought merrily & carelessly about you. I am six years older & I think sadly – perhaps something more! The time will doubtless arrive when I shall think *calmly & contentedly* – would it were come.

Caroline told Melbourne that she did not mean to reproach him, but while they were both in town she was tormented by 'knowing I am so *near* you & may not see you'.

It was a sad way for their affection to end. She would, she said, 'never feel the same thing for any one else'. Only he knew how falsely she had been accused; and yet he had never – as surely anybody else would have done – written her a kind word when the trial was over. Silence for her was not possible; she had to tell him 'no one either in the past or the future will have loved you more earnestly, more completely – & I may say more *steadily* than the woman whose threat of passion you pretend to fear – & who has been made to appear a painted prostitute in a Public Court.' Caroline's words, like Byron's, perhaps run away with her; she too was a writer. It sounds as if she regretted that their relationship had been unconsummated. 'In the sight of Heaven my crime is the same as if I had been yr mistress these five years,' she wrote later.

No wonder she felt wronged and indignant. The year 1837 was a very black one for her. Melbourne's sister, Lady Cowper, in spite of those years when she had been Palmerston's mistress, was one of many society hostesses who would not invite Caroline to their homes. It was also the year of the Queen's accession and the start of the extraordinary closeness between her and Melbourne. Not till 1840 was Caroline again received at court. A year later Melbourne resigned. After he had a stroke, in 1843, she was writing affection-etly to him. 'Dearest old Boy,' one letter began, and it ended 'God bless you – Ever Yrs   Caroline.'

The Duke of Wellington was more skilful in his management of relationships with other men's wives. In 1822, the year after he decided he could no longer bear to live with his wife, he was sufficiently intimate with Harriett Arbuthnot to tell her about his marriage problems. She was a granddaughter of the Earl of Westmorland and the wife of a colleague, Charles Arbuthnot, and in 1824 both she and Mrs Lane-Fox, another of Wellington's women friends, were sent anonymous letters accusing them of being in love with him. The Arbuthnots discussed the letter with

Wellington, who recognized the writing as that of the diarist, Charles Greville. He had an old grievance against the Duke because his mother, Lady Charlotte Greville, had had a love affair with him a few years earlier. He was to attack again at the end of Wellington's life.

He was not the only one to suspect Mrs Arbuthnot of being the Duke's mistress. Her husband too received an anonymous letter, threatening to reveal discreditable facts about several public figures if he did not arrange an official appointment for its sender. Arbuthnot's refusal brought him a 'vulgar placard' and the further threat to accuse his wife of having an affair with Wellington. Creevey, too, referred to her as 'the Beau's flirt'. But Lady Shelley, who knew them both well, was certain that they were not lovers. Mrs Arbuthnot, handsome though she was, had no 'womanly passions' and was 'above all a loyal and truthful woman', she said. She was also devout, the dutiful second wife of a man nearly thirty years older than herself. Intensely interested in politics, she enjoyed hearing and discussing the problems of the day with Castlereagh and Canning as well as with Wellington. Lady Salisbury, the young first wife of the second Marquess, who was Wellington's closest woman friend from Mrs Arbuthnot's death in 1834 until her own, five years later, described his relationship with her predecessor during those last years.

Whether there is any foundation or not for the stories usually believed about the early part of their *liaison*, she was certainly *now* become to him no more than a tried and valued friend to whom he was sincerely attached – her house was his home, and with all his glory and greatness he *never had a home*. His nature is domestic and as he advances in years, some female society and some fireside to which he can always resort become necessary to him.

So even she was not sure about the early years of their intimacy. There is no ambiguity about the word 'liaison'.

They certainly spent – and were seen to spend – a lot of time together. The Duke brought Harriett Arbuthnot Eau de Cologne and gloves from Germany; and for her birthday in 1822 he sent her a 'petit Cadeau', a bracelet made from emeralds and pearls which had decorated a sword presented to him in 1800 by a grateful

Mahratta chief, hoping it would remind her of someone who had a sincere regard and affection for her. When he was away he wrote frequently to her, often asking her to pass on snippets of news to her husband. 'My dear Mrs Arbuthnot', his letters usually began, and they ended 'God bless you and believe me ever yours sincerely'. He wrote very warmly and affectionately. Just before going abroad in 1822 he told her that he hoped she would

> think of me sometimes, and whenever you think of me wherever I may be, you may feel certain that my thoughts and wishes are centred on you, and my desire that every action of my life may please you. God bless you.
> Your most devoted and affectionate Slave.

The best letters carry the imprint of the person to whom they are addressed as well as that of their writer, and Harriet Arbuthnot must have been a remarkable woman to be given such affection and admiration from the great men in her life. That laid her open to criticism, of course, and some of Wellington's other friends thought that in company she monopolized and bossed him. When he went to Oxford for his installation as Chancellor of the University, they thought that the dons might be put out by seeing her parading so openly with him. He for his part never liked women to be deferential and submissive. They both enjoyed their jokey nicknames for each other: he was her 'slave' and she was 'la Tyranna'. On one occasion Harriett wrote to Lady Shelley that 'the slave (poor creature!) has asked my leave to invite you to dinner', and she had magnanimously agreed.

The proof of Wellington's deep affection for Harriett Arbuthnot is his reaction to the sudden news of her death, from cholera, in 1834. He was staying at Hatfield when the express reached him, and his shock and grief were beyond his control. He threw himself on the sofa, and almost sobbed as he walked distractedly up and down. Then he left the room. The following day he went away, leaving a note to explain to Lord Salisbury that he had to go to Mr Arbuthnot. After Wellington's visit Harriett's widower wrote at once to him about the affection his wife had had for him.

> She had no friend to whom she was so much attached as She was to you. . . .I believe I may say that you never had such a friend before & you will never have such a one again. . . . I am writing

'A Sketch in the Park'. The Duke of Wellington and Mrs Arbuthnot.

all my thoughts to you, for we were *three*, & you will understand – O my dear Duke you feel for me I know – you feel for yourself also.

Their grief drew the two men together. Wellington had so often been welcomed in the Arbuthnots' home, and now he took Harriett's widower into his. It was said to be his care that kept Arbuthnot alive for the remaining fifteen years of his life.

Harriett's earlier friendship with Castlereagh had also been intimate and loving. Secretary of State for Foreign Affairs during and after the war with France, he succeeded his father as second Marquess of Londonderry not long before his suicide in 1822. It was after his death that Harriett described what Castlereagh's friendship had meant to her. He had been

> the man who, for eleven years that we have been known to each other, has taken the most affecte [sic] interest in all that was a subject of joy or sorrow to me, who from the hr I married to the day of his death has been the kind & affectionate adviser to whom I have ever had recourse in every annoyance, and whose place in my fond remembrance I feel can never be filled up. . . . He used to call on me almost every other day, come at my breakfast hour, used to call his visits to me jokingly, 'coming to take his orders', talked to me of the debate of the night before, & took the opportunity to discuss business with Mr Arbuthnot; & nothing ever happened to me of importance, either private or in our public situation, I never had any annoyance or distress that I did not consult him & receive from him the most friendly advice & the kindest sympathy.

How many friendships, Platonic or not, are as strong as that?

At Lord Salisbury's wedding in 1821 to Frances Gascoyne, Wellington has already been seen honouring the occasion by giving the bride away. It was to her that he turned for friendship after Harriett Arbuthnot's death, until Lady Salisbury too died, five years later, in 1839. She was endearingly surprised to be granted his affection. 'I sometimes think how can I be worthy of the friendship of such a man,' she wrote, 'what have *I* done to deserve the highest honour a woman can attain to be *his* friend?' Yet she had the confidence to give him her outspoken opinions of his colleagues in 1837, at a time when he had survived public hostility and risen to peaks of national prestige. Peel and Aberdeen, she told him, she considered 'thoroughly honest and honourable, Ellenborough without political principles, Fitzgerald a jobber, Harding for whichever side he would make most by, and Lyndhurst a double dealer.' What did the Duke make of such straight verdicts? 'He said nothing, but seemed to assent,' she thought. It is an intriguing conversation-piece.

So firmly married a woman friend as Lady Salisbury might be expected to be beyond the range of mud-slingers, but even in her company Wellington had to be on his guard. When he invited her and her children to visit him at Walmer Castle, when he was Lord Warden of the Cinque Ports and nearly seventy, he had to urge her not to come without Lord Salisbury. 'One would suppose that you might hope to go through the world without giving reason for scandal,' he wrote; 'and that I am beyond the age to afford any ground for it. But it is not so. There was plenty of it last year. There will be more if your visit should be repeated this year without the company of Lord Salisbury.' Wellington valued their friendship no less than she did. When she died, two years later, he wore mourning for her and sealed his letters with black wax in token of his grief. It is said that no one else quite replaced her as his confidante.

Curiously enough, the woman who probably most nearly did this was her successor, who married Lord Salisbury after he had been a widower for eight years. Wellington and the second Lady Salisbury both enjoyed what they called their 'quarter-deck exercise', walking together almost every day along the north side of the Green Park. A footman, within call but out of earshot, followed behind them. Once again he had a lively correspondent who told him how happy she was to receive the little notes he sent off to her. 'God bless you. Ever yours most affectionately', he ended these, and he told her his letters amused him as they did her. 'I laugh while writing them, thinking of the amusement they will afford you.' She too treasured the Duke's affection as the earlier Lady Salisbury had done. In her old age he had 'first and foremost' place in her list of the remarkable friends she had had.

It was Wellington's last important relationship with a woman that really threatened to get out of control. This time his lady friend was unmarried, and she complicated matters by falling in love with him and proposing to marry him. Angela Burdett-Coutts had been born in 1814, and had inherited the vast fortune of her grandfather, the banker Thomas Coutts. She was devout, intelligent – she was a member of the Royal Society – and like Florence Nightingale she dedicated her life to the relief of poverty and distress. Her youth and fortune made her fair game for fortune-hunters; Disraeli as a young man is said to have been one of the many who set his cap – without any encouragement – at her. But it was not her fortune that made Dickens and Wellington her close friends. In 1846, when she was twenty-two and the Duke was seventy-seven, she was clearly falling in love with him. And he was devoted to her, writing to her at least once every day when they did not meet. Angela's family had a curious history of lop-sided marriages. Old Coutts the banker had been eighty when he married the young actress Harriot Mellon; and after his death, although she took her first husband's love-letters with her wherever she went, the middle-aged and somewhat raddled widow Coutts married, as has been told, the vapid but noble Duke of St Albans, twenty years her junior. So to Angela Burdett-Coutts a difference of fifty-five years between her and the man she wanted to marry was at least not unthinkable.

He explained his reasons for refusing her offer. His first duty to her was that of friend, guardian, and protector, he wrote.

> You are Young, My Dearest! You have before you the Prospect of at least twenty years of enjoyment of Happiness in Life. I entreat you again, in this way, not to throw yourself away on a Man old enough to be your Grandfather, who, however strong, Hearty and Healthy at present, must and will certainly in time feel the consequences and Infirmities of Age.

It is said that Angela went on hoping that one day they would marry. Wellington gave her an apartment of her own at Stratfield Saye, with a private staircase so that she could come and go as she pleased. During the summer of 1847 they were seen everywhere together, and of course the scandal-mongers sharpened their quills. That was the moment for Greville to return to the attack. In July he entered in his diary that the Duke was 'astonishing the world by a strange intimacy he has struck up with Miss Coutts with whom he passes his life, and all sorts of reports have been rife of his intention to marry her'. The sting lay in the words which followed. 'Such are the lamentable appearances of decay in his vigorous mind.'

Angela Burdett-Coutts, Wellington's last intimate woman friend, asked him to marry her when he was seventy-seven and she was twenty-two. The painting is by W.C. Ross.

The mind in question was still vigorous enough to smile at the rumours. 'It does amuse me mightily to find at times a veteran eighty-two year old, deaf with all! turned into a lover!' he wrote four years later. That year Angela gave a magnificent birthday banquet for Wellington. In 1852 he died, and was mourned by the whole nation as well as by the young woman who had wanted to be his wife. Almost twenty years afterwards she became the first woman to be created a baroness in her own right. She also followed her strange family marriage-pattern – but this time in the opposite direction – by marrying, when she was sixty-seven, a man of thirty with whom she lived happily for her remaining twelve years.

So Wellington's women friends spanned the years from the failure of his marriage to his death. Was he ever really at risk from feminine birds of prey, on the alert to swoop down and pounce on him? One of the least alluring of them has still to be to mentioned. Greville would have had some sharp words to say if she had won the day. In 1834 Miss Anna Jenkins called at Apsley House with a Bible and the intention to bring about the Duke's spiritual rebirth. After the shock of Harriett Arbuthnot's death Wellington felt drawn to meet Mrs Jenkins, as he thought she was called, not realizing that his visiting evangelist was young and pretty. He explained that he was not 'in the habit of visiting young unmarried ladies with whom he is not acquainted', but he overcame his scruples and did call on her. Miss Jenkins was struck by the sight of the Duke's 'beautiful silver head' and read to him from St John's Gospel about Nicodemus the Pharisee being told by Christ that he must be born again. At that point Wellington seized her hand and told Miss Jenkins he loved her.

He had other matters to think of, however. He was then sixty-five, acting Prime Minister, and with other political responsibilities. His relationship with Miss Jenkins was confusing although – in snatches – ardent. She was concerned for his spiritual salvation, which did not seem incompatible with her chance of becoming a duchess. He was torn between his public duties, visits to his evangelist, hours and reams of correspondence, and eventual retreat. But during their ten years of skirmishing he wrote Miss Jenkins nearly four hundred letters. It is a solemn thought that the great man's old age might have been lumbered with a marriage as silly and oppressive as that of his youth.

PART TWO

11

Fair Game

So much for long shots of the nineteenth-century inhabitants of the great country houses as they made their way in and out of love and marriage. As the camera now zooms to close-up it still catches the poetry and splendour of the setting, which could not fail to affect the lives and loves it harboured. Sometimes past history heightened the drama. Byron's flirtation with Lady Frances Webster took place partly at Newstead Abbey, his family home, where remains of the ancient priory which Sir John Byron bought in 1540 still remain. But by a curious coincidence the other backcloth to their philandering was a house which also had a link with his family. This was Aston Hall, in Yorkshire, which James Wedderburn Webster had leased and where Byron visited him.

As his carriage drove up to the door he had no idea that beyond it lay the promise and the danger of a love-affair with his host's pretty young wife. At first it seemed that the lady in question and her husband almost forced it upon him, although his initial reluctance was certainly fairly soon overcome. And at the back of Byron's mind was the amused awareness that he was following in his father's footsteps, for Aston Hall was the house to which his father, Captain John Byron, had eloped with a youthful love. It was odd, Byron wrote to his old friend Thomas Moore, that he should find himself 'a visitor in the same house which came to my sire as a residence with Lady Carmarthen (with whom he adulterated before his majority – by the by, remember, *she* was not my mamma)'. Byron's progress reports on his flirtation with Lady Frances are as entertaining as all his letters (but not all his poems) are. They are also instructive, if only as a blueprint of amorous expertise. Each move in the perilous game is described in his letters to Lady

Melbourne. The story begins in 1813, two years before Byron married Lady Melbourne's niece, Annabella Milbanke, and about the time when she was warning him urgently of the dangers of his incestuous passion for Augusta.

In September of that year Byron stayed in the country with the Websters. Lady Frances had been very young when she married James Wedderburn Webster, Lady Holland's son by Sir Godfrey Webster, her first husband; and the stage was set for a flirtation between her and Byron – by her youth (she was twenty) and good looks, by Byron's allure for all women, and by Sir James Webster's provocative and quite unjustified certainty that his wife adored him. Byron told Lady Melbourne that Webster was 'passionately fond of having his wife admired' and sure that she would never be unfaithful to him. Added to that he could not resist telling other men about his successes with women. He could hardly have offered Byron a more inviting challenge. 'I think any woman fair game,' "Bold" Webster (as he was called) was unwise enough to say. Byron carefully ascertained what he meant; that Webster 'might love where he liked but that no one else might like what he ever thought proper to love'. What could be clearer? The red light turned to amber.

The next scene is the Websters' billiard-room, where Byron and Lady Frances, both experts at one at least of the games they were playing, managed to make their 'declaration' while they concentrated on their breaks. Byron's next move was to hand her a letter, which she coolly placed 'not very far from the heart which I wished it to reach'. There it was and there it stayed after Webster joined them. Byron added a stop-press postscript to his earlier account: 'This business is growing serious – & I think *Platonism* in some peril.' Any scruples he might have had disappeared that evening when Webster offered to bet Byron that he 'for a certain sum wins any given *woman* – against any given *homme* including all friends present'.

He was asking for trouble, and trouble came. When Webster paid Byron a return visit at Newstead, he went on boasting, this time – curious claim – 'congratulating himself on possessing a partner without *passion*'. No wonder Byron had to tell someone about all the ironies of the situation; and who would share his enjoyment more delightedly than Lady Melbourne? Byron wrote that he was not yet certain of Lady Frances's desires, but he 'never

Lord Byron looking dashing
in travelling dress.

Lady Frances Webster,
whose husband told Byron
he thought any woman was
'fair game'.

saw more decisive preliminary symptoms'. When he told her that he was willing to be hers on her own terms she 'burst into an agony of crying', in spite of the danger of her husband and sister being not far off.

She must have had a very steady nerve. She managed to give Byron a note and to take one from him, as well as a ring, in front of her husband's eyes. And yet, Byron noted, 'she is a thorough devotee – & takes prayers morning and evening'. Webster's grumble about his wife's 'aversion from being beneficial to population & posterity' made Byron wonder whether he might be wasting his time, but he was encouraged by her showing more inclination than he had 'ever heard from any woman within the time'. She was so adept at pulling the wool over her husband's eyes and clearly enjoyed doing this so much that Byron decided that Webster did not have much idea of his wife's feelings. At dinner she openly manoeuvred a change of place for Byron and achieved some skilful *double entendres* in her conversation with Webster. She wanted her sister to share her bedroom, she said. Only husbands had the right to 'divide their spouses' pillow', Webster amused them by replying.

The campaign went on. 'She is – you know – very handsome – .. . & singularly warm in her affections,' he told Lady Melbourne: 'but I should think – of a *cold* temperament – yet I have my doubts on that point too.' Knowing him and his weaknesses so well, he said, Lady Melbourne would not be surprised to hear that Byron was 'totally absorbed in this passion'. He admitted that his treatment of Webster was decidedly wrong; and yet the man had almost provoked Byron to seduce Frances by boasting that he himself went after other women and that she was so passionless.

His next bulletin told of Webster 'attacking' his wife and her sister at the breakfast table in front of the servants and another guest. Byron now decided to 'try to make an "affaire reglée", and if that did not succeed they would probably go off together. 'As for him he may convert his Antlers into *powder-horns* – & welcome,' as he had always promised he would. A duel held no terrors for Byron. Meanwhile the drama deepened, and one day when they were left entirely on their own was 'nearly fatal'. Frances said she was entirely at Byron's mercy. 'I am not *cold* – whatever I seem to others,' she reassured him. He 'spared her' – at two in the morning – and she seemed to be grateful. By now Byron loved her and was willing to face divorce, a duel, or a getaway together. That she would not do, she said, 'on Byron's account'. She declined it. On one important score Byron felt he had nothing to answer for. 'She *don't* & *won't* live with him'; they had been 'separate for a long time'.

The mechanics of their affair are good to watch. Byron described how they sat and looked at each other and 'the most amusing part was the interchange of notes – for we sat up all night scribbling to each other'. He would never forget 'the quiet manner in which she would pass her epistles in a music book – or any book', looking calmly at Webster or Byron as she did so. Once she offered Byron a note as he was taking her in to dinner at Newstead, with the servants all around and her husband and sister just behind them. It was as impossible for him to take a note as it was for her, 'without *pockets*', to keep one. Bluff and boldness were their only chance, and they both enjoyed the danger. On one occasion Byron slipped his note into the 'cover' of a letter he had, saying openly that it was the frank she had asked for. The deal was clinched by Webster grumbling that 'women did nothing but scribble'.

In the end even he realized that something was going on, and Byron reported that the two of them had 'subsided into a mortal coldness'. All Byron blamed himself for was 'a few kisses for which she was no worse – and I no better'. Webster told his wife that she had made an explanation between Byron and him necessary, although he still went on declaring that they loved each other so much, that he was the best and happiest of husbands. 'Don't you see how the poor girl *doats* on me?' he asked Byron. The only time she had a chance to give practical proof of this, Frances took refuge in 'tears & tremors & prayers'; she was more concerned with fearing the devil than welcoming her lover. Her letters told how she blamed herself for being deceitful and how she dreaded being discovered. And yet it seemed to Byron that she was asking for this, writing to him as she did and sending some of her notes by a third person.

So how would it all end? Probably in a duel, Byron thought, and that would not displease him as 'all the sex would be enamoured of my Memory' – except for Caroline Lamb, who would 'go wild with *grief*' that he had not died for her. Or perhaps Webster would let his wife choose between them? Or, a third possibility, he would decide that after all Byron's friendship was 'not inconvenient' and they would all be 'happy ever after'.

As usual, there are gaps in the story. At all events, four months after the start of his flirtation Byron was writing to Webster with Olympian calm that he had 'long passed the happy time when one's heart is turned by a pretty face'. He now felt able to give his opinion about beautiful young women 'as impartially as I would of a Statue'. Had Webster become equally dispassionate and cool?

Evidently not, as in 1821 he was once again jealous, although this time not of Byron. Mrs Arbuthnot told how Webster suspected his wife of carrying on with Lord Petersham, and one night when she was going out he felt sure they were going to meet. So he got up behind her carriage, and sure enough it drove to the stable yard, where Lord Petersham came out to speak to her. 'While he was standing with his head in at the window, Mr Webster dismounted from behind & beat him most furiously', calling the servants to come. Lord Petersham challenged Webster to a duel, with the classic outcome of shots being fired into the air, honour being bloodlessly satisfied, and the two men reconciled. Was Lady Frances tempted to 'go wild with grief', as Byron had imagined Caroline Lamb would, because no one was killed?

12

Discreditable Connexions

Love and marriage sometimes succeeded in bridging the gap between the great country houses and the working-class world. On at least two occasions in the 1820s the Two Nations, as Disraeli was to call them, came together as romantically in real life as they later did in the pages of his *Sybil*.

The first of these caused a rumpus in the state rooms of Longleat, recently modernized by Sir Jeffry Wyatville. The second Marquess of Bath was a distinguished man in his own right, Fellow of the Society of Antiquaries as well as Lord Lieutenant of Somerset, and he may well have considered that he had made good provision for a family inheritance that dated from the reign of King John and included the rolling, wooded acres of one of Capability Brown's most imaginatively landscaped parks, with the magnificent Elizabethan house at its heart. By his marriage to a daughter of Lord Torrington he had seven sons and three daughters.

But in 1820 his heir, Viscount Weymouth, ran away with Harriet Robbins, the beautiful daughter of a tollgate-keeper on the turnpike road not far from Longleat, and married her. His parents had other reasons for disapproving of their son; he drank too much and got into debt, but it was what they called his 'discreditable connexions' that displeased them most. Thomas and Harriet went off to France together, lived happily near Paris, and travelled in France and Italy, making do – with difficulty – on his income. They hoped that Lord Bath would forgive him, but he was obdurate and did all he could to debar Thomas from the succession. He had six other sons, after all. Could one of them not inherit Longleat? And bring a worthier Marchioness to preside over it?

His lawyers advised that this was impossible. The right of primogeniture, which had kept the family fortune and estates intact throughout the centuries, prevented all attempts to exclude the rightful heir from the succession. Lord Bath sent his lawyers to France to parley with Thomas and to offer him £10,000, the Irish estates and £3,000 a year if he would give up his claims to Longleat. Thomas refused to sell what he correctly looked upon as his legal rights. When his father died, he declared, he and Harriet would come back to England and live at Longleat.

As it happened, they never did. Thomas died childless in Paris in 1837, shortly before his father, so the succession went to his brother Henry. Once again the lawyers scratched their heads. Harriet could be pregnant – she might even pretend to be pregnant and in due course turn up with a son for whom the succession could be claimed. So they advised the third Marquess not to take his seat in the House of Lords until nine months after Thomas's death. However, Harriet made no awkward demands. (The family would certainly not have granted them if she had.) They docked her income, and refused her modest request for a loan so that she could buy back some paintings that had belonged to Thomas and were held in store at Longleat. The family did not want the pictures but they would not let Harriet have them, so they were sold at auction. Harriet stayed on the continent, eventually married an Italian count, and died in Rome in 1873. The third Marquess had made up for his brother's misdeeds and misfortunes by marrying the daughter of a baron, but he died the same year as his father and brother. So his six-year-old son, John, became the fourth Marquess of Bath.

The second instance of 'discreditable connexions' had as its setting Uppark, the delicately furnished and decorated seventeenth-century house high on the South Downs, between Petersfield and Chichester. From the middle of the eighteenth century it was owned by the Fetherstonhaugh family, and it was young Sir Harry who was later to commission Humphry Repton to landscape the grounds. But in his salad days he was no less embarrassing to his family than Lord Weymouth, and he is believed to have been diplomatically dispatched abroad on his travels because he had fallen in love with the daughter of a miller who, like the Longleat tollgate-keeper, lived dangerously near the family home. This time at least a marriage was prevented, and it seems the splendours of the continent helped him to forget his girl, although soon after arriving back at Uppark he was in trouble again. This time his choice was a beauty who was to be famous as Emma Hart, Lady Hamilton, and Nelson's great love. At Uppark she was only fifteen and then called Emy Lyon. She was pregnant and penniless when she was sent away nearly a year later.

Fetherstonhaugh must have been a man of complicated passions – his loves always came from outside his own class – as it seems some ten years later he had an affair with an Uppark footman called Joseph Weaver. The family papers include correspondence and a heavy bill from London solicitors, mentioning large payments made to induce someone – always unnamed and referred to as '*him*' – to go away to Ireland. There is also a record of £10,000 being paid to another man, as well as a local tradition that there used to be strange homosexual goings-on up at the big house. Not long ago, old men in the village at South Harting remembered that when they were lads they were warned not to go near the grounds of Uppark after dark. All that now remains of these excesses is a curious classical urn which stands on a wooded rise, over the lawns which slope gently down to the house. Its sculptured sides illustrate with explicit Roman gusto a homosexual orgy. It was known locally as 'Sir Harry's Shame', and the story goes that bushes were planted discreetly around to camouflage the lurid detail of its scenes, but villagers came along at night and cleared them away so that the 'Shame' would be exposed.

However that may be, the next record of Sir Harry's amours dates from 1825, when the pretty Uppark dairymaid caught his roving eye. He was over seventy by then, and perhaps the gracefulness of the setting as well as that of its central figure encouraged his romantic thoughts, suggesting that this time his love might be installed permanently in his home. The dairy, probably part of Humphrey Repton's design, was unusually elegant and charming. Sir Harry would bring his guests to enjoy its rustic sophistication as well as fresh cream from his Guernsey herd which was offered to them there. It was a delicate white building, with slatted seats, slim pillars, and a curved roof. A door led to the brightly tiled dairy where marble tables held the earthenware crocks and bowls of cream. The head dairymaid was Mary Ann

Bullock, daughter of the Uppark keeper and poulterer. Sir Harry's last amorous adventure began when one day he heard Mary Ann singing as she worked.

The story, handed on from a later dairymaid who had heard it from Mary Ann's contemporaries, is that Sir Harry at last decided to call at the dairy and ask Mary Ann to marry him. Seeing how surprised and flabbergasted she was, he told her to take her time, think about his offer, and then send him her answer. But how? She could not write, and of course had no contact with the 'above stairs' part of the house. Sir Harry hit on an ingenious code. Mary Ann of course had the entrée to the kitchen at Uppark, so if she agreed to be his wife she should cut a slice from the leg of mutton that would go from there to the dining-room that day. The slice was duly cut, and before long the news was flying round the country. 'I hear Sir Harry Fetherston [sic] is to marry his cook', the Duke of Wellington was told, not altogether accurately, by Mrs Arbuthnot. Such things did happen, although Sir Harry was unusual in arranging for his wife to be given some education before she married. He sent her to Paris, where she was taught to read, write, and embroider. Then in 1825 she came back to Uppark, and they were married in the magnificent Saloon by the Vicar of Harting. The bridegroom was seventy-one, his bride twenty.

Inevitably the story caused amusement as well as some questions. Why did Sir Harry marry Mary Ann? Was it because in his old age he wanted an heir? Or had she played an old trick on him by telling him that she was already pregnant? Most of the evidence suggests that the marriage went well, although certainly no heir was born. Together the Fetherstonhaughs founded a school, at Sir Harry's expense, in the village; and he arranged for arms for his wife to be registered with the College of Heralds so that they could be quartered with his own. They are still to be seen on the hatchments in the church. Those were not the only ways the marriage broke through the class barrier. On one occasion the couple were driving through the park when a little girl opened one of the gates for the carriage and threw a bunch of flowers into Lady Fetherstonhaugh's hands. Who was that child? Sir Harry asked. When he heard that she was Frances, his wife's sister – but surely he might have discovered that before? – he is said to have brought her to the house and arranged for her to be educated. A nineteen-year-old illegitimate daughter of his also joined them there, and the three women

Sir Harry [Henry] Fetherstonhaugh, of Uppark.

The marriage certificate of Sir Henry Fetherstonhaugh and Mary Ann Bullock.

lived together for the rest of their lives.

The story has come down mostly by word of mouth and not always convincingly, but two written records also survive. Inside a book can be seen what look like some of Mary Ann's early attempts at writing and at signing her new name. 'Mary', she has written, and 'Lady', 'Mary Bullock', 'Lady Featherstonhaugh' [sic] and 'Darling'. There is also an account, believed to have been written by Lady Fetherstonhaugh at a time when she was more accustomed to her quill, giving a detailed and caring description of her husband's last illness.

But there may have been problems. It is said that soon after his marriage Sir Harry confided in his old gamekeeper. 'I've made a fool of myself, Legge,' he said. On another occasion the footman who was standing at the door to receive them laughed at his mistress showing how unaccustomed she was to her new position, and was immediately dismissed. Society could hardly be expected to take the marriage seriously, and local county families did not invite the Fetherstonhaughs. There is also a somewhat mysterious rumour that £10,000 was bequeathed by Mary Ann to the son of Joseph Weaver, the footman who had been her husband's lover. It was suggested that Mary Ann at one time was young Weaver's mistress. Certainly his initials, J.W., have been discreetly added to her coat of arms in South Harting church.

At all events the strange *ménage à quatre* carried on at Uppark until Sir Harry died, aged ninety-two, in 1846. He left all he had to his widow, who died nearly thirty years later. Neither history nor local tittle-tattle relate whether anyone was singing in the dairy then.

13

Adieu till We meet for Ever

Chevening, on the southern slopes of the North Downs not far from Sevenoaks, was the home of the talented and public-spirited Stanhope family for over two hundred years until in 1967 the seventh Earl died and with him the family came to an end. Generation after generation of Stanhopes were born and reared in the house, and 'homed' to Chevening from far-off campaigning, travels, and government appointments. Their affection for the place is hard to parallel, even among the home-loving country house families. The tragedy that is the subject of this chapter took place almost exactly a hundred years after General James Stanhope, later the first Earl, bought the house. It had been rebuilt in the seventeenth century, almost certainly to plans by Inigo Jones, on the site of a much older building, and the new owner at once set about making extensive improvements.

The dangers of childbirth prompted many wives to write farewell letters, to be given to their husband in the event of their death. One of the most touching of these was left to James Hamilton, son of the third Earl, and half-brother of Lady Hester Stanhope. He was exceptionally happily married, having fallen in love with Lady Frederica Murray, the third Earl of Mansfield's daughter, when she was still a girl in the schoolroom. He waited for her for five years, and married her in 1820, just after her twentieth birthday. The following year a son was born to them, and it was before the birth of their second child two years later at Chevening that she wrote the letter to her husband which is still kept in the silver case that he had

SACRED T·
THE RIGHT HONOURABLE LADY
DAUGHTER OF
AND WIFE OF THE HONOU
WHO DIED IN CHILDBED JANUAR
HER LIFE WAS ALL PURITY AND HAPPIN·
HER OWN PRAYER WIL·
THE MOURNERS SHE HA
"TO BE A PIOUS CHRISTIAN; A FAITHFUL A
"GRATEFUL DAUGHTER, A KIND SISTER; TH
"WAS TO ME; THE FRIEND OF THE POOR A
"LIFE ON EARTH AND TO DIE IN THE B
"FORGIVEN AND THAT I SHALL ENTER TH
"OR WAIT FOR THOSE I LOVE; THE
TO HIS ALLWISE AND ALLRIGHTEOUS W
A RESIGNED, AFFLICTE
CHEERED BY HER ME
HE WAITS IN HUMBLE HO

The memorial to Lady Frederica Stanhope and her baby, in Chevening Church, Kent. It was commissioned from Sir Francis Chantrey by her 'resigned, afflicted, but grateful husband'.

made for it. It was written on 9 January 1823, two days before the baby was born. He lived for only one day, and the day after he died his mother followed him. She was twenty-two and, like Laura Lyttelton in an earlier chapter of this book, she seems to have been certain that she was going to die. Her letter shows that she had thought very carefully about what lay ahead for her husband and children – she hoped of course that there would be two – after her death.

> My dearest and best Husband my own beloved James, I write this to express my gratitude for the happiness you gave me happiness dearest James such as no mortal ever felt. . . . I am sure [it] will be a consolation to you to reflect that by no thought or action did we ever disturb that felicity which it has pleased the Almighty to permit us to enjoy. I do not repine at my death dearest James. . . I feel more for the grief that I know you will suffer, than sorrow at quitting all I love.

Like many wives of her time and class, she was encouraged by her unquestioning faith and by the certainty that those she was leaving would all join her again in a future life. Meanwhile there would be problems for her husband and children, and she wanted to leave him her advice and instructions. Her requests are extraordinarily selfless. Almost all she asked on her own behalf was that the baby, if it were a girl, should be given her name. She had some practical advice on the choice of a governess, and then concentrated on how things could best be arranged for her widowed husband. First of all she wanted him to marry again – in order to 'preserve his virtue,' and 'therefore I earnestly wish it,' she said.

> Do not let the wordly idea of it being a want of affection to my memory deter you. I do not expect any one will make you as happy as I trust I have done but I earnestly wish such a person should be found. Whenever you have found such a person likely to suit you, disclose the state of your heart *truly* if you do not fall in *love* do not pretend it but avow that esteem and attachment are all that you feel.

She imagined her husband's relationship with his second wife, almost seeing it through the eyes of her successor as she warned him of possible dangers. 'Should you ever disagree or should anything be disputed never say what *I* should have done or felt,' she advised him. It would help him if after her death he thought of her as of a sister, and spoke to his second wife as he had spoken to Frederica of his own sisters.

> Do not be surprised or hurt if you should discover any jealousy of me or my memory, her very love for you would excuse it. Do not continue to wear the Locket if it should seem to hurt her if you wear it but let her hair be worn on the same chain as mine it is my wish. I trust you will consult my Parents as you would your own in the choice, they shall know it was my wish you should remarry.

She did not forget that the woman she was writing about would be a mother to her own children as well as to those she would probably have herself.

> I am sure the Wife you will chuse will be fond of my Children and I feel no fear or anxiety in their having a Stepmother. If she should have Children make no difference between them and take care no one else does through the mistaken notion they are not cherished as they ought to be. This is not written with forced feelings but on mature serious and I trust religious considerations. Trust to no one but yourself the religious education of our Children.

All that was left was to say goodbye.

> And now my husband my Friend my own James Father of my Children Adieu till we meet for ever. I trust this letter will not have given you pain but comfort as it has done me in writing.

She ended with a prayer. Five days later she died, having seen her baby both live and die.

James never recovered from her loss. He commissioned Sir Francis Chantrey to design a memorial for Chevening church. An appealing figure, the sculptor's own favourite, the young mother lies in her nightgown, asleep on a couch with her baby, also asleep, at her breast. Left alone, James and his son went to live with his wife's parents at their home at Kenwood. It seems that he tried to obey the instructions he had been given, as in March 1825 a young lady whom he was expected to marry was also staying there. But the wedding did not take place. James had been severely wounded years before his marriage at the battle of San Sebastian, and for the rest of his life was often in great pain from a musket ball that could not be removed from his shoulder. Was it because of the pain, the insomnia it caused, because of his grief for Frederica, or because he could not face a second marriage that James left his family that evening in their splendid Adam mansion on the edge of Hampstead. Heath, walked out into the grounds and hanged himself? Frederica's courageous plans for her husband's life without her deserved a happier dénouement.

14

Beautiful Woman neglected by her Husband

Death is a great mender of broken marriages. After a lifetime of neglect and irascibility, Edward Stanley apologized to his wife and family shortly before he died. He and Henrietta Maria Dillon met and married in Florence in 1826, and they proceeded to have ten children. Stanley, who in 1850 succeeded his father as second Baron Stanley of Alderley, was absorbed in social and political life in London, where they had a house in Grosvenor Gardens, and for months on end left his wife and children on their own in the country. Henrietta later recalled how, soon after his marriage, Palmerston noticed that Stanley was showing very little interest in his wife, and decided to take advantage. He came up to her, she wrote, 'in his impudent, brusque way, with a "Ha, ha! I see it all – beautiful woman neglected by her husband – allow me, etc." '

The neglect continued, but so did Henrietta's devotion. Her letters to him are almost always loving. 'My dearest love', they start; 'God bless you my darling', they usually end. In between comes a rag-bag of family news – children's illnesses and naughtinesses, and what should be done about both; what they want for Christmas; local gossip. Then she is brought up with a start as she imagines her husband, far away in London, faced with her long, uninteresting letter. 'I hardly like to write half I have to say to you for I feel yr mind must be so engrossed with yr present anxious work.' And again: 'I have written to you every day & begin to fear you will tire of my letters as I have little to say that is agreeable.'

The Stanley home in Cheshire had been destroyed by fire in 1799, and after that they lived at Park House, which had been the bailiff's home. In September 1845 the family in the country were settling down to the cold dark months ahead when Edward Stanley's letters from London seemed to take longer than usual to reach his wife. 'I have been fidgetted all the week at not hearing from you,' she wrote. But she had more than the fidgets: she was jealous as well. 'I am really vexed not to have heard fom you. . . Poor ensnared man you have been basking in the charm of that wicked woman. Pray write.' That time she signed herself 'Your affect & irate wife H.M.S.'

It sounds a charmless, chilly marriage. The letters between Edward Stanley's wife and his mother admit to all its failings. 'Having been obliged to ask him for money to pay a bill this morng. I have not had much conversation out of him since,' wrote Henrietta. She had a lot to grumble about, but of course her grumbles did not spark off loving reactions in her husband. Her mother-in-law did not attempt to make excuses for her son. 'The truth is,' she wrote to Henrietta, '& an unpleasant truth it is, that Edward has no taste for the company of Wife & Children by themselves & that you are afraid of being set down at Henwood & left there when he is amusing himself in Town.' It was a check-mate situation for Henrietta, particularly as Edward's rare visits to his wife and family often seemed to result in an addition to their number.

From time to time she was tossed a few crumbs of affection. Perhaps it was his pleasure at being offered – and accepting – the position of Under Secretary of State for Foreign Affairs by Lord John Russell in 1846 that prompted him to send his wife a few warm words. 'I am very glad you miss me a little & still more flattered at your saying so,' Henrietta replied. But she was still uneasy about 'that wicked woman'. She could not agree, she wrote to her husband, that Lady Harriet was not dangerous, for he seemed to have been entirely occupied with her. But of course 'people who have only to amuse & be amused have great advantages over unfortunate women who have as many children to see after as I have'. They did have a house in London, but Edward did not exactly press them to come. He was so much freer on his own. He looked forward to their visits much less than his wife did. 'I am getting very weary of my widowhood,' moaned Henrietta. 'I have now been alone three months out of four – I shall be so glad when the time comes for going to London, I have quite settled in my mind how I shall locate the children without you being aware they are in the house.'

Month after month her reproaches droned on. Henrietta welcomed the chance of Edward being sent as Minister to Florence because if they were there together he 'could not get away'. Did she really imagine that would throw him into her arms? Or even encourage him to get the job in Florence? Meanwhile would he please send her some money; 'this is the third time of asking'. When Edward wrote from a brilliant house-party at Panshanger his letter was not well received by his wife, as she and 'half a dozen of the children' had colds and if he did not get them a small stove she would die. 'I am glad you have been so well amused at all your visits,' she added, not altogether convincingly, 'but I had better say no more & be content to enact the part of nurse & housekeeper without meeting help or sympathy.' That brought a protest from Stanley that his wife's attacks were unjust, and the only way to avoid others was for him not to tell her about the people he met and the things he did. 'If I express myself in favour of a married woman you are jealous, if of a girl, I am a Monster to my own children.' It had been her choice, he reminded her, to live in the country rather than in town.

There was always something to mark up on Henrietta's scoreboard. After her birthday – which of course he had not remembered – she wrote: 'My dearest love, So you forgot my birthday well peace be with you.' It was only one small addition, she said, to 'the heavy list' of his sins. And when he spent Christmas Day away from the nest: 'You can hardly think my dearest Love how very much your children miss you this day.' He was impervious to her reproaches. On one occasion when she suggested coming to London, he replied: 'I have no objection to your coming to Town when Parliament meets provided you leave the children in the country.' That was too much. 'Thank you for your invitation to London,' Henrietta riposted; 'it is not pressing enough to make me decide upon coming.' The sharpness of the letters is entertaining now, but each one must have been a crucifixion for the loving but unloved Henrietta.

It seems surprising that after such bitter exchanges, not to mention Edward's enjoyable social life and dangerous attentions from 'wicked women', on the few occasions when they did meet they still slept together. In 1847, when their eldest son was twenty, Henrietta wrote to Edward that she was pregnant once again. He scolded her for her carelessness. Of course the fault was hers. 'What can you have been doing to account for so juvenile a proceeding?' he asked, and hoped it was not 'the beginning of another flock for what to do with them I am sure I know not'. However she must just make the best of it.

Henrietta was more resourceful. 'A hot bath, a tremendous walk & a great dose have succeeded,' she wrote, 'but it is a warning.' The extraordinary thing was that in spite of everything she still loved her husband, and was still able to tell him so. 'I do not feel a day older in the love I have for you, & even after my long experience that tenderness is not given to me I often feel my heart overflow with love & the hope of living some day together.'

Every summer Edward went off to Scotland for two months without his wife, who was left 'fretted and in suspense'. Her friends sympathized with her, but she knew it would be useless to try to make him stay against his will. She knew too that she had been a good wife and a good mother. She had 'loved him supremely' all her life. In 1854, after his father's death, Lady Stanley (as she then was) wrote to her husband in case they did not meet on their wedding-day that year. She would always consider it 'le plus beau jour de ma vie' and believed truly that her love had been 'ever increasing & will I trust never cease to do so as long as I live'. Lord Stanley for his part attributed all the troubles of his life to want of money – 'not for superfluities or fancies, I do not even think of them, but for things essential to that position in which we are placed'.

Even so, he had a gay, sociable life, was a Member of Parliament for years, and had several important government appointments, including those of President of the Board of Trade and Postmaster-General. While he was alive Henrietta was overshadowed as well as neglected by him, but in her widowhood she blossomed, attracting the most distinguished personalities of the day to her house in Dover Street, and forcefully pioneering the movement for women's education. The years of loneliness and self-pity must have tempered her steel.

15

Every favourite Plan upset

Marriage of a young girl to an older, widowed man with a ready-made family happened so often that it is worth following the well-documented step-by-step pattern of one important case. Crabbed age and youth? That is certainly how it looked at one point.

Lady Frances Elliot, one of the ten children of the second Earl and Countess of Minto, had a happy childhood at Minto House in Roxburghshire in a family which was strongly marked by Whig politics and the Scottish Presbyterian Church. So she was used to hearing about Lord John Russell, and in 1835 she noted in her diary that she had been glad to see him and his wife at a party which she had found otherwise 'very tiresome'. Fanny (as she was called) did not shine at parties, although one partner admired her 'engaging manners and sweetness of disposition . . . even more than her admitted beauty'. She was shy and diffident, convinced that it was 'impossible for anybody ever to admire my looks or think me agreeable'.

In 1838 Lord John Russell's wife died, and two years later, when he was forty-eight and Fanny twenty-four, they met at 'rather solemn dinner-parties' and he came to stay with her family at Minto. He was then Colonial Secretary, popular, and well known for his part in the fight for electoral reform. When he came to stay he went out of his way to bridge the generation gap by joining Lord Minto's older and younger children in their games of trap-ball and shooting. He had his reasons for doing this. Fanny noted in her diary that before going away he 'said quite enough to make me tell Mama all I thought'.

It was evidently a shock to them both. Lady Minto was glad that

Fanny 'did not like him in that way', although she was sure she did in every other. Next morning he went off early, leaving a note for Fanny, which she answered at once, 'begging him not to come back, but also telling him how grateful I feel'. Two days later he wrote her a very abject, self-pitying note.

DEAR LADY FANNY, – You are quite right. I deceived myself, not from any fault of yours, but from a deep sense of unhappiness, and a foolish notion that you might throw yourself away on a person of broken spirits, and worn out by time and trouble. There is nothing left to me but constant and laborious attention to public business, and a wretched sense of misery, which even the children can never long drive away. However, that is my duty. . . . So do not blame yourself, and leave me to hope that my life may not be long.

In spite of that letter – could it possibly be because of it? – Fanny began to change her mind. There was gossip in the Press of their engagement. Lady Minto, although she contradicted this, began to think it would happen in the end. Her own feelings were ambivalent. She wrote to her married daughter that she would be unhappy if Fanny accepted Lord John, but she would also be wretched, if Fanny never married at all, to think that she had refused him. There were long family discussions. Fanny's uncle, although strongly against 'disparity of years', greatly admired Lord John and thought she would be very wrong to turn him down. But the age gap remained a big one. Fanny's father, away from home, wrote that 'his eyes were only just opened to Lord John's being an old man, when he looked on him in this new light'.

In London, early in 1841, Fanny agreed cautiously that they should meet so that she could have a chance of getting to know him better. And gradually she began to wonder whether her earlier decision had been a mistake. She told her mother that she was 'too old to think it necessary to be what is called desperately in love'. She also admitted that if he had been younger she would have accepted him. (Her grandson, Bertrand Russell, with hindsight was to guess that her 'Puritan inhibitions' probably made her incapable of passionate love. But after all, he only knew her in her old age, and he was fortunate to enjoy an above-average freedom from inhibitions himself.)

210

Lord and Lady John Russell.

Lady Minto spoke frankly to Lord John about Fanny's feelings, and was touched by his reactions and by his agreeing to spend less time with them all. A month later he distinguished himself by a brilliant speech in Parliament. And a month after that he and Fanny became engaged. Everyone – Fanny first and foremost – at once forgot any doubts or disadvantages there might be. Lady Minto wrote of 'Fanny's happy face . . . how perfectly satisfied and proud she is of the position she has put herself in'. Her future son-in-law was everything Lady Minto's proudest wishes could have wanted for Fanny, who would never have been suited by an ordinary person. He treasured every word she said and appreciated her interest – so unusual in a girl – in all the great events of the day. Lady Minto's anxiety that Lord John's four stepchildren and his own two young children would 'overload' Fanny was dispelled by their being so good, so healthy, and so 'disposed to love her'.

They were married in 1841 in the drawing-room at Minto. When Lord John arrived there the age gap again made itself felt, although this time it was not between him and Fanny. She wrote to her sister that the younger children were 'so much too respectful to Lord John. Not to me, for they take their revenge upon me, and I am unsparingly laughed at, which is a great comfort.' After the wedding they went off for their honeymoon at Bowhill, lent to them by the Duke of Buccleuch, and Fanny was soon launched on the excitement and ordeal of an official reception with bands playing, bells ringing, and banners flying. After that they went to London, to Lord John's house – and his children – in Wilton Crescent.

Fanny's new life had certainly begun. They visited the seventh Duke of Bedford, Lord John's brother, at Woburn and experienced a Whig defeat in the general election. The Duke put the family home at Endsleigh at their disposal, and they lived there when Parliamentary affairs did not keep them in town. At the end of 1842 their son John (later Viscount Amberley) was born, and it was then that Fanny admitted to being 'overloaded'. She wrote in February 1843 to her sister, envying her because

great lady as you are, you lead a quiet life; how far from quiet mine is and always must be, and how intensely I long that it could be more so, how completely worn out both mind and body often feel at the end of a common day, none can imagine but those who have become in one moment mother of six children, wife of the Leader of the House of Commons, and mistress of a house in London.

Her load was soon to be heavier. In December 1845 Lord John wrote to her from Osborne to say that the Queen had asked him to form a government. Fanny was far away and the family had all been ill, but she wrote, 'like a Spartan', as she put it, to encourage him, 'with all my regrets – with the conviction that private happiness to the degree we have enjoyed it is at an end if you are Prime Minister'; still she hoped he would let no one dissuade him. He had spoken of the 'desolation of our domestic prospects', but she bolstered him up by telling him of her ambition that he should be 'the head of the most moral and religious government the country has ever had'. Once again it was to her sister that Fanny wrote her less courageous thoughts. If ever she had wished herself not married to her husband, she said, it had been during these last days when the highest honour in the land had been within his reach. Proud though she was and convinced that he must go ahead, 'still to myself it is all loss, all sacrifice – every favourite plan upset'. To Lord John too it was a total 'sacrifice of private happiness to public duty'.

She seems to have caught the tone of voice and mood of the letter Lord John had written after she refused him. On this occasion the 'highest honour in the land' was not to be Lord John's. But Fanny's mettle had been tried and had stood the test. Thirty years of public life and marriage lay ahead.

16

It must have been Agony every Time

No one could say that her daughters' marriages came about without careful planning by the loving but neglected Lady Stanley of Alderley who was dumped with her family in the country while her husband was enjoying his work and the company of 'wicked women' in London. The first to get married was Blanche, and every move she made was watched and anxiously commented upon. Her grandmother, old Lady Stanley, did not like Blanche being 'surrounded by *clever* men'. She wrote to her daughter-in-law, warning her that that was 'setting-up for a character' and seldom 'ends well for matrimony'. It is a curious argument, perhaps not unconnected with a story that Blanche had loved a charming young painter, Richard Doyle, but had been steered by her mother away from him and into the arms of the less charming but certainly noble seventh Earl of Airlie. He was twenty-five, and had only lately succeeded his father. Lady Stanley accepted him as a suitable match for Blanche, although she admitted that he was not brilliant. Perhaps that was something of a relief after the undesirably clever men who had been surrounding Blanche so recently. She also considered him to be poor, which seems a strange assessment of a young man who owned four Scottish castles as well as two other houses. Airlie Castle, in Angus, had been the home of the Ogilvy family since 1431, and he also had Cortachy Castle, Cluny Castle, and Keltie Castle, as well as Auchterhouse, in Forfarshire, and a London home in Bolton Street.

Lord Airlie visited Alderley in the spring of 1851, when Blanche was twenty-two, and followed her adoringly wherever she went. Lady Stanley wrote to her mother-in-law that he had not yet proposed although Blanche assured her that she had given him every chance. The trouble was that Blanche enjoyed her present life and was in no hurry to marry. As for Airlie, Lady Stanley had never seen a man so completely mesmerized. Perhaps it was because her feelings were so cool that Blanche could discuss them openly with her mother. She was disappointed that she cared so little for Airlie, Lady Stanley told her husband; she would 'so like to be desperately in love'.

In spite of that, when he did at last propose, Blanche accepted him. They had gone walking together and it was of course a perfect opportunity. But Airlie said not a word. Then at last he had to. He was neither as good nor as clever as she was, he said, but he loved her very much. This time it was Blanche who was silent, and it was more than he could bear. He seized her hand, spoke in agony, and told her that she frightened him. Blanche then managed to answer that she would try to make him happy. Her voice sounded cold, and different from his, she later told her mother.

Then she asked Airlie a leading question. Could he, for her sake, give up the thing he loved best? This was an allusion to his passion for racing. Yes, he promised, he would do that. Then came her second question. Had he ever loved Lady Rachel? That broke the ice, and Airlie burst out laughing. No, never, he answered. Had he ever 'liked anyone'? Blanche asked. Yes, he had certainly been in love with Martia Fox. Oh well, she did not object to that, said Blanche generously, since Martia was now dead. But Blanche felt she should warn him that she was 'ill-tempered'. Airlie admitted that he knew she had faults, but they were not bad ones.

Blanche told her mother all that had happened, and she in turn sent on the news to Lord Stanley. The first feelings of the couple seem to have been terror and embarrassment. Blanche said that 'she was afraid when she met him something dreadful would happen, meaning he would kiss her which he has not yet ventured to do'. He had already managed to call her Blanche, 'which she will get used to'.

After that, the atmosphere became a little less tense. Airlie told Lady Stanley that he had loved Blanche for two years but had few hopes that she would ever care for him. He was soon 'not shy at all now with any of us', managed to call Blanche by her name 'quite naturally', called Lady Stanley 'My Lady', and wanted them all to call him Airlie – not Lord Airlie any more – which they did not find easy. He was specially upset when Blanche called him Lord Airlie.

She, however, was still very capricious and changeable, and her mother would be relieved when she was safely married, she told Lord Stanley. As for Airlie's past life, since he seemed to be passionate he was not likely to have lived like a monk during the two years of his love for Blanche. (At this point she could not resist reminding her husband that their own wedding had been postponed because of an illness he contracted while he was courting her.)

So she was content with her future son-in-law and felt sure he loved Blanche faithfully. Soon afterwards the fairy-tale transformation took place, and Blanche discovered that she was very fond of Airlie. He did not consider her handsome, she said, and she was glad of that as she thought he would not then get tired of her. But she was thawing at last. They went into the wood together and cut their names on two trees. Lady Stanley found herself liking Airlie more very day. He was happy to give up his racing and gambling, and was 'very good about letting himself be seen. . . on the whole the people are pleased & think it very fine he shld. be an Earl'.

A few days after the wedding in September 1851, a radiant letter came from Blanche. They had been magnificently welcomed in Scotland with bonfires, cheers, and torches all the way from Glamis. She had walked into her new home at three in the morning to the deafening shouts of a large crowd. The castle was floodlit, and 'Airlie looked so happy & handsome, it was a perfect moment, never to be forgotten, & I hope neither he nor his people will ever regret my being here.'

But honeymoon problems lay ahead. Blanche got a book called *Hints to Mothers*, which Airlie too was seen to read – 'for his ignorance is surprising'. Reading was not enough, and they consulted the celebrated Dr Simpson, who had pioneered the use of chloroform in childbirth. He operated on Blanche, for whom 'it must have been agony, every time', he said. When she was well again, three months after the wedding, her mother wrote to Lord Stanley that she hoped Blanche would not allow herself foolish fancies that she did not love her husband. No one could be more devoted and considerate than Airlie, and it would be Blanche's fault if he changed. Three years later, when Lady Stanley stayed at Cortachy Castle with Blanche, now the mother of two girls, she did not find her daughter 'nearly as amiable in her own house as her husband'. Had marriage then not succeeded in making her any less 'ill-tempered, capricious and changeable'?

17

Expunged from the Peerage

Even before his marriage to an unknown Spanish woman who had what the Stanley family considered the even greater disadvantage of being a Roman Catholic, Blanche's eldest brother Henry was something of a cuckoo in the nest. He was born in 1827, and when he was still a boy he became passionately interested in Arabic. This led him on, after Cambridge, to various diplomatic postings and to becoming a Mohammedan. So he had been out of England for some time when in 1869 his father died and Henry succeeded as the third Baron Stanley of Alderley. He then had to tell his family some important news: seven years earlier, he had married Fabia, the daughter of Señor Don Santiago-Frederico San-Roman, of Seville.

It was a bolt from the blue and the Stanleys did not take it well. They were an affectionate, close family whose view of Henry as a queer fish probably made him all the odder, so that he felt misunderstood and persecuted. A packet of family letters tells of the family's dismay and the self-righteous and angry reactions of Henry and his wife.

The first of the letters was written by Henry to tell his Aunt Ellen about his marriage and his happiness during the past seven years. His mother, he said, had been startled by the news at first, although less than he had expected. His aunt replied with a kind letter, very different from the one he had from his other aunt, Louisa. What the family did not like was that, by keeping the marriage secret, Henry had been living for all that time 'in a doubtful position', as if Fabia was his mistress. Henry assured his aunt of 'the respectability of my wife in character before and since our marriage, and of her being a lady by birth and education'. It had been as 'a sacrifice which she made for me' that she had lived with him without their making a public announcement of their marriage. If society chose to take offence at that, they would not complain, Henry said. But his family had no right to 'throw it in her face'.

It was not the first time Henry's private life had suffered from his family's interference. Ten years before, he had wanted to marry a lady in Wallachia, he now reminded them, but then too the Stanleys had objected. His mother had refused to mention the matter to Lord Stanley, and eventually the lady had thrown him over 'on perceiving the aversion of my family'. There had been at least two other occasions when Henry was strongly advised against a marriage he was planning. His taste and theirs had never agreed. Another early love affair is described in a bundle of letters he kept all his life. This time his love was a French girl, Claire, who lived in Paris. It would undoubtedly have been another mésalliance. He had always hoped to free her from having to earn her own living, and would never fail her if she were in need, he said. But her scenes and lamentations had ended by destroying his love for her, and above all he begged her not to come and find him in London. It would be useless, and sad for them both.

And now he was still being harassed by his family, who this time were attacking his wife as well. 'If the rest of the family go on boring me,' he told his aunt Ellen, 'I shall give up the house at Alderley to them, as that is what they seem to want, and send them all to the D---l saving your presence.' It never came to that, but the harassment went on.

Henry did attempt to conciliate his family, assuring them that Fabia had 'completely adopted my country and its interests'. It was understandable that they should want to know more about the marriage. It had been 'a civil one according to the law of the Ottoman Empire', he explained; his wife's relations, being also Roman Catholics, would have objected no less than the Stanleys, so they decided to go ahead without consulting them. They had been married in Algiers, in the presence of 'Mussulman witnesses', but they were not sure of the validity of the marriage certificate because Algiers was then a French province, subject to French laws. For that reason, when they were in Constantinople a contract had been duly drawn up by two lawyers and a former attaché of the Turkish Embassy in London; and the marriage was entered in the register of the Imam of the mosque, who was one of the witnesses. Henry assured them that this compliance with Turkish custom made the marriage 'good in English law', but the circumstances did not inspire confidence. They must have sounded very heathen and outlandish to the Stanleys.

Fabia tried to win them over, but she had not managed to learn much English during her seven years with Henry. The letter she sent to his aunt in November 1869 must have been translated and written by him, and the wording was probably also his. It began with diplomatic appreciation of the friendliness shown by Aunt Ellen and her husband, comparing this with the very different attitude of most of the family. Henry's brothers, she wrote, were planning to disinherit any children he and Fabia might have. Meanwhile they had complied with Aunt Ellen's suggestion that there should be yet another marriage formality – at St George's, Hanover Square, this time – and this had now taken place and been witnessed. But she had to point out – and surely it is Henry's voice which is heard here? – that this English marriage discredited the earlier one and therefore threw doubts on her status during the last seven years. They hoped it would avoid lawsuits and annoyances for any children they might have, but it had created a permanent rift between Fabia and her husband's family.

The quarrels and arguments rattled on. Henry disapproved of what had been done on the estate while he had been away and was endlessly finding new signs of his brothers' hostility. Fabia – or was it Henry again? – wrote about their past happiness, when they had no need of wealth or inheritance. She wished Henry had been a third or fourth son; how much easier life would then have been for them. Old Lady Stanley enclosed a lawyer's letter when she wrote questioning the legal validity of the marriage. What concerned her most was whether Fabia and any children she might have would be entitled to inherit. If they could legalize their marriage, she wrote, she would 'receive' them and the family quarrels would end. The Stanleys had always prided themselves on Whig traditions of open-mindedness and tolerance, and Henry's unmarried aunt Louisa stood by these. The family's acceptance of Fabia should depend, she wrote, on Henry's providing proof of his marriage as well as information about Fabia's antecedents. If she were proved to be a virtuous woman, 'let her Birth be what it may, there is no disgrace'.

Aunt Ellen explained to Henry why the family needed to be reassured. 'You are allied to one of the highest families in England

and it is natural we should feel anxious that all should be clear.'
Henry and Fabia had been right to blame their troubles on his
being his father's heir, but the Stanleys were also right to have
doubts about the marriage. In 1941 a note was added to the family
archives, recording that long enquiries had led to the discovery by
the fifth Lord Stanley of Alderley that Fabia in fact already had a
husband, and that he was alive and in Spain at the time of her
London marriage. The note states that her name had therefore been
'expunged from the peerage'.

At this distance it may seem a storm in a teacup, occasioned
mainly by the fact that the teacup rested on so splendid a silver tray.
Henry and Fabia had no children, and the family qualities of
exceptional intelligence and character were handed on mainly
through Henry's sisters. (Bertrand Russell was Henry's nephew,
one of his nieces married Gilbert Murray, and the Mitford sisters
were great-nieces.) The family had plenty to be proud about. How
could they guess that a hundred years later the barony would be
extinct, the old house at Alderley burnt to the ground, and the park
now a busy industrial headquarters?

18

My Fred

The unpublished as well as the published pages of the diary which Lucy Lyttelton began in 1854, when she was thirteen, are needed for a three-dimensional picture of the steps which took her and Lord Frederick Cavendish from casual acquaintance to marriage. Lucy was the daughter of the widowed Lord Lyttelton, whose wife Mary, the sister of Gladstone's wife, died in 1857 after having had twelve children in seventeen years.

Although her diary is candid and explicit about the development of her attraction to the man she was to marry, it does not manage to get him clearly into focus. He remains a shadowy, blurred figure in spite of being in the foreground of her picture. Perhaps the Cavendish reserve which troubled Lucy was one reason for this. Writing about them both, it has been easy to call her by her first name but it has taken a long time to follow her in referring to him as 'Fred'. Even Lucy found it difficult, it will be seen. Yet there can be no doubt that he was a lovable, admirable man, sufficiently open-minded to hold much more liberal ideas than his wife and his eminent brother. From 1865, the year after his marriage, until his death he represented the West Riding of Yorkshire in Parliament. In 1873 he was appointed Junior Lord of the Treasury, in 1880 became Financial Secretary to the Treasury, and two years later for a few fateful days he was Chief Secretary for Ireland. But facts and official appointments cannot breathe life into the portrait of a man who has been dead for over a century. In Lord Frederick's case this comes from the affection and admiration he inspired in his wife, and from the fact that half the House of Commons is said to have made the long journey to Derbyshire for his funeral.

Lucy's first mention of her future husband comes in 1862, when she stayed at Chatsworth for four days with her aunt and her cousin. It was a rather formidable experience. 'I can't judge of the house yet, only it seems immeasurable,' she wrote on the day they arrived. The remote and intimidating seventh Duke of Devonshire had a family party which included his son Frederick staying with him, and each day more relations and friends turned up. Lucy's own home at Hagley was large and stately, but the company as well as the grandeur of Chatsworth, with its state rooms and sculpture gallery, its splendid park and gardens, Paxton's conservatory and the rocketing Emperor fountain all gave her 'an oppressed feeling, which is my form of shyness, I suppose'. This lessened a little each day that she was there, 'but be at my ease I cannot'.

The Lytteltons and the Cavendishes were related, and Lucy and Lord Frederick were in fact third cousins, so she might be expected to feel less strange at Chatsworth. But there were important differences between the families. Religion was all-important to the Lytteltons, less so to the Cavendishes; and Lucy's inherited politics were Conservative before her marriage won her over to follow – some but not all of the way – her husband's radical liberalism. But it was in mood and temperament that the families differed most. Along with their devoutness, the Lytteltons were unconventional, ebullient, talkative, noisy, and light-hearted; while the Cavendishes were reserved, quiet, and awe-inspiring. The gap was bridged by Gladstone, whose family was so close as to be almost one with their Lyttelton cousins, and who was, of course, the leader of the Liberal Party. The Gladstone connection must have helped Lord Frederick's political career, bringing him various public appointments, including the one which was to cost him his life.

At all events he next turns up in Lucy's diary a month or so after her Chatsworth visit. This time it was at the Gladstones' home at Hawarden that they met, and Lord Frederick was a partner of hers at 'one of the very best and liveliest balls' she had known. It had begun at nine-thirty and ended five hours later. After that came some seven months in town and country during which Lucy was offered and accepted an appointment as Maid of Honour to the Queen, before Lord Frederick is again mentioned as one of her dancing partners, this time at two July balls. In September 1863 her royal duties began, taking Lucy to Windsor and Osborne, and that December she and her father paid another visit to Chatsworth. Again Lord Frederick was one of the party, and at dinner on the day they arrived Lucy and he got into an argument about the Church which 'excited and interested' her. They took very different views of the subject. 'I don't think I was wrong,' wrote Lucy, 'as I did not introduce the topic on purpose.' But she did wish she 'had been somebody who cd have convinced him!'

Convinced or not, he was evidently interested and charmed, for he was Lucy's neighbour at dinner the next night and followed her a few days later to Hawarden, where again they discussed Church matters. Perhaps what Lucy called 'the most delightful ball I have ever had' owed some of its delight to the fact that 'F. Cavendish' was again listed among her partners. She still did not divulge much in her diary – 'I feel in something of a dream', was the most she allowed herself, the week after the ball – but there is a whiff of excitement in the air. She also wrote revealingly to her married sister: 'I could not help having my head turned by Lord Frederick seeming rather to like me. He is so very pleasant that this did put me into a state of mind. I know this may be stupid and that it may all come to an end: but Oh dear!'

It soon became clear that it was all not going to come to an end. When Mrs Gladstone asked Lord Frederick to buy some photographs in aid of one of her charities, he asked her for one of Miss Lucy Lyttelton. Characteristically, Lucy turned to prayer and to trusting in heavenly guidance at this solemn turning-point in her life. On the last day of 1863 this was her mood as she summed up the events of the year that was ending. 'There is much in my heart to make me thoughtful, and to give me a sort of awe, in looking forward.' In April she went to London, and they met almost every day. After Lord Frederick came to luncheon, Lucy and Mrs Gladstone and he went together to see a fresco that was being painted in one of the Chambers of the Houses of Parliament. Two days later they went with him to the Privy Council Office to see Garibaldi being given a great spontaneous welcome from crowds of London working people as he drove past. The next day Lucy was invited to a luncheon given to Garibaldi by the Cavendishes at Chiswick House, and afterwards Lord Frederick came back with her to high tea and the theatre. That was 12 April, and the next day they both went to a splendid party, again in honour of Garibaldi, at Stafford House. It was there that he proposed and she accepted. What she confided to her diary gave away no secrets. 'It was to be a never-to-be-forgotten evening to me,' she wrote.

Next day Lord Frederick (as she still called him) came to breakfast, and in the afternoon his sister Louisa called to see Lucy. Her mood was a mixture of happiness, piety, and fear. 'I seem frightened, in spite of the strange happiness. God make it right for me! God guide me in my decision! I am so foolish and bewildered.' It was probably helpful that the next day she had to go to the Queen at Windsor. Her young brothers, who were at Eton, came to tea in her room at the Castle, where she fed them on 'unlimited eggs, etc.', but she resisted her longing to tell them of her 'wonderful secret'. Not until the Sunday did she begin to feel calmer. 'Today my doubts and fears (which have been many) began to melt away.' Back in London, Lord Frederick came to dinner with his father, brother, and sister, and the following day all was settled. 'We are engaged, and my doubts and fears have been all absorbed in the wonderful happiness and peace. . . .I will try with all my heart, my very best to deserve it all; but I never shall!' Lord Frederick had endeared himself to Lucy's grandmother and sisters, asking the girls if they would forgive him for taking Lucy from them. And that afternoon he brought her the first of her wedding-presents – a locket framed with diamonds and pearls, which was to hold a twist of his hair.

What the Lytteltons called 'a Sunday talk' brought them together the next day. 'He told me all his opinions that he thought I shd not agree with him about. I don't – but he has built his house on the Rock; and I can't but trust him!' Fred stayed to dinner and afterwards they went to see *Henry IV* at Drury Lane. 'I believe now everybody knows it,' wrote Lucy. Friends and relations began to call with jewelry and other presents, and that evening she wore the locket with Fred's hair in it, hanging it next to her mother's little pearl chain. 'It felt to me as if I was telling her about it'; throughout all the excitement Lucy's only regret had been that her mother was not there to share it. Coming to breakfast was a pleasant way to begin the day, and the next morning Fred brought his sister with him, and stayed for the rest of the morning, again 'talking on serious subjects'. He understood how important her religion was to Lucy and gave her 'the *deepest* feeling of happiness' she had yet felt by saying he would like to go with her and her father to Communion. After the serious talk they went to Devonshire House, where 'even the being taken to the Duke's study didn't much frighten me! He kissed me *very* kindly.'

Next day Fred saw Lucy off to her royal duties at Osborne. Each of them hurried to put pen to paper. 'I wrote my first letter to *Fred*: O how strange that looks!' When did she first call him Fred? In her diary until then he had always been 'Lord Frederic [sic]' or simply 'He', and she found it difficult to change. Next day she received her 'first letter from *him*: such a dear one! grave and simple, like himself. It makes it all *very* real to me.' Everyone at Osborne was interested in her news. The Queen kissed her affectionately and said 'I must congratulate you, but I must scold you a little too!'

There were still realities she had not faced. In a letter Fred 'discoursed a little about housekeeping. O dear me! I don't believe I yet realize *what* a new life is before me.' Even so, Lucy had a head start on most other young brides who were faced with the prospect of stately housekeeping and managing a large staff and 'establishment'; her mother's death gave the older Lyttelton daughters practice in such things. Her royal appointment and the knowledge that she had given satisfaction as Maid of Honour must also have brought her a reassuring measure of self-confidence.

Then came the news that the Queen was to hold a Privy Council at Osborne and that Lord Granville would bring Lord Frederick, who was his private secretary, with him. Lucy had always been inclined, like the Queen, to exclamation-marks and underlinings, and she seems to have caught something of the Queen's tone of voice now when she speaks of her love. 'Oh what it will be to me to see his dear face!' she cooed. It was a 'golden day' for them. 'We had all the afternoon to ourselves, in the ugly little ladies' room, who will never look ugly to me again.' Fred brought with him a diamond 'betrothal ring'.

Planning and fittings for her trousseau caused some daunting misgivings. 'At times the bewilderment of all the unknown new clothes, and the vague state of mind I get into as to where they will all go, what new places I myself am going to, make my poor addled head spin; but through it all, the sunshine is bright over the future!' She chose an onyx signet ring for Fred, and he was delighted with the crystal locket she gave him 'with a scratchy bit of my hair in it'. She chose lockets for her twelve bridesmaids and went with Fred to be photographed. It was a comparatively unfamiliar and lengthy ordeal at that date. 'I fear we shall look like fools.'

A great family dinner and party followed at Devonshire House. She was gradually feeling more at her ease there. But for Lucy, home would always be the Lytteltons' house at Hagley, where she went for a week with Fred and her father the day after the Devonshire House party. There they could relax, going for rides together, playing whist, and reading aloud in the evening. A diary entry for one of those Hagley days brings the only mention she made of any shortcomings in Fred, and even that she quickly cancelled out. She tells how he 'read aloud to me with fervour and feeling enough to counteract the *slight* disadvantage of his funny inability to pronounce either "r" or "th".'

There was a great send-off from friends, tenants and village, and a presentation of a Bible and Prayer Book, bound together, from the under servants. Back in London, they rode together in Rotten Row and Fred came 'in his uniform' to a big birthday-party for the Queen. Fred had a sitting for the miniature that his sister was giving Lucy, who went to dinner 'all by myself' – meaning that everyone else was a Cavendish – at Devonshire House. They were all 'kind and nice, setting me at my ease; but I cd. not quite say I *was* at my ease! though very happy after dinner with my Fred holding my hand.'

It was a society convention to leave engaged and newly-married couples deliberately on their own during social occasions. A week before their wedding, Fred and Lucy at a little musical party were glad to be 'treated with such respect as to be left in one of the drawing rooms by ourselves most of the time'. Then the two fathers-in-law with their lawyers came together for the signing of the marriage settlement, and the wedding-day dawned. It was 7 June, a specially important date for Lucy as it was the anniversary of her first Communion.

After the splendid wedding in Westminster Abbey, the bride and bridegroom drove to Chiswick House, nearest to London of the Duke's homes, and then very rural and peaceful. There they stayed for four days, during which Lucy received her first letter in her 'pretty new name' and they read poetry to each other – Milton from Lucy, Tennyson from Fred. Back in London, she steeled herself at last to call her sister-in-law and brother-in-law Lou and Eddy – both actually and in her diary. 'I may as well smash the ice at once!' She was still an unsophisticated country girl at heart, married though she was to the son of a duke.

So far she had been to only three of the family homes. Their next visit was to Bolton Abbey in Yorkshire, where they found them-

A portrait of Lady Lucy Cavendish by George Richmond, painted at
about the time of her marriage.

selves driving under a miniature triumphal arch, inscribed with the message 'Welcome to Bolton'. At church on their 'first married Sunday' there were 'knots of people' eager for a sight of them. It was at Bolton that they started at last on some of the rather solid books they had chosen to take with them on their honeymoon – Carlyle's *French Revolution*, Joseph Butler's *Analogy of Religion*, and Kingsley's *Westward Ho*! And Fred gave Lucy 'a little lecture on ferns'.

After their fortnight's honeymoon and a month travelling abroad they came back to London – 'Devonshire House is a little wonderful to arrive at!' – and then '*home* to dear old Hagley'. There they had another festive village reception with cheers, flags, and more triumphal arches. Fred made a little speech of thanks, Lucy holding his hand – perhaps to make up for those missing 'rs' and 'ths' – as he spoke. Coming back to her home as a married woman brought her the novelty of being 'handed in' to dinner by her father and proudly taking her place at the head of the table. At a dinner party at Hagley a few evenings later she wore two of her most splendid wedding presents – a necklace from the Queen and a bracelet from her brother-in-law. But she felt she 'looked just like Lucy Lyttelton nevertheless!'

Holker Hall in Westmorland also had to be visited. Again the men took the horses out and themselves drew the carriage up to the door; and again she and Fred held hands as he thanked them. At Hardwick Hall, the Devonshire home a few miles over the hills from Chatsworth, they had another week on their own, this time with what Lucy described as 'the ducal circumstances of a special train, twenty-two servants, six horse-boxes and two carriages'. After that to Chatsworth. 'I needn't describe my curious feelings on coming to this stately place as my Fred's wife.' It had been during her visit in 1862 that Fred had first thought that they might marry; and on her second visit that she for her part 'began really to like him'.

She still felt awkward with the Duke and with Fred's brother, Lord Hartington. Very slowly her father-in-law's reserve began to melt. Not until nine months after their wedding did he call her Lucy; and it was over a year before she could tell herself 'I think the Duke is a little fond of me now, and at all events I have ceased to be terrified at him!' Even so, on occasions when Fred had some engagement which left his wife and his father alone together for the day, Lucy suspected that the Duke wished her 'at the bottom of the Baltic'.

So gradually the temperamental differences of the two family backgrounds were smoothed away. And gradually they adjusted and matched their attitudes to the two subjects – religion and politics – which were most important to them both. It seems they achieved this by recognizing that religion was paramount to Lucy, politics to Fred, so each adapted to the positive lead given by the other in his or her own sphere. It was a big step that Lucy took when she crossed from right to left in politics to become a Liberal. She was amused to see this happening while they were still on their honeymoon. 'I am come to a pretty pass when I find myself crowing over the Whig victory!'

Occasionally Fred's radicalism clashed head on with Lucy's religious principles. It was not 'for want of many a talking to' that he insisted on voting in Parliament for the new Burials Bill, which aimed at allowing dissenters to be buried in Anglican churchyards. She was also as strongly against legalizing marriage with a dead wife's sister as she was against the movement to allow women the vote. 'The subject of female suffrage (odious and ridiculous notion as it is),' she wrote, 'is actually beginning to be spoken of without laughter, and as if it was an open question. I trust we are not coming to that.'

There are few such unselfconscious accounts of the coming together of a couple in the world of the great country houses. Their marriage stood the test of time as well as that of the childlessness they so regretted. It came to a tragic end when Lord Frederick was murdered – by mistake, it seems, as the assassins were out to kill his colleague – in Phoenix Park, Dublin, in 1882, a few hours after taking up his appointment there as Chief Secretary to the Lord Lieutenant of Ireland.

Then and Now

Interesting as it always is as well as often distressing and amusing to share for a few hours the experiences and feelings of people whose lives were so different from ours, it must surely be a relief to home back to the 1980s. Would anyone choose to put the clock back? And if so, how far? Was there ever, will there ever be a golden age of love and marriage?

This picture of one aspect of one class in one country during one century can be no more than an impression, a sample taken hopefully from the mass of evidence that has been handed on. Even a carefully chosen sample cannot give a fair cross-section, as history and records are both unavoidably élitist, concerned almost exclusively with the famous and the talented. Only occasionally and accidentally do windows open on the personal lives of non-eminent Victorians and Georgians.

So how does the past compare with the present? How does it all add up? There was certainly less freedom during the last century – even for the men, even for the aristocracy. But freedom is a tricky horse to ride and even today sends people flying over its ears, whereas in the unliberated past they managed to keep jogging along, uncomfortable and insecure but still in the saddle. There was also less understanding of emotions, less chance to get to know another human being before tying two lives together. And there was far less control of circumstances – physical, social, legal, and financial. Appearances were all-important. Relationships were often as tightly corseted as all the women and some of the men. There were couples who never confronted each other completely naked. It took courage as well as passion to exorcize all the taboos and inhibitions.

The mass media of today masochistically gives pride of place to the disasters and miseries of the world. Perhaps that is one reason why it is a pleasure to retreat back into the past and in chandeliered ballrooms and spanking carriages to meet men and women with emotions and instincts recognizably like our own, with personal problems that were different from ours but perhaps even more oppressive. How would the Upper Ten Thousand of the last century make out in ours? Would any of us go back to theirs?

Bibliography

Abdy, Jane and Gere, Charlotte, *The Souls*, Sidgwick & Jackson, 1984

Acland, Alice, *Caroline Norton*, Constable, 1948

Acton, William, *Prostitution*, second edition, John Churchill, 1870

Airlie, Mabell, Countess of, *In Whig Society, 1775–1818*, Hodder & Stoughton, 1921

Alsop, Susan Mary, *Lady Sackville: a Biography*, Weidenfeld & Nicolson, 1976

Anglesey, Marquess of (ed.), *The Capel Letters*, Jonathan Cape, 1955

One-Leg, Jonathan Cape, 1961

Arbuthnot, Harriet, *Journal, 1820–1832*, ed. Frances Bamford and the Duke of Wellington, Macmillan, 1950

Askwith, Betty, *The Lytteltons*, Chatto & Windus, 1975

Balsan, Consuelo Vanderbilt, *The Glitter and the Gold*, Heinemann, 1953

Battiscombe, Georgina, *Mrs Gladstone*, Constable, 1956

Bédarida, François, *A Social History of England 1851–1975*, Methuen, 1979

Bessborough, Earl of (ed.), *Lady Bessborough and her Family Circle*, John Murray, 1940

Blakiston, Georgiana, *Lord William Russell and his Wife*, John Murray, 1972

Woburn and the Russells, Constable, 1980

Blunden, Margaret, *The Countess of Warwick*, Cassell, 1967

Burnett, David, *Longleat*, Collins, 1978

Bury, Lady Charlotte, *The Diary of a Lady-in-Waiting*, John Lane, 1908

Byron, Lord, *Letters and Journals*, vols 3 and 4, ed. Leslie A. Marchand, John Murray, 1974 and 1975

Calder, Jenni, *Women and Marriage in Victorian Fiction*, Thames & Hudson, 1976

Cavendish, Lady Frederick, *Diary*, 2 vols, ed. John Bailey, John Murray, 1927

Cowles, Virginia, *The Rothschilds*, Weidenfeld & Nicolson, 1973

Cox, Millard, *Derby*, J. A. Allen, 1974

Creevey, Thomas, *The Creevey Papers*, ed. John Gore, John Murray, 1948

Eden, Hon. Emily, *Letters*, ed. Violet Dickinson, Macmillan, 1919
The Semi-attached Couple, Folio Society, 1955

Egremont, Lord, *Wyndham and Children First*, Macmillan, 1968

Egremont, Max, *Balfour: a Life of Arthur James Balfour*, Collins, 1980

Eliot, Elizabeth, *They all married well*, Cassell, 1960

Elwin, Malcolm, *Lord Byron's Wife*, Macdonald, 1962

Fairfax-Lucy, Alice, *Mistress of Charlecote*, Gollancz, 1983

Farington, Joseph, *Diary*, 8 vols, ed. James Greig, Hutchinson, 1923

Foster, Vere, *The two Duchesses*, Blackie & Son, 1898

Glendinning, Victoria, *Vita*, Weidenfeld & Nicolson, 1983

Granville, Lord, *Private Correspondence*, ed. Castalia, Countess Granville, John Murray, 1916

Greville, Charles, *Memoirs, 1814–1860*, 8 vols, ed. Roger Fulford and Lytton Strachey, Macmillan, 1938

Gronow, Captain, *The Reminiscences*, Bodley Head, 1964

Gunn, Peter, *My dearest Augusta*, Bodley Head, 1968

Harrison, James Fraser, *The Dark Angel: Aspects of Victorian Sexuality*, Sheldon Press, 1977

Healey, Edna, *Lady Unknown*, Sidgwick & Jackson, 1978

Henley, Dorothy, *Rosalind Howard, Countess of Carlisle*, Hogarth Press, 1958

Hewett, Osbert Wyndham, *Strawberry Fair*, John Murray, 1956

Holland, Lady Elizabeth, *Letters to her Son, 1821–1845*, ed. Earl of Ilchester, John Murray, 1946

Holland, Lord, *The Holland House Diaries*, ed. Abraham D. Kriegel, Routledge and Kegan Paul, 1977

Howell-Thomas, Dorothy, *Lord Melbourne's Susan*, Gresham Books, 1978

Huxley, Gervas, *Lady Elizabeth and the Grosvenors*, Oxford
    University Press, 1965
  Victorian Duke, Oxford University Press, 1967
James, Robert Rhodes, *Rosebery*, Weidenfeld & Nicolson, 1963
Knowlton, Charles M.D., *Fruits of Philosophy*, J. Watson, 1850
Lerner, Laurence, *Love and Marriage*, Edward Arnold, 1979
Longford, Elizabeth, *Wellington: the Years of the Sword*,
    Weidenfeld & Nicolson, 1969
  Wellington: Pillar of State, Weidenfeld & Nicolson, 1972
Lovelace, Earl of, *Astarte*, Christophers, London, 1921
Lyttelton, Edith, *Alfred Lyttelton*, Longmans & Co., 1923
MacCarthy, D. and Russell, Agatha, *Lady John Russell: a Memoir*,
    Methuen, 1910
McGregor, O.R., *Divorce in England*, Heinemann, 1957
Martin, Ralph, *Lady Randolph Churchill*, Cassell, 1969
Masters, Brian, *The Dukes*, Blond & Briggs, 1975
Mavor, Elizabeth, *The Ladies of Llangollen*, Michael Joseph, 1971
Meade-Fetherstonhaugh, Margaret and Warner, Oliver, *Uppark
    and its People*, George Allen & Unwin, 1964
Mill, John Stuart, *The Subjection of Women*, Longmans & Co., 1906
Milner, Viscountess, *My Picture Gallery*, John Murray, 1951
Mitford, Nancy (ed.), *The Ladies of Alderley*, Hamish Hamilton,
    1938
  The Stanleys of Alderley, Hamish Hamilton, 1939
Montgomery Hyde, H., *The Londonderrys*, Hamish Hamilton, 1979
  The Other Love, Heinemann, 1970
Mosley, Nicholas, *Julian Grenfell*, Weidenfeld & Nicolson, 1976
Nevill, Ralph, *Life and Letters of Lady Dorothy Nevill*, Methuen,
    1919
Newman, Aubrey, *The Stanhopes of Chevening*, Macmillan, 1969
Nicolson, Nigel, *Mary Curzon*, Weidenfeld & Nicolson, 1977
Norton, Caroline, *Letters of Caroline Norton to Lord Melbourne*, ed.
    James O. Hoge and Clarke Olney, Ohio State University
    Press, 1974
Oman, Carola, *The Gascoyne Heiress*, Hodder & Stoughton, 1968
Pearson, John, *Stags and Serpents*, Macmillan, 1983
Pickering, A.M.W., *Memoirs*, ed. S. Pickering, Hodder &
    Stoughton, 1903
Pullar, Philippa, *Gilded Butterflies*, Hamish Hamilton, 1978
Raikes, Thomas, *Journal*, Longmans & Co., 1856

Raymond, E.T., *The Man of Promise: Lord Rosebery*, T. Fisher Unwin, 1923

Ridley, Jasper, *Palmerston*, Constable, 1970

Roberts, Brian, *The Mad Bad Line*, Hamish Hamilton, 1981

Roberts, Charles, *The Radical Countess*, Steel Bros, 1962

Rose, Kenneth, *The Later Cecils*, Weidenfeld & Nicolson, 1975

Rowse, A.L., *Homosexuals in History*, Weidenfeld & Nicolson, 1977

Russell, Bertrand, *Autobiography*, George Allen & Unwin, 1967

Russell, Bertrand and Patricia (eds), *The Amberley Papers*, Hogarth Press, 1937

Russell, George W.E., *Collections and Recollections*, T. Nelson, 1903

Schmidt, Margaret Fox, *Passion's Child*, Hamish Hamilton, 1977

Stafford, Ann, *The Age of Consent*, Hodder & Stoughton, 1964

Surtees, Virginia, *Charlotte Canning*, John Murray, 1975

Thompson, F.M.L., *English Landed Society in the Nineteenth Century*, Routledge and Kegan Paul, 1963

Tomalin, Claire, *The Life and Death of Mary Wollstonecraft*, Weidenfeld & Nicolson, 1974

Tuchman, Barbara W., *The Proud Tower*, Hamish Hamilton, 1966

Victoria, Queen, *The Girlhood of Queen Victoria. A Selection from her Majesty's Diaries, 1832–1840*, 3 vols, ed. Viscount Esher, John Murray, 1912

Warwick, Countess of, *Afterthoughts*, Cassell, 1931

Wellington, 1st Duke of, *A Great Man's Friendship: Letters to Mary, Marchioness of Salisbury, 1850–1852*, ed. Lady Burghclere, John Murray, 1927

Wellington and his Friends, ed. 7th Duke of Wellington, Macmillan, 1965

Wilson, Harriette, *Memoirs of Herself and Others*, Peter Davies, 1929

Wohl, Anthony S., *The Victorian Family*, Croom Helm, London, 1978

Wollstonecraft, Mary, *A Vindication of the Rights of Woman*, J. Johnson, 1792

Woodham-Smith, Cecil, *Florence Nightingale*, Constable, 1950

Wyndham, George, *Life and Letters*, 2 vols, ed. J.W. Mackail and Guy Wyndham, Hutchinson, 1925

Young, Kenneth, *Arthur James Balfour*, G. Bell & Sons, 1963

Ziegler, Philip, *Melbourne*, Collins, 1976

Index